WHY
AM I
LIKE
THIS?

T0326149

WHY
AM I
LIKE
THIS?

A Journey into Psychological Astrology

Judy Balan

**SIMON &
SCHUSTER**

London · New York · Sydney · Toronto · New Delhi

First published in India by Simon & Schuster India, 2023

Copyright © Judy Balan, 2023

Text illustrations by Tanvi Shivam.

1 3 5 7 9 10 8 6 4 2

Simon & Schuster India
818, Indraprakash Building,
21, Barakhamba Road,
New Delhi 110001.

www.simonandschuster.co.in

Paperback ISBN: 978-93-92099-43-4
eBook ISBN: 978-93-92099-44-1

Typeset in India by SÜRYA, New Delhi
Printed and bound in India by Replika Press Pvt. Ltd.

FSC
www.fsc.org
MIX
Paper from
responsible sources
FSC® C016779

For my brother, who generously shared the meatier portion of the family neurosis with me; and without whose relentless cheerleading ('You should call the sequel: Why Am I *Still* Like This?'), I may have never needed to write this book.

CONTENTS

But First...

I grew up believing I was created by God but sometimes it's more plausible that I was created by Ricky Gervais.

Tonight is a classic. I can't fall asleep because I find myself compulsively replaying and reliving in horror, those chart-topping cringe moments of the last two decades of my life. I can barely wrap my head around some of these. Like that phase when, in the throes of the Catholic Charismatic movement, I invoked the name of Jesus with so much ferocity, that it scared not only Satan but also anyone in the vicinity. And how I swung directly from that phase into the arms of more than one militant atheist who blamed organised religion for all the world's problems. Then there was that brief period when my overwhelming need to defy convention made college dropouts seem sexy. And of course that low point in the 2000s when everyone was into 'casual relationships' and I emotionally contorted myself into this trend in the hope of becoming 'a chill person'.

'What possessed me,' I mutter as vivid memories of a person who was apparently me but went about behaving in ways that were decidedly not me, streams in HD with background score and surround sound. Some of these scenes casually switch genres from full-fledged drama where the stakes are so high that you want to reach into your television screen to deliver a tight slap to the protagonist, to Emmy-winning cringe-com—like that time at a party in London when I tried to overcome social anxiety by talking, long after I should've stopped talking; that one time I made a string of sweeping statements on a news panel and woke up to a sudden burst of dodgy followers; and that night out with people I didn't know too well, when right after texting a friend 'baby', my brain did a thing and I accidentally addressed one of the straight males in front of me baby and to undo the horror, spent the rest of the evening calling everyone else baby.

The sound of sudden pelting rain on the roof snaps me out of this rude reverie and brings me back to my tiny ten-by-ten bedroom. Exhale. I may always be a bit of a social disaster but at least I am no longer that woman making reckless decisions with her emotional life. 'Yes, nowadays it's financial life,' says a voice in my head that sounds uncannily like my father, but I mute it for the time being.

I turn to my right and take in the empty space on my queen-sized bed that by now, feels like a presence all by itself. This empty side of my bed has been the silent witness to my becoming, long before therapy became cool. It has been around since those days when I'd cry through the night and pass out from exhaustion, that one time I made a Shawshank-Redemption-style exit out of my Dark Night of the Soul, numbed myself with food, alcohol, television binges, online shopping, more messy emotional entanglements, used comedy to dissociate from the intensity of feeling, analysing, writing, analysing, back to square one, all the way to praying, praying, pleading, why am I like this, why am I like this, *why am I like this*, giving up, dying, tumbling into the void, dead, drinking of the cup of silence, keeping vigil with the darkness until the first spark of light begins to emerge both within and without, my equilibrium returns, and I feel held by the creation myths in a way that I cannot articulate.

Through all this and more, this empty right side of the bed has been a most reliable presence. So you see why it feels wrong not to personify it. I will call him *Strange Bedfellow*.

My phone blinks. A text from a friend who has had a particularly bad week and sounds it. 'What the fuck is going on in the skies?' she wants to know. 'Is it mercury? Is the bastard retrograde again? Or is it saturn? It must be saturn! When does this stop? Make it stop!'

I want to *astrosplain*. Astrology through the lens of depth psychology is about taking responsibility, not blaming the stars, your circumstances or other people. It's a symbolic language that holds up a mirror to your own unconscious material, and the best way to work with it is by looking within. But I resist the urge because Strange Bedfellow (SBF) makes a face that says, 'Look who's so put together now, that she can't let her friend have a human moment.' And if there's anyone who knows exactly how *unputtogether* I am, it's him. So I send commiserating emojis instead. Along with approximate dates for when she can expect the intensity to subside. SBF approves.

But how did this happen? How am I suddenly not the one spiralling as much as the one people reach out to while spiralling?

'That does not sound smug and braggy at all,' SBF says. 'You should totally go ahead and put that in a book.'

Except that's not what I'm saying (I still spiral). And this does not come from anything resembling self-satisfaction as much as an acknowledgement of the strange and fascinating journey I've been on since my encounter with astrology and Jungian psychology.

1

Why Don't I Come with an Instruction Manual (and Other Questions)

I have been curious about the human psyche for as long as I can remember. Long before I was conscious of it; long before I had heard the word 'psyche'. In my tweens, I devised my own kiddy version of the famous Swiss psychiatrist Carl Jung's (pronounced Yoong) Word Association test so I could understand 'what people are *really* like'. Of course, I had no idea who Jung was or that there was such a thing as the unconscious. This was still several years before the internet so no one was as yet asking 'What kind of cocktail am I' or 'Which Disney Princess am I,' let alone 'What's going on in the deeper recesses of my psyche that makes me this one of a kind, uniquely fucked up masterpiece.' At least, no one in my immediate environment was.

As a child, I assumed my parents and the other adults in my life knew what they were doing because they were so put together, with all the icky emotional bits neatly tucked in. My parents never really had serious fights. Not to my knowledge anyway. There were arguments that got loud at times, sure, but never any dramatic displays of outrage, hurt or betrayal. Instead, it was in the atmosphere. Every time someone bit their tongue, held back tears or swallowed their anger, a dense, invisible, emotional-charge-laden cloud would descend upon the room. I instinctively knew not to prick this cloud for fear that it might rain bile. So I developed strategies to navigate it whenever it showed up. I could pretend it didn't exist like my parents did all the time, I could make a joke about it like my mom often did (this was tricky and could go several ways), I could go for a smoke (no I couldn't) or turn on the TV like my dad, I could bury my nose in a book and be oblivious to it like my brother often was, or I could distract myself as I waited for it to pass. All good strategies that eventually became my go-to defence mechanisms but only after two decades of living all the way on the opposite extreme.

Unlike my family and extended family, I had big feelings that were beyond my capacity to contain. When I loved, I was consumed, reckless and obsessive. When I was happy, I was euphoric, when I was angry, I had outbursts and when I was sad, I despaired. It's not that I didn't try holding them in, as I was taught to, but they had a way of erupting in the most theatrical ways and at the most inconvenient times. Before I knew it, they became my whole personality.

My parents worked hard to give my brother and I, a stable, drama-free childhood and I know that that early sense of stability and security continues to sustain me in the most difficult phases. It also gives me the courage to chase my curiosity even when it leads me into dark caves guarded by giant three-headed dogs because something rock-like inside says 'everything works out in the end.'

But for the longest time, I hated my drama-free life. I felt like a character in a novel where nothing happens. And for reasons only melodramatic teens would get, this felt worse than being cast in an outright dark novel. I had too much dramatic flair to be wasted on a life of quiet contentment. And so I despised the ordinariness of everyday life that my parents seemed to enjoy and embrace. Even my brother and my peers who came from similar backgrounds, didn't struggle as much as I did with accepting it as a necessary part of being human.

School, or the idea of school, was particularly hard to make peace with. I simply couldn't accept that I had to wake up at a certain time every day and spend anywhere between six to eight hours at this place, for fourteen years of my life, and I had no say whatsoever, in the matter. It had nothing to do with learning difficulties because I rarely got anything less than 96% in any subject. So when I was eight and developed mysterious stomach aches (and all the tests came out normal), my parents tried to find out what was making me so unhappy. Maybe I was being bullied. But I wasn't. They even suggested changing schools but I refused, because it wasn't the school as much as the system I had a problem with, though I didn't have the vocabulary for it at the time.

By the time I was twelve, I simply couldn't absorb anything that I wasn't interested in. It didn't matter that I *had* to study; it didn't even matter that I was repeatedly told how brilliant I was and that this was a piece of cake for me. I went from 100%, 99%, 96% and maybe occasionally, 88%, to flunking in three to four subjects in each exam. Given the high premium south Indians place on conventional education, and how much pride my mum took in my academic excellence, this phase was particularly disconcerting for her. But it did nothing to ruffle my self-assurance. 'Please,' I'd roll my eyes. 'I could beat the whole class hollow if I wanted to. I'm just not *interested*. Besides, if I'm so brilliant, why do I need a report card to validate it?' Whether or not this was true, I completely believed it at the time, so I continued to ignore academics until my final exams, because failing in your finals meant spending another insufferable year in the same grade and I couldn't bear the thought of that. 'She has so much potential' my teachers would bleat over and over at the PTMs. 'She's doing this deliberately,' one was convinced, and I agreed. My plan was to somehow get through the boards, after which I'd never have to study math, physics and chemistry again. Again, I was particularly excellent at math till I decided it was 'boring.' And part of the reason it was boring was also because my entire family (both sides) was into it and I was driven by some inner compulsion I couldn't understand, to go down a completely different path.

Grade 10 finally came and the pressure I was under was nothing like what my classmates experienced. They wanted to excel, while I couldn't bear the thought of going through the year itself. I wasn't sure I could survive it emotionally. Again, my body produced a curious symptom. My nose was blocked through that entire academic year and I went through at least twenty-five bottles of Otrivin (nasal drops). It was like I literally couldn't breathe through that year. The nose block mysteriously disappeared once I was done with the boards and I was back to being the teacher's pet in Grade 11 'because I love this teacher and I love her subject (Advanced English)'.

But academics aside, it's not like my life was boring in any objective sense. There was plenty of love, laughter, conversations, music and art. We were into everything, my brother and I, and my mom enthusiastically signed us up for all kinds of music lessons, sports, art and gardening that we of course took for granted and gave up halfway as my dad had predicted, and they kept me creatively stimulated.

But my big feelings were still left without outlets because nothing extraordinary ever happened to us. Nothing wild, exhilarating, horrible, strange or mysterious ever touched us or so it seemed. So I invented a fantasy world where I was sometimes the martyr, sometimes the heroine and lived in it most of the time. In martyr mode, I wrote bad song lyrics and pretended I was an emo musician. In heroine mode, I fought passionately for my ideals even if it meant fighting alone. Neither of these modes was ideal of course, because I desperately wanted to belong. And I wanted to understand why I found ordinariness so unbearable, to the point of feeling miserable and isolated while my peers didn't, or at least seemed to have more grace available to them to navigate these hormonal years.

In the early to late nineties when I was a teen, nobody went to therapy. Not in my part of the world at least. The only person I knew who came close, was someone who was diagnosed with a psychotic disorder and even she was mostly medicated and sent away. The concept of seeing a psychotherapist for non-clinical reasons was unheard of. In fact, any word that sprung from 'psyche' (which, by the way, means 'soul' in Latin) was regarded with suspicion, omitted from everyday conversation or spoken in hushed whispers as if it was the Dark Lord's name and by mentioning it, you could accidentally summon him. Instead, there were books on the subject of personality that didn't seem to elicit the same fear-based reactions. I remember having one on the four temperaments (choleric, melancholic, sanguine, phlegmatic). I coerced everyone I knew into taking the test so I could get a handle—however broad—on who they were and how they worked.

I just wanted to know how people worked. Both individually, and as a species. I wanted to know how *I* worked. I couldn't understand why this was not a part of our curriculum at school. Instead, I was being asked to learn the parts of a computer when I couldn't even find the 'off' button to my emo spells. Also, if something as clunky and unsophisticated as a 90s PC could come with an instruction manual, why was I, in all my human complexity, expected to figure myself out?

2

Something Freaky This Way Comes

When I was thirteen, there was a lot of buzz around this Catholic retreat centre in Kerala. We heard all kinds of stories from people who had been there—the blind could see, the lame could walk, people spoke in strange languages and so on—but I think it was this obvious energetic shift we noticed in the people themselves, that made us want to go. People who returned from this place just seemed...different. In a good way—they seemed kinder, calmer, more joyful, and excited to be alive. And my mom decided we had to go as a family and find out just what was going on in this small town in our sister state. So my parents did something out of character and acted on impulse—they booked our tickets! But there was one little hitch. This was a week-long charismatic retreat, which meant that there'd be loud cries of 'Hallelujah', 'Praise the Lord' and Bible verses, and the Holy Spirit would be involved.

This made us uncomfortable because we practiced Catholicism Lite—basically, our spiritual practice involved going to Sunday mass (often late), family prayer at night, and not much else—and this was all a touch unhinged and Pentecostal for our taste. We were good with Jesus and Mary but the Holy Spirit we liked to keep at a respectful distance because my family placed a high premium on normalcy, and the Holy Spirit had a reputation for disrupting that. We associated the Holy Spirit with those Bible-wielding, white-saree-clad Pentacostals who, like Jehovah's Witnesses, went door to door asking random strangers to accept Jesus Christ as their lord and saviour and we wanted nothing to do with that.

But then again, the people who reported these things had also been like us, and they hadn't gone cuckoo from what we could tell, so maybe we could just go there and observe. We could check out these alleged miracles and return with our normalcy intact. That was the plan.

Before we left, my mom prepared us. 'We won't have access to TV or the outside world for a week.' Which meant I'd be skipping *90210*, *X-files*, *21 Jump Street*, *Doogie Howser*, *Picket Fences* and so much more. Not to mention hours of MTV (Or was it Channel V by then). For India in pre-internet times, that was a lot of good television I was sacrificing to be here (not that I was given a choice). I wasn't sure I could survive it but I had to admit I was curious. For once in my life, something bizarre and freaky had touched us and I wasn't going to treat it like it was nothing.

Except it turned out that my mom hadn't given us the full picture:

1. We'd be woken up at 5-something in the morning and the only thing available to drink before we hit the hall for 'praise and worship' would be black coffee without sugar.

2. For lunch, we'd have fat Kerala rice with some dubious gravy and sides and we'd have to wash our own plates (gasp).

3. There'd be thousands of people attending the retreat simultaneously in seven languages and sometimes the Malayalam crowd (thousands of people) would beat us

(less than nine-hundred) to the lunch or dinner queue, which meant the longest queues I'd ever stood in (though to be fair, they moved miraculously fast).

4. There'd be one whole day of compulsory fasting for everyone except the old and the sick. Until that point, the only kind of fasting I was familiar with involved skipping a meal on Good Friday (breakfast) or giving up something I liked.

5. While the centre was a massive expanse of gorgeous green land, in May of 1995 when we visited, there was barely any infrastructure yet, which meant sleeping in dormitories with no mattresses (though a kind soul had helped us find a small room) and toilets without seats (I remember making a serious attempt to hold it in for the week). The priest who ran the centre, whom I shall call Fr. Zen, apologised to us on Day 1 for the 'sub-human conditions'.

Fr. Zen was a small man but he had a large aura. I don't mean that in a new-age sense because I have no idea how to read auras. But there was that strange 'something' I couldn't put a finger on. His accent was a peculiar mix of Malayalam and American English, and when he preached the 'Woe-d of Gaaahhhd' I listened, transfixed. He was a relatively young priest, about forty at the time though he looked much younger—clearly too young to be enlightened so why did his face seem lit from within?

But the day got going and I stopped wondering about the priest's aura because we had finally got to the part we most dreaded: being asked to lift our hands to heaven and praise the lord out loud. Thankfully, we weren't the only ones who had trouble engaging with this. Most of the eight-hundred-something people gathered in this small space for the English retreat seemed to be charismatic virgins too and equally self-conscious. I particularly recall a group of cute college boys who looked like a boy band. Those of us who didn't get to the hall early enough didn't have seats so we sat on the stairs leading up to the hall on the first floor, hidden from the preacher's view. The boy band sat with us there on the first couple of days singing that Boyz II Men song ('I Swear,' was it?) that used to play on a loop at the time. It was good to know that there were others here who felt trapped like I did.

My joy was short-lived because very soon, another Mallu gentleman with the blackest beard I had ever seen, stepped on to the stage and started playing his keyboard, drowning out the boy band's a cappella. He invited everyone to clap and join in as he burst into a song that seemed too vibrant and celebratory to be a gospel song (in Catholicism Lite, we only sang sleepy hymns that were at least a hundred years old and accompanied by an organ so this was a little too-cool-for-school for me).

Black Beard had a deep voice that was nice enough but he was no James Hetfield, and he sang in English with a thick Mallu accent (sacrilege, in my thirteen-year-old universe) and yet there was that mysterious 'something' again because by Day 3, we were all clapping and singing along. They called this the anointing of the Holy Spirit—it wasn't about talent or skill but the presence of God moving through a person.

The retreat was divided into praise and worship (music), talks on the word of God and the key aspects of the Catholic faith (love, forgiveness, sacrifice, repentance, surrender, faith etc.), testimonies (where people from all backgrounds and faiths shared their respective Road to Damascus stories), and mass.

On Day 3, just as we were warming up to Black Beard, another musician took the stage. Unlike Black Beard, this one was a legit musician who had been the lead singer of a legit Indian rock band so we couldn't tell how much was talent and how much was the anointing, but every young person in the room was riveted. He shared the story of his personal experience of Christ at this very retreat centre, the visions he started seeing, and how he heard the call to serve God and eventually chopped off his long hair, quit the band and decided to become a full-time gospel musician. His talk also suggested that I must be wary of rock music. I was moved by Rockman's story and I wanted the God experience he had had, but this last bit made me feel unsettled because I loved my rock music; it had got me through so much and the idea that it could be bad for me just didn't sit right. Also, I had come here with a lot of expectations and while it had been interesting so far, this wasn't going to cut it. Where were the miracles we had heard so much about?

By Day 4, we were all quite used to hearing people break into tongues (as in the Acts of the Apostles where the Spirit of God descended upon the disciples as tongues of fire and everyone spoke in strange languages). This was freaky at first and I was skeptical because no two tongues sounded the same so you could basically make up your own language and call it the Spirit. But then it happened that someone—I don't recall who—started praying and singing in tongues as we worshipped and it was the most enchanting, other-worldly sound. It wasn't just a few random syllables either, but a whole language and as these canticles in strange languages continued, Fr. Zen—arms wide open and body swaying ever so gently (as was his style)—called out random names from the crowd and proceeded to deliver a message to each one of them from God.

Had he memorised our names from the registration forms? Even so, how could he know someone's specific situation, confirmed by that person sobbing uncontrollably? Granted, some of these messages were generic and some, Bible verses. But there were plenty of specific ones on the lines of, 'Cynthia, you have felt abandoned by your birth parents all your life and now you're being given the grace to forgive them. As you do, the stomach ulcers and migraines you've been suffering from, since the age of ten, will be healed. The heat you feel on your head right now is the Spirit of God descending on you.' This was then followed by Cynthia breaking down somewhere in the crowd or even stepping up on stage later that night to share her experience. And since this was Day 4, Fr. Zen invariably called someone seated next to us or someone we had grown familiar with over the last few days, and I felt left out.

'Call my name, call my name, call my name,' I prayed. 'I know there are a lot of sick people here and I'm not sick, and my parents didn't give me up for adoption like Cynthia's but please God, call my name. Just once. I just need to know you can hear me.'

But God didn't call my name. Not that night anyway.

We had heard a lot about Days 5 and 6. Day 5 was Inner Healing and Day 6 was the Infilling of the Holy Spirit. In a sense, all the other days were softening us to become more receptive on these last two days. Inner healing was a lot like inner child healing in therapy that is quite commonly practiced today, but done in a concentrated way and in a group setting, accompanied by music, prayer, prophecy, 'Rhema' (the spoken word of God conveyed to an individual as in the example of Cynthia; this is different from 'Logos', the word of God as it appears in the scriptures).

I'm not sure what changed on this day. Maybe we *had* become receptive but I vividly remember the very first time I felt God—which, for me, is a word that sums up this Being that I can only describe as 'entirely Other'—enter a physical space that I was in. As the Being moved, the atmosphere felt charged with something that resembled an absurdly high voltage of electricity, and love with a capital L. I wept like I never had before as this Love penetrated what must have been my soul, and it felt as if I might physically die, if I was loved any more.

[I had always assumed that it was growing up on 90s romcoms that set me up for all the wrong expectations of love. But now, as I write this, I realise it wasn't Meg Ryan movies, Notting Hill *or Colin Firth, it was God. How was the love of a mortal man ever going to suffice after this?]*

I thought I was having a special visitation but when I opened my eyes, I could tell some version of this was happening to many people in the hall because they were also weeping from rapture like I was. Some of them were shaking, some laughing, some appeared to have fallen to the ground in a trance-like state and another, clapping gleefully like a toddler at the circus. I realised this was precisely the kind of thing that would have seemed batshit crazy to me earlier, but in this moment, it just made sense. What is the right response to a supernatural encounter anyway?

By Friday night, I'm not sure there was even one person among the eight-hundred-something of us who hadn't been moved in some way. The boy band had halos on their heads by now and their energy felt so different, as I'm sure mine did. There was a couple from a different religious background who had come seeking healing for the wife. I don't remember her specific condition but I want to say she had a tumour in her brain that had impaired her speech among other things. I do know that she couldn't speak and the husband had taken her everywhere. I remember the woman's face quite clearly. Her head was tonsured from a pilgrimage somewhere and her face was the colour of turmeric. On Friday night, as we gathered together one last time, this woman was not just speaking, she was singing along with us as tears streamed down the husband's face. I even remember the song:

Listen, let your heart keep seeking
Listen, to His constant speaking
Listen, to the Spirit calling you.

I don't know if her tumour had shrunk like the many people who had shared stories of their miraculous healings from prior visits to the centre. I remember one boy from the Malayalam group that week, who said he was born with one leg significantly shorter than the other. In the one combined mass we had, this boy went up on stage to throw away his crutches and tearfully share the story of how his leg basically grew that week. Now, I had not seen his leg before but it didn't really matter. By then, I was saturated with miracles and while that was what I had come here seeking, it wasn't what I was carrying back with me.

In the end, it didn't matter how God had shown up for someone else. And as much as I wanted a more theatrical experience of God like most people seemed to be having—tongues, seeing visions, being able to prophesy, feeling a flame of fire on their head etc.—what I received that week was more than I could hold in my thirteen-year-old consciousness.

The Infilling of the Holy Spirit was the crescendo of the retreat but my crescendo already happened the night before. I had already been a receptacle for Love in a freakishly high voltage, so how much more could I possibly take? It suddenly made sense why Moses was asked to hide in the cleft of the rock when God passed him by. Or why in the Old Testament, God always showed up as a cloud, wind or fire. Not because he was trying to be mysterious but because a human being cannot survive seeing God; or as I would learn more than two decades later in my Jungian Studies: the individual ego cannot contain archetypal energy in its fullness without being annihilated.

The last night of the retreat was in many ways similar to the previous night in terms of the electricity, the miracles, the healing and the supernatural charge in the atmosphere but I wasn't waiting in expectation for something to happen. The something I had already received would take years to unpack and understand. So you can imagine my surprise and delight when on the last night, Fr. Zen called my name when he was relaying messages from God.

'Judy, I have called you by your name. You are mine. You are precious to me.'

The message was a Bible verse (Isaiah 43:1) and I could've brushed it off as too generic. Also, it was quite likely that there were more Judys in the room. But as I recalled, this is exactly what I prayed for—'Call my name, call my name, call my name. I know there are a lot of sick people here and I'm not sick, and my parents didn't give me up for adoption like Cynthia's but please God, call my name. Just once. I just need to know you can hear me.'

I wept when it was time to leave. 'We can always come back another time,' my mom said.

'But it won't be with the same people,' I sniffed. I had an awful habit of forming strong emotional attachments to people in a short period of time, but that wasn't what I was crying about. My real problem was a bit more complex: Now that I had witnessed the extraordinary—the magical, the supernatural— that I had been aching for all my life, how was I supposed to go back? How does one transition from this state of consciousness back to caring about school, boys, gossip and TV shows?

Again, there were no instruction manuals.

3

That Thin Line between Madness and Mysticism

'The psychotic drowns in the same waters in which the mystic swims with delight.'

—Joseph Campbell

In the years that followed, I returned to the retreat centre several times (and promptly showed up to the three-day retreats they held in my city) not unlike a drug addict, perennially in search of his next high. I wanted God to show up in my room in the same way he had shown up at the retreat but he didn't. I missed the goosebumps, the electricity and the undeniable sense of this wondrous, magnificent Being so close to me, but there was nothing. I was told this God cared about having a relationship with me but so far, he had only come across as a rockstar who needed an audience in order to make an appearance.

We were warned about this at the retreat; that while the sensational aspect of the experience was wonderful and even necessary at the beginning, this was about initiating a lifelong relationship with the Divine. And any real relationship takes time and effort to build, and is never all thunder and lightning. I didn't appreciate this. Why couldn't it be all thunder and lightning? The way I saw it, if you took the thunder and lightning out of the equation, then communing with God basically looked like psychosis: It was just me in my room, talking to myself. This felt pointless and uninspiring, not to mention, boring. What made anyone—of any faith—want to talk to God at all, if they weren't actually expecting God to talk back? How was this even normal?

I had a richly textured emotional life as a teen, and I felt the full gamut of feelings that went with this experience of longing for, and being denied an audience with God. If you think being ghosted by some guy you hooked up with a few times is painful and humiliating, I want you to imagine what it must be like to fall in love with someone with everything you've got, trust that they're all in too as they said they were, and then randomly get ghosted by them for so long that you wonder if any of it was real. *Then,* I want you to multiply that feeling by 100000000000 and you may still only scratch the surface of God ghosting.

I am of course, speaking for my melodramatic teen self here but suddenly it's obvious why I've had such a frustrating level of tolerance for the crap people pull in romantic love. In other words, I may have just stumbled on the answer to the question that's been echoed back to me several times by concerned friends through my teens, twenties and early thirties 'How can you let him yank you around like this?'

I may have felt yanked around by God but I couldn't replace him, as I found after much searching and heartbreak. So for several years, I swung between the polarities of my own psyche, though at the time, the only language I had for this was God and the devil. I felt a profound sense of disquiet with this clear and definitive line that my faith drew for me between the sacred and the profane, leaving no room for life's ambiguities. But I dismissed it because I was led to believe that even questioning the line was a sin and separated me from God.

This went against all logic of course, because the Being that I experienced as God, was beyond my capacity to fathom, let alone distil into any clear definitions. All I knew was that it was 'wholly Other' and 'wholly Love'—meaning, there was no frame of reference, none at all. I also knew that that was my specific experience and others described it differently. So I figured maybe this numinous Being allowed glimpses into different aspects of its nature to different people, and they were all valid even when they apparently contradict each other because by definition, it was beyond any finite comprehension.

So to me, the only thing that really felt wrong, arrogant and 'sinful', was any attempt to speak for this Being on what was sinful and what wasn't. But while I couldn't see eye to eye with the church on most matters, it was still through the church that I had even had this life-changing encounter, so maybe I was wrong and they were right.

This tension between the black or white God I was taught to please, and the Being I *knew* was beyond such duality, was impossible to hold within (not that I had read Jung back then to even know that I was supposed to hold it). So I swung from one extreme to the other; embracing one while rejecting the other. When I got back from a retreat, I was Team Black or White God so I was lopsidedly 'good'. Like pray-at-all-times-turn-the-other-cheek-will-myself-into-asexuality good. I then became unconsciously inflated from all this 'goodness', which invariably showed up as a holier-than-thou attitude that made me disconnected from people and by extension, my humanity. While I was insufferably kind, forgiving and generous (as I was expected to be), I compensated by turning into a judgemental bitch with impossible moral standards.

Evil, meanwhile, became a powerful hook—both for my fascination with the dark and mysterious, as well as my need for a larger-than-life purpose. With the devil as my nemesis, life was anything but ordinary. My peers were preoccupied with what they wanted to do in college, while I was poring over books on spiritual warfare—hardcore fasting, intercession, exorcism etc. Needless to say, this made me very difficult for most people to relate to. But it didn't matter because we, the Chosen Few, were like Dumbledore's Army. While most young people my age were busy doing young people things like exploring their sexuality and using fake IDs to sneak into pubs, I was busy training to take down powers and principalities in the invisible realms.

When the high wore off as it invariably did, I was once again in touch with my human needs and longings, but they were far more amplified and compulsive, thanks to prolonged periods of repression. So I swung to the other extreme, often giving into things that were previously wrong, sinful or taboo. I felt deprived of a chance at a normal life because this early experience of God seemed to have hijacked my teen years, so I unconsciously compensated by holding on to those years well into my twenties.

But even as I wrestled with the need to rebel against Black or White God and judged myself harshly when I did, something else had changed: My view of the sacred softened, and the lines between sacred and profane started to blur. I could connect with people again thanks to my full participation in the human experience, and my willingness to be broken by it; my friendships thrived and I enjoyed being in *this* world. In these phases, I couldn't bear to be around 'the charismatic prayer group type'. As if I hadn't been one of them just a while ago. And not just any one of them but the most zealous of them. They, in turn, saw me as the prodigal daughter and I suspect, prayed for my return. I usually kept my participation in this movement under wraps because I couldn't explain it, and it embarrassed me. Suddenly I was the one who favoured normalcy over the extraordinary.

But participating in the human experience without the Divine, meant quite a bit of suffering and no electricity-charged cloud to seek refuge in. And the way I saw it, it was an either-or, and I had chosen my humanity.

But as fate—or what I now understand as my own complexes—would have it, in the August 0f 2001, when I was in the final year of college, there was a three-day retreat happening at my college, and it was compulsory for Catholic students to attend. I knew the preacher who was going to be leading it; I used to love his talks on spiritual warfare. He had basically been my favourite Defence Against the Dark Arts teacher. I knew the couple who was going to be leading praise and worship as well. I had been a huge fan of the singer—her voice and general charisma. But it had been so long since I was in that world, and I felt ambivalent about revisiting it. This time, I was going with my closest friends, two of whom came from non-Catholic backgrounds (so they were under no obligation to attend) but wanted to go. I suppose we had all been searching for a spiritual anchor in our own way, and having been through everything else together—separating our own values from those that were our parents', the boys, the heartbreaks, the hopes and dreams—we decided to do this together too.

I don't recall the details of the three days but I remember my friends being deeply moved. Thank god they were, because I was once again jolted out of blissful normalcy—this time, with visions and 'messages' about things I couldn't possibly know—about the future, what was going on behind the scenes, and even other people's lives (in the same way that Fr. Zen and so many others had). I had spent years asking for these very 'gifts' and a more sensory experience of God but it hadn't happened. This time, I was protective of the normal life I had built so I didn't want the thunder and lightning to disrupt it, and yet here it was.

I want to be clear: I did not experience these gifts as a burden then. Not consciously anyway. I fully embraced them because they were a direct line to the Divine and this way, I didn't ever have to be separated from the Magnificent Being again (spoiler: wrong).

This sudden upgrade to oracular status fetched me a fair share of attention which I pretended not to enjoy (because it would be so wrong to hijack God's glory *gasp*). My spirituality had always relied heavily on the sensational which meant that it lacked any real roots to survive life's uncertainties and hardships. Of course I didn't know this then. I had assumed that I was given these gifts because I had made some kind of spiritual progress. Like a video game where I could collect super powers for reaching a particular level. Except they were rightly called 'gifts' and not 'rewards' so they were random (or so it seemed), unearned and had nothing whatsoever, to do with me. And as is often the case with good things that come easily or when one is not ready, I handled it recklessly and it harmed me more than anyone else.

For starters, I assumed that any 'message' I received was the infallible word of God and questioning it was lacking faith.* My trust in what I received was sincere and to be fair, I had a pretty good track record. I couldn't possibly go into every vision and message I received during this phase because a) I didn't document everything b) many were generic/Bible verses so maybe I imagined them, and c) it is not relevant to this story.

But I do want to mention a couple of experiences that have stayed with me through the years; long after I pledged total

---

*I had struggled with trusting these messages and visions initially but after a number of them turned out to be spot on—both in relation to me and others—I decided to go all in.

allegiance to the rational mind, decided to tear out the chapters of my life that involved this mortifying character arc, and dump them in some desolate part of my psyche so I'd never have to deal with them again (aka the definition of psychological ignorance).

God Hijacks My Career Plans with a Prophecy

As graduation day drew closer, my friends were all busy sending in their applications to the finest colleges in India and abroad. Those who didn't care for a master's degree, seemed to have a solid career plan that didn't require it at the time. Meanwhile, I was in the throes of my mystical union with God, and completely dissociated from these earthly pursuits. I couldn't see the point of it all. With no exaggeration, it felt as if Voldemort was at large, and instead of letting me get up to speed on the horcruxes, my dad was busy persuading me to do my master's. I had said no but I needed to have a plan and I didn't. So I took this up with God who promptly gave me a vision. I saw the number 21 with a crown over it. I don't recall the exact words but I was told that by my 21st birthday, I would be in ministry; which meant I'd be doing what these people at the retreats did, except I was terrified of the stage and while I could sing, I was not a singer. There were other roles too, but none that caught my attention and at the time, it didn't matter. I was overjoyed; I didn't have to be separated from God again by pointless academics. And I had heard it from the horse's mouth! Now everyone had to shut up. Except they didn't because they were understandably concerned that I was making big life decisions based on these visions. Besides, time was running out. If I was going to do my master's, I needed to start applying yesterday. So I went to God again, not because I couldn't trust the vision but because I felt pressured by everyone's anxiety—including fellow charismatics who feared I was going a bit overboard with this. This time, I got a clear instruction. 'Wait; do nothing for three months.' But now my friends and family had more questions. 'Where would you go for this ministry?' 'Who would you go with?' 'Do you know anyone at all?' 'What would you even do?' I told them I had no answers but that I trusted what I was given. Some admired my faith and were curious to see what might happen, but most were just worried that I had completely lost it. As time went by, I felt restless too. There was no sign of any ministry yet and I felt the first pangs of anxiety. When I asked God about this again, I didn't receive any more messages or visions or signs. It was almost as if he was offended by my lack of trust.

About two and a half months into my wait, a preacher from Secunderabad I had never heard of, along with two of his protégés, were in Chennai for a retreat they were facilitating. My brother had known one of the protégés from a retreat he had attended at the centre several years ago, but had never met the preacher. So he invited them over for lunch and it just so happened that we all hit it off instantly. While they too subscribed to the Catholic Charismatic brand of spirituality, their vibe was noticeably different. They were far more grounded, fun, irreverent even. They effortlessly switched between spiritual warfare and jokes about spiritual warfare. They were still interested in watching movies, going to places, meeting people, having hobbies, spending time with their friends and they were always laughing. This was oddly soothing for me because I had been frighteningly intense and one-dimensional about my spirituality so far. It was all or nothing, and this felt like...permission. They were only here for a day; that afternoon, after lunch, as we were all gathered together in the living room, joking around and singing new gospel songs, this preacher whom I shall call Toronto, suddenly looked me in the eye and said, 'Beta, what are you doing right now? Are you in college or working?' I said, 'Nothing. I just finished college and...' I didn't get to finish. 'You're coming with us on ministry for the next trip. Be ready.'

A collective gasp swept through the living room because everyone in the group except Toronto and his protégés, knew about my ministry prophecy.

I turned 21 on September 2nd, 2002. We left for my first ministry trip with the group to Calcutta, on September 3rd, 2002 (yes, we went the day *after* I turned 21, not before but I didn't feel like giving God grief over that technical error).

Over the years, for what seemed like good reasons then, I went to great lengths to reject and disown my mystical experiences along with church teachings I simply couldn't accept. But even in the face of blind denial, this piece has remained; quietly challenging me to explain it rationally.

The Diabolical Presence

I want to tell you about one more experience from this time that has stayed with me (among others) despite my best efforts to explain it, deny it and turn away from it.

It was about seven in the evening, and I was in the living room of my parents' old house, praying the rosary. My parents were in the bedroom to my right and there was no one else in the house. I faced the dining room from where I sat and the dining area led to the kitchen on the left, which had a small sit-out area attached to it. The entrance to the house was to my left in the living room and the door was wide open. As I prayed the rosary, I received a 'message' instructing me to close my eyes quickly. After which, the impression I received was that some form of evil was about to 'pass through' in a physical way and I wouldn't be able to handle it if I were to see it. My instinct was to close my eyes immediately as instructed and wrap my fingers tightly around the rosary because the impression had come suddenly and urgently and there was no time to process. In almost the same instant, I heard the sound of footsteps approaching from the kitchen (it was coming from the door that led to the sit-out area); it got louder as it got closer, making its way through the dining, and to my left in the living room, and out the front door. It happened so quickly, almost as if this being was in more of a hurry to get away from me; but as I sat there, heart pounding, the hair on my neck bristling, eyes shut and fingers clutching the rosary, I knew I had to re-think my interest in spiritual warfare. And though it only lasted a few seconds, I felt this presence almost as palpably as I had first experienced the Being at the retreat centre; and I can only describe it as the embodiment of all that was evil.

Now this story by itself can be quite easily dismissed as a psychotic episode if one is looking for a rational explanation as I was, within a few years. In fact, I was so desperate for normalcy that I was more than willing to be diagnosed with a psychotic disorder if it meant none of this was 'real'. But it wasn't a psychotic episode as you'll probably agree in a minute when I tell you what happened next.

As I heard the eerie presence exit through the front door, I received an impression again that it was safe to open my eyes. Except I couldn't. I wanted to run to my parents in the room right next to me but I sat there frozen; and then the phone rang, making me jump. Eyes still closed, I reached for the phone. It was a fellow unhinged charismatic friend who prayed with me on an almost daily basis. She'd come over, we'd have our own praise and worship at home, intercede for others, for the world, exchange visions and prophecies and what not. If I was out of balance, she was at least ten times worse but as I mentioned before, the accuracy of these 'gifts' seemed to have nothing to do with one's spiritual maturity, capacity for discernment or even character development.

'What just happened there?' she demanded with the urgency and confidence of someone who had been right about these things so many times before.

'Oh my god,' I felt my voice shake as relief swept over me; relief that I wasn't in fact losing it but something had actually happened. 'I'll tell you, but you tell me what you know first,' I said. I needed her to spell it out for me.

'I was told that you were going to have a personal experience of evil and to call you immediately,' came the response.

I am going to leave these fragments here with you as inconclusively as they left me; till about thirteen years later, I stumbled on the story of the famous Swiss psychiatrist, who had also been curious about the paranormal from a young age because of visions and dreams he couldn't explain; thought he was having a psychotic breakdown in his thirties but instead, it ended up being his initiation into the mysteries of the 'collective unconscious'—which would go on to become one of his unique contributions to depth psychology.

But more on Jung later. For now, I want to depart from the world of mystical madness, to a more widely relatable form of madness—human love; specifically, what the Greeks called Eros.

4

Tension of the Opposites

Before we go into the subject of romantic love, I must mention just how many levels of sexual repression I was born into so you have context. There was the Indian level, Tamilian level, middle class level and Catholic level. And as the ordained black sheep of a large close-knit family, I was psychologically set up to have strong reactions to this. So, when satellite television made its way into India in the early 90s and my wide-eyed tween self got a window into teen life in America, I felt mad with betrayal. These kids were only a couple of years older than I was, and they were not only partying, dating and wearing shorts to school, they were *gasp* having sex, while we hadn't even got to the sex part in our biology class. Also I went to an all-girls convent, while kids on the other side of the world were actually sharing a classroom with the likes of Jason Priestley and Luke Perry and living the 90210 life. Oh, and the parents—they seemed quite happy to send their teens off on dates while the very mention of a boy's name at home might have got me in trouble for weeks. Where was the justice!

This east-west dichotomy not only angered and frustrated my raging hormones, it confused me. The way I saw it, America's response to adolescence was to openly acknowledge it as the rite of passage that it was and do their best to go with it, while

India chose to be in denial about it. The idea that any form of physical intimacy prior to marriage was dirty and shameful was repeatedly reinforced, while nobody batted an eyelid about marrying complete strangers for societal approval, and having sex and babies with them right after. I may have only been twelve, but based on the two views I was exposed to, I instinctively chose Team America. This set me up for a long and arduous battle, not only with my family and larger cultural background but, unbeknown to me, the parts of myself that sprung from this background.

Again, all I was asking for, was a logical explanation for why things were the way they were. And if there were none, I could've made my peace with, 'Hmm...I'm not sure, but let's find out together.' Instead my questions, which, to be fair, got lost in teen tantrums, were met with non-answers on the lines of 'because that is their culture and this is ours'. This only infuriated me because unlike my family and so many of my peers, I had no natural loyalties or sympathies for my own culture. I just wanted some well-argued principles to live by that would help me make sense of myself and my very complicated pre-teen life. It didn't matter who or where it came from. It just had to make sense. So the whole idea of communal pride just made me want to bang my head against a wall.

If my family had been as unloving as they had been illogical, I may have suffered much less conflict over my choices. I may have walked out of home and never looked back like so many people I later met. But I was deeply loved even as aspects of my inherent nature were deeply rejected.

So I acted under an inner compulsion to rebel against everything that came with a Tamilian/Indian/middle class/Catholic tag (often throwing out the baby with the bathwater), and I suffered acute guilt, pain and shame over those very choices.

This battle that started to erupt in the mid 90s, continued well into the late 2000s, culminating in a marriage and divorce that wrecked my peace of mind for a good long time. But more importantly, it made me face an important question: How the hell did I go into this marriage when literally every person who knew me expressed serious discomfort over my decision? What had made me so blind? It wasn't quite love because my instincts clawed at my insides the entire time—from the moment I said yes, all the way down to the aisle—in the form of nightmares when asleep, and as hyper-vigilance when awake. But I dismissed them because after all that I had been through with signs and messages from God, I wasn't about to trust another thing that was not backed by solid facts.

I must pause here and go back to the events that led to this Big Fallout with God, which directly influenced this decision (and the subsequent hyper-rational phase). Between 1995 and 2001 (the years that marked my on-again-off-again dynamic with God), I was two people: the mad mystic who wanted nothing more than constant communion with the electricity-charged cloud that was God; and the teen who felt cheated out of the American teen life and rebelled against everything her family/cultural background stood for. Sometimes, these two people overlapped despite my best efforts to keep them compartmentalised, and I started to find in romantic love, a hook for my longing for transcendence and union.

So it wouldn't be an exaggeration to say that I was quite literally looking for divinity in the mortal men I fell in love with. You can imagine how this went. All that intensity that was directed into my relationship with God, now went into an ordinary human being. Except my longing for what I had once touched was so real, that I always looked past the ordinariness, into that tiny spark of divinity that lurked somewhere deep inside of him, and I latched onto it and magnified it until I couldn't see the rest of him. I then became so engulfed by this image of him (as opposed to the real him) that everything he actually was, felt like a personal betrayal.

And because this was a flesh and blood god that I could touch and hold, Eros became the container in which my two selves (mad mystic and American teen) could merge. Like an inverted fairytale, I'd kiss the prince and to my horror, he'd morph into a frog or a beast; which would wake me up from my enchanted sleep, so I could break up with him, only to do it all over again with another potential god. But I couldn't break the cycle because a) it takes a while of repetition before you create a pattern that you can recognise as problematic and b) this was the only thing that had even come close to that ecstatic mystical union I had once experienced and I couldn't imagine living without it.

So when I started seeing those visions and receiving impressions and 'messages' in 2001, I had already tasted this human love; which wasn't quite God (in the Christian sense that I had experienced) but 'divine' nonetheless, in its capacity to possess even otherwise rational humans with its longing, ecstasy, fear, madness and downright despair. And while I had promptly transferred all allegiance to God now that he was back again in my life, I hadn't quite forgotten what it had felt like to have a god I could see and touch. And so, one day, when someone (wrongly) interpreted a vision I had as a prophecy about the one true love of my life who was about to make an appearance real soon, I fell for it. And I fell so hard for it, there was no way this was going to end well.

I mean, I could have both God *and* a human love? And God himself was going to handpick him for me? The same God who had been right about so many concrete things in my life so far, including the ministry at age 21 and the run-in with the diabolical presence? What could possibly go wrong? This was peak arranged marriage. For all my seeming western-mindedness, I was unconsciously quite Indian—I may have been in love with Love but I also wanted guarantees.

Anyway. Before I knew it, this mysterious love became the whole focus of my conversations with God. The fact that God not only had no objection to this but totally indulged my questions should've struck me as suspicious, but I was too far gone. Soon, I had a whole dating profile for this man, along with a date on the calendar marked out for when I'd meet him. Again, there was no sign whatsoever that this could happen (you have to remember that it couldn't be just anyone, he had to fit the specifics of the profile *and* show up on the day). Again, the people around me were most concerned. But after having witnessed my last few prophecies come true, they didn't put up a fight. Not that it would've made any difference because I was sure this time. Surer than I had been all the other times because by now, my faith was on steroids. This was also much more high-stakes for me than everything else because there was nothing I wanted more than for my two selves to co-exist in peace.

D-day finally came and the anticipation reached a fever pitch. Morning turned to afternoon to evening and, nothing. Nothing happened. No one showed up. By bedtime, I was a complete wreck. If God did speak, I didn't hear a word anymore. This wasn't so much about being promised a fairytale love and then denied it; this was about everything I thought I was seeing and hearing for the last couple of months. If that was wrong, then everything had to be wrong. How could the same visions and messages be so impossibly, freakishly accurate all those other times and completely off the mark this time? Where were these visions even coming from? Who was it that was speaking to me?

Again, I was very open to calling this psychosis if it meant there was a way out. But that couldn't explain all those other times.

I felt angry, betrayed, confused, abandoned, ridiculed and terrified and all these feelings fused and blurred into one unbreakable resolve to never again trust *anything* that wasn't factual, concrete, solid, and provable. And so I did the closest thing I could to surgically remove this mystical part of my personality—I refused to engage with it, denied its existence both in me and in others and refused to trust anything (dreams, visions, impressions, hunches, gut feelings, intuition, synchronicity) that wasn't backed by facts and evidence.

So when I decided to get married and every person who knew me closely, expressed their concerns about it, I refused to listen unless said concerns were also backed by facts. And when friends and family gave up, my own instincts took over by day—I felt plagued with suspicion and hyper-vigilance though I was never known to have trust issues. But I brushed it off as my own 'issues'. By night, I had nightmares with recurring themes of being in danger and the urgent need to escape. But I ignored them all because I felt I'd rather die of this hypothetical danger than venture down that mystical path that I saw as certain (psychological) death.

I'm not going into the gory details of this marriage and divorce for the sake of everybody's mental health. But let's just say that the instincts, dreams and other people's intuitions were soon validated, and my situation got progressively worse until it started mirroring the themes of my earlier dreams. And though it only lasted three years, I couldn't help but feel the same sense of anger, betrayal, confusion, abandonment, ridicule and terror—only this time, with rational thinking. I had relied entirely on the factual this time and look what happened! What was I supposed to do now? How was I supposed to navigate my present circumstances if I couldn't understand how I got here? If I couldn't trust both the right (God, intuition, signs, dreams, visions, etc.) and left (facts, reason, logic) sides of my brain, how the hell was I supposed to survive this and more importantly, not repeat it?

5

Comedy as Healing
(and a Defence Against Feeling)

I was too numb to even be aware of my inner conflict, so instead of taxing the tangled ball of yarn that I apparently had for a brain, I sought refuge in comedy and writing. I had always been writing—in some form or the other—since I was a child but I had never taken it seriously enough to pronounce myself a writer. Back in the 90s when I was a teen, it meant something to be a writer. And since I didn't come from the kind of background that usually produced writers (we mass produced engineers and mathematicians, and it took gumption to even suggest that you wished to pursue the humanities in college), I didn't take myself too seriously when I started a blog. I was flat broke, so I couldn't afford most forms of distractions, and there was no Netflix at the time; and living through a period that would produce PTSD symptoms for the next decade and longer, which meant I couldn't even focus long enough to read.

So writing a blog seemed like the only form of amusement, catharsis and self-help I could afford and I dove headlong into it as a way of coping with my circumstances. But a curious thing happened as I started to write. Instead of sounding like the train wreck and colossal failure that I felt I was, the voice that emerged from the rock-bottom I found myself in, possessed an aliveness

I had never known before. It was light and decidedly un-rigid; honest, open, and most surprisingly, funny. I had never known myself to be funny until then. I was intense, high-strung and had no capacity to see the humour in difficult times.

And yet funny seemed to be the defining tone of this emerging voice. Suddenly, everything was funny; my swinging from one extreme to the other, my hyper-religious-weirdo phase, the hyper-rational phase, the wilful turning away from instincts, my completely unrealistic expectations of love, suffering at my own hands, even the symptoms that trauma produced, were strangely, darkly funny. This was profoundly liberating because once you metabolise your suffering and can get yourself to a place where you can laugh at it no matter how painful (you really have to find it funny though, you cannot fake this), it can no longer have power over you. And so I laughed at everything—societal norms, being a young divorcée in India (I was only twenty-seven), well-meaning relatives, single-parenting, unsolicited advice, but most of all, I laughed at myself. And everyone laughed with me because they saw themselves in my story. Soon the blog brought wonderful real people into my life and eventually, the idea to write a novel, which would go on to become a bestseller and at least temporarily, give me a fairy-tale turnaround.

And so like Narcissus, who had never seen his own reflection before, I gazed deeply into mine as it showed up in my writing, fell in love with this voice, and latched on to it as if I was nothing, if not funny.

And for years, I used comedy as a crutch to manage and often deny, my capacity to feel, and feel intensely. I think by now we all know enough pop psychology to acknowledge that we all carry unconscious beliefs and ideas that we inherit from the psychic pool of the families we spring from; and that they go on to influence our behaviour, sabotage our relationships and script our demise until we wake up and take responsibility for our own collusion with these unconscious forces.

And in the particular psychic pool that I come from, feelings (particularly the kind that produced tears) were generally not welcome. And while no one explicitly told me I wasn't allowed to have feelings as a child, it was repeatedly reinforced in the way everyone handled their own feelings and mine. So the general take-away for me, was that feelings were:

- icky
- uncomfortable
- embarrassing
- the enemy of peace and quiet
- caused drama
- something to be disowned
- something to be distracted
- something to be hidden

And the Freudian cliché that I was, I was almost exclusively attracted to men who reinforced these unconscious beliefs and generously topped it with some of their own. It went something like this. Feelings:

- made you 'crazy'
- manipulative
- too needy
- too clingy
- too suffocating
- too much

To be clear, I was definitely at least some of those things but I'm trying to establish my difficult relationship with the feeling function, and why I was compulsively drawn to those I was drawn to, and not to suggest that the men in question were cold, or anything but regular human beings with their own psychological baggage.

By the time I was in my thirties, I had learnt how to get a handle on my emotional intensity (for the most part) and comedy had everything to do with it. It felt good to come across as a 'chill person' for a change. So every time my feelings— which were always triggered by romantic involvements—got the better of me, I'd take it to my writing and let comedy work its healing magic in transmuting that suffering. I'd laugh, everyone would laugh, and suddenly, I didn't feel quite as unmoored. And I obviously didn't notice this as it happened, but instead of suffering my suffering and allowing comedy to bring me perspective at the right time as it originally had, I started to use it as a defence mechanism to short circuit the process and avoid the intolerable feelings altogether.

But during this period that I relied exclusively on writing and comedy, I was neither hyper-religious nor hyper-rational so all was well, or so I assumed. I also loved how sane and put-together I felt when I wasn't romantically involved with anyone, so I decided to take it up a notch and commit to quitting relationships altogether. I was thirty-three, and I knew I only had a few precious years before my daughter was going to have her own boy drama, and I felt this pressure to get this part of my life together before she got there.

I had been in and out of relationships since I was sixteen and I was ready to admit that I was somehow, despite my best intentions, getting this all wrong. For starters, I was stuck in a pattern I couldn't break. My specific pattern was an attraction to men who had the emotional bandwidth of a small rodent, and either couldn't or wouldn't commit. There was also a recurring theme of lies, betrayal and power struggles in varying degrees (from garden-variety gaslighting to full-blown violence) and all the comedy in the world couldn't distract from the fact that I simply didn't have the emotional endurance I once did. So quitting relationships to focus on my long-suffering career seemed like a logical first step in the right direction and I threw myself into my work in every way possible. The result was the most productive year I've ever had. All the energy that went into longing, waiting, needing, missing, fighting, arguing, making up, analysing, breaking up, analysing, having heart wrung out and cooked in high heat in my own tears till it reached noodle-like consistency...you get the picture, now went into work and I was unstoppable and life was good. Or at least it was drama-free.

6

Curiouser and Curiouser

So I'm not sure why, in the middle of one such drama-free day of that super-busy, drama-free year, I felt the need to ask my friend about that astrologer who had written that freakishly accurate forecast she had sent me years ago. While I had had a brief Linda Goodman phase in high-school (because I was always on the hunt for a system that could explain human nature), I had never been the type to read astrology forecasts even as entertainment. But this Susan Miller, as my friend had promised, had spooked me by the specificity of her predictions. I don't recall much now except that it was an annual forecast and I happened to read it towards the end of that year (2007? 2008? 2009?), when everything she had predicted had already played out. But impressed as I was, I hadn't followed up with Susan Miller or astrology until the end of 2014, following this vague curiosity that seemingly 'popped out of nowhere'. Vague curiosity soon turned into guilty pleasure as I lapped up Susan Miller's monthly reports even when they were way off point, because those occasional accurate predictions were still specific enough to have me hooked. But unlike most people who read these forecasts to find out how their month was going to turn out, I found myself drawn to dig deeper: What is a natal chart? What is the ascendant? What are conjunctions, squares, oppositions, trines and sextiles? Why do my life's biggest turning points coincide with eclipses in certain signs or transits of outer planets? Why is Jupiter entering a new sign such a cause for celebration? What is a stellium? What are houses in astrology? And finally, if so much could be gleaned from just knowing your sun sign (which is about 2% of a person's horoscope), what might a closer look at my natal chart with nine other heavenly bodies, reveal?

And then of course, one link led to another, and by the time I realised I was in the rabbit hole, more than two years had passed, my astrology book collection had spread from Kindle (where I kept it a secret) and onto my physical bookshelf (which it soon outgrew), and my entire worldview had undergone a massive reconstruction. I would also learn very soon that Carl Jung, the legendary psychiatrist and founder of analytical psychology, spent a great deal of his time studying astrology and had much to say about the 'psychological truth' that the natal chart pointed at. This was the closest thing to a scientific validation of astrology, which was extremely important to me at the time, given my baggage.

> *'My evenings are taken up very largely with astrology. I make horoscopic calculations in order to find a clue to the core of psychological truth. Some remarkable things have turned up which will certainly appear incredible to you.'*
>
> —C.G. Jung, in a letter to Sigmund Freud, 1911

But though I spent all my time poring over books and charts, it never once felt like I was learning astrology. To me, it was a language, and one that felt like my native tongue. It was as though I recognised it and 'remembered' it. I realise this sounds woo-woo but it's just how I felt. It moved me profoundly and made me feel seen in my entirety as no system, person, theory or religion, ever had. Suddenly, my whole life made sense through the lens of my natal chart (more about what a natal chart is, later). It put everything in context—the good, the bad, the befuddling, everything!

Predictive astrology—which is a broad term for a number of astrological techniques that focus on the 'what's going on in the here and now, and later' question—added to the fascination. Because now I could look back on the key events and periods of my life through the lens of predictive astrology, and get—not a friend's perspective, a family member's advice or a shrink's analysis but—COSMIC COMMENTARY on the meaning of that time and event, what it was trying to accomplish in me, how I could have responded to it and so on. How utterly, insanely cool!

I then dug out the charts of family members, friends and ex boyfriends to understand relational dynamics and interpersonal conflicts. And then looked up key events from *their* lives and like I said, before I realised it, more than two years had passed. Of the many ways astrology moved me in those early days, these in particular, stand out:

1. Astrology consistently blew my mind with its accurate symbolic portrayals of the multiplicity within a person's psyche. We like to think of ourselves in the singular—a definitive 'I'—but the 'I' I saw reflected back to me by my natal chart was a richly textured plurality with all its cracks, holes and contradictions that I had spent so much of my life grappling with. It not only gave me a vocabulary for the aspects of myself I couldn't get a handle on, it was in every sense, the map of individual nature and destiny I had always wished existed.

2. I had always believed that we all have our unique paths and by extension, individual timelines but astrology

became proof of that. So this whole idea that you must accomplish something by a certain age or even comparing ourselves to others, just made no sense. While there are certain astrological cycles common to us all (meaning, we all go through them at a particular age), the rest is entirely individual as dictated by the individual patterns in our charts. It is one thing to believe, and quite another thing to actually know and thanks to astrology, I could 'see' that we're not all headed in the same direction, so why assume we have to take the same route?

3. I remember reading somewhere that there comes a moment when you're looking at a person's natal chart, when your eyes get drawn to one or two specific points that make you go 'how do you live with that?' It's true. Every chart, without exception, has this. Which brings me to my point about how astrology made me a lot more empathetic than I was before.

4. While for most people, prediction is synonymous with astrology, I found that astrology was actually an excellent way to stay in, and make the best of the present, by understanding the meaning of the time I was in and the particular cosmic currents I was navigating.

5. I'm the kind of person who needs to understand how things work in order to feel safe. It's a coping mechanism. If my child or dog is sick, I want to know everything there is to know about the illness so I can be prepared. If I have PTSD, I want to research trauma thoroughly from every possible angle so I know what I'm dealing with. If I love you, I want to know you in and out so that when that moment invariably comes when you start unleashing your demons at me, I'd like to be able to have a sense

of humour about them, instead of retaliating or running scared. Having an in-depth understanding of the things and people that matter to me is central to managing my own sanity. So you can see how astrology also quickly became a defence against the seeming randomness of the cosmos. I know I cannot control life or what happens to me, but if I can understand it, then I can find meaning in it. And meaning can go a long way in helping me relate to, and manage my suffering.

She Had Me At 'Complexes as a Psychological Model of Fate'

But even as staggeringly insightful and mind-altering as astrology was, I couldn't shake off the feeling that something was missing. Now that I knew why I was the way that I was, what was I supposed to do with it? And if I could do nothing and this was all set in stone, then what was the point of all this? I mean, why even study astrology? Some of the traditional approaches to astrology (both in the Vedic system as well the Western traditions) involved 'remedies' for 'malefic' planets and transits but at an intuitive level, this didn't sit right with me. So I kept looking until I found Liz Greene, astrologer, psychologist and Jungian analyst, and one of the pioneers in Psychological Astrology (which is a synthesis of astrology and depth psychology, specifically analytical or Jungian psychology).

You know that feeling when you've gone years looking for something but didn't know what it was and then finally found it? For me, it was Liz Greene's entire body of work. Her scholarly voice soothed my specific anxieties—'What if this whole thing is woo-woo and I just can't see it?' 'This is all great but I would feel a lot safer if there was some scientific basis or empirical evidence to back it up' etc.—and introduced me to the next phase of my astro-journey: Jungian Psychology.

All this obviously meant that keeping astrology a secret was no longer an option. I was going to have to 'come out' to my super-Catholic family and my hyper-rational friends.

Fuuuuuuuuuccccckkkkk.

This was going to be even more exhausting and isolating than the evangelical phase (when I could at least lean on fellow unhinged religious people) and the divorce phase (when I was supported by friends whose lives had also been derailed by bad decisions or tragedy or both, and felt the need to act out). But as much as I was in love with astrology, I couldn't see how it fit into my personality. Because, thanks to American pop-culture, I had this distinct image of 'the kind of people who like astrology and tarot'—the kind that said things like 'we live in a friendly universe' in that shrill voice and sent you love, light and good vibes instead of real birthday presents—and it just made me so *uncomfortable.*

But even as I was wrestling with my need to openly embrace my strong feelings about astrology and the need to keep my world from spiralling into chaos, the universe thought it would be hilarious to introduce a romance sub-plot (read emotional crisis) at this inconvenient time. Especially given how recently I had sworn off relationships and regained my equilibrium.

The One that Led Me to Jung

In every obvious way, he was different from my type (my type being exciting, mentally stimulating and emotionally stunted with no respect for boundaries) so I didn't see it coming. But then again, I had major uranus transits and progressions at the time and 'didn't see it coming' is sort of textbook uranus. Had I been less caught up in the intense and confusing feelings this person stirred up in me, I may have noticed that I also had some heavy-duty pluto and neptune transits as well as eclipses coming up, but I missed them all. Not that I could've helped myself under such unrelenting cosmic weather because one look at my chart at the time and any astrologer would've gone 'Ohhh, HONEY.'

From Day 1, I felt an effortless, instinctive closeness with him that I couldn't explain, especially given that he was not my type. I mean, he possessed an emotional depth that was always palpable even when so far away, and carefully tucked under a *brightsunshiny* persona. In my experience, emotional depth was in itself hard to come by but especially so in people who presented as hyper-rational, witty and relatively social. But if that combination was rare enough, he also had strong boundaries (gasp) and was respectful of my own boundaries (what sorcery!) and possessed a dignified air and this old-world charm that I wholly adored in the specific way I had adored Jane Austen novels as a girl.

The fact that he somehow always saw the best in me and generously overlooked my annoying traits (which are many), only made the instinctive attachment stronger, and the Austen feelings louder; and like most people in this phase of attraction, I fell partly (and narcissistically) in love with the version of myself I could only see through his eyes. But most of all, he didn't scare easily and had a surprising tolerance for my own emotional range, which I found super attractive.

BUT. While *he* was different, the pattern was much the same. He was in a 'complicated situation' and needed time to 'figure things out' which meant that we couldn't really be together. There were other reasons too, I just couldn't see it at the time. And the fact that he could, obviously made me feel short-changed and not wanted enough. I should've recognised by now that this feeling was usually the password that woke up my specific demons and it did.

And out came insecurity, jealousy, obsession, fear of abandonment, anxiety, insatiable emotional hunger and as if these weren't a handful, there was also shame. Shame was different. He was always the plus one. So, every time I gave in to one or more of the others, he'd just let himself in and bash me up for falling so short of all my values; which, by the way, was this overwhelming need to be balanced, rational, reasonable and put-together with zero tolerance for excessive emotionality and all this dark, primal stuff, until I was reduced to a puddle of powerlessness and self-loathing.

Now I was very familiar with all these demons and their whole routine through the last two decades of being in and out of relationships. But I had always chalked that down to the old toxic type. I mean if you're in a relationship with a narcissist, then maybe that has something to do with why you feel like shit all the time.

But this one had given me no reason to feel threatened and yet here I was.

There was a concerning level of compulsion, attachment and emotional fusion in the dynamic (which was mutual, though I experienced it at a much higher degree) that made me constantly aware of his presence in the absence. And all this amplified by sexual tension. I should probably mention at this point that this 'relationship' was entirely digital. For almost a year, before we met in person, it felt like we were always connected by some invisible electrical cord and I could tell every time the connection was interrupted. This was a lot, and in some ways more unsettling than those mystical experiences from all those years ago because I had no frame of reference for this level of fusion with an actual person. I felt like a psychic sponge, absorbing feelings, moods and fleeting thoughts that were not my own (and that I concluded were his) and I felt unmoored as I felt my boundaries dissolve without my conscious volition. For the most part, I kept these experiences to myself or let him in only partially, because while he knew I was somewhat batty, I didn't want him to find out just how much. But anytime I did let him see me in the throes of these cycles of need and anguish, he always responded with love, and even had a way of lulling shame into a temporary comatose.

In retrospect, it feels like a nightmare in the making that we actually decided to meet because our dynamic had all the ingredients of a volcano waiting to erupt. And as the needy one in the equation, I obviously had a lot more to lose.

I was understandably nervous because meeting someone you already have such an all-consuming connection with, is likely to be a let-down. It's just a lot of pressure to stack up to the version of yourself in the other person's imagination. How do you compete with that? And yet, incredibly, it exceeded all our expectations and any sense of self I still had left was completely dissolved in those 20-something hours that we spent together. Love was declared and promises were made. And by now, the rational part of my brain had been off its game for so long that I didn't realise that said promises were made in an oxytocin rush (astrologer note: it was also mercury retrograde).

Fast forward to six months later: Everything was exactly as it was before we met. We hadn't met again and there were no discussions on meeting again, and yet he wasn't avoiding me or shutting me out or growing emotionally distant. I was confused and wanted an explanation as was my right; an explanation that I probably would've got had I been in any position to have a conversation. But I was also unravelling because you know that 'I' at the centre of the personality that we all rely on, in order to be functional? I had completely lost that. My 'I' was swallowed whole in the oceanic oneness that was 'Us' and while it seemed as though I was crying out for him, I was actually just crying out for my own lost centre. The fact that he was so self-contained only made it worse. As if my 'I' had dissolved into a gazillion granules that had been absorbed by his 'I' and the only way I could get in touch with myself was by fixating on him.

I felt robbed, untethered and entirely undone. And when I called him that night, I probably sounded like it. And for the first time, this guy who had repeatedly assured me that intense feelings were nothing to be ashamed of, suddenly seemed to have changed his mind. It wasn't so much what he said because I remember it being a very short conversation. But I felt him recoil from me as if he couldn't stand to be around what I had become. This was not an unreasonable response given the state I was in. But if you remember my difficult history with feelings and how, only recently (and thanks to him), I stopped hiding behind comedy and let myself be seen in these 'uglier' moments, you can see why this rejection felt like death. To me, there was a finality about it that nothing could undo because it wasn't about him. It was about the gradual effacing of my 'I' over nineteen years of emotionally charged romantic involvements. And all this particular relationship did was create enough psychic impact for what remained of the 'I' to be blown to smithereens.

Rabbit Hole: Part Deux

And this is the thing about rock bottoms: you don't get to choose when you've hit yours. I thought I had hit it when I swore off relationships but the fact that I was making an informed decision meant that the 'I' was still in charge and I hadn't reached the end of myself. But this one had to be it because now my consuming need was not for him to fix me, but to get to the bottom of my patterns so I could find the wholeness I was looking for, within. Also, I had been through some legitimately traumatising experiences in past relationships and I had somehow bounced back from them quite quickly. Why did this one, the nicest of anyone I had been with, and the one I had spent less than 24 hours with, hit me so hard? And how could *one* conversation be the thing that tipped me over the edge and make me emotionally freeze when he had been consistently good to me? Was he not allowed to run out of patience or have a bad day? But it wasn't about all those things. I knew even before I read Jung that it wasn't about the facts. I knew I was having a ridiculously disproportionate reaction and yet I was helpless to do anything about it. It's a truly unsettling moment when it hits you—I mean, really hits you—that you are not a singularity, you are a multiplicity; and some of these 'others' inside of you, are not on your side.

In my studies of Liz Greene so far, I was already quite familiar with the terminology and key concepts of Jungian Psychology. And though I had always meant to explore this further, pain turned out to be a far more compelling motivator than curiosity. And in that state of complete nothingness, something in me pointed quite clearly in Jung's direction; so much so that I 'knew' that this was going to save me. So over the next year, I threw myself into Jungian psychology in the only way I knew how: books. I knew no Jungians, couldn't afford to see a Jungian analyst and had zero guidance on where to start, so I let intuition and a sense of adventure be my guide and they didn't disappoint. Over the next year and longer, I read every great Jungian analyst I could find on Amazon (not that I knew who was great then)—Marie Louise von Franz, Barbara Hannah, Clarissa Pinkola Estes, Robert Johnson, Edward Edinger, Marion Woodman, Jolande Jacobi, June Singer, Murray Stein, Sylvia Brinton Perera, you name it.

I even read them in the 'wrong' order so not everything made immediate sense, intellectually. But hunger and desperation made up for lack of structure, and I absorbed what I read at a much deeper level where it acted like medicine on my frazzled soul.

I became fascinated with the unconscious as Jung understood it, and determined to explore it with whatever tools I could access at the time. I started listening to my dreams, keeping a dream journal, working with them as much as I could on my own. The way dreams, astrological transits, relational dynamics and my own 'symptoms' (I'm using this in a broad sense to describe anything I experienced as a problematic pattern) came together to offer me commentary on what was going on in the unconscious, blew my mind. But of all the tools available to me, astrology proved to be the most insightful, especially used alongside dreamwork.

I experimented with the principles I read about. With the help of astrology, dreams and Jungian theory, I made a map of my symptoms to see where they led me in the unconscious. And while I'm sure I made a ton of technical errors (not to forget that one cannot analyse oneself), some mysterious inner force that I can only call the Self—the transpersonal centre and totality of the psyche—seemed to be firmly on my side and carried me through it. Here is how Jungian analyst June Singer describes the relationship between the ego (the 'I') and the Self and I think it captures beautifully how I experienced this inner force:

> *'I cannot describe what it is, for I do not know, but I can tell how it feels. It feels as if one were being drawn inward toward a center of great luminosity, yet to fly straight into it would be like a moth darting into a flame or the earth hurtling itself into the center of the sun. So one moves about the center instead, close enough to see the brightness, to feel the warmth, but maintaining the orbital tension, a dynamic relationship of a small finite being to a source of light and energy that has no limits.'*

—June Singer

And somewhere between the time I came undone after that phone call, and started burrowing myself in the mysteries of the unconscious, something happened. The compulsion I felt in the relationship was gone. Not the pain itself (which I could live with) but the compulsion. The heat and tightness in my chest, the sense of someone else living in my head, the circular, obsessive train of thoughts that had the capacity to build up in intensity and derail my whole day—it felt as though the 'I' was beginning to return to me, but this was a poised, upgraded version. And though I had initially turned to Jung to get better and fix myself, clasping those books as if they were a lifejacket, I started to realise that 'getting better' and 'curing symptoms' was never the point at all. Fascinating as all the theories were, Jung had always drawn me like a magnet with one word: wholeness. And wholeness, is not about becoming better or perfect, nor is it about aspiring to some collective standard of what is good, beautiful or successful. In the Jungian sense, wholeness is about becoming yourself or all that you potentially are, by facilitating a dialogue and a connection with your unconscious, and all the parts of you that are trapped in there. This time, I turn to Jolande Jacobi, to capture the essence of Jungian psychology:

'To relieve the isolation and confusion of modern man, to enable him to find his place in the great stream of life, to help him gain a wholeness which may knowingly and deliberately reunite his luminous conscious side with his dark unconscious side—this is the meaning and purpose of Jungian psychological guidance.'

—Jolande Jacobi

So while the quicksand of 2017—like other years that stand out—plunged me into an encounter with the less attractive parts of myself, it turned out, as these things usually do, to be a blessing in disguise; an initiation and an invitation into a world that would keep expanding, and grow more fascinating and meaningful with time. Jung's model of the psyche and what he defined as individuation—the lifelong process of realising our innate wholeness—became exactly what was missing in my practice of astrology. And if I had to do those nineteen years all over again to find both these gems, I absofreakinglutely would.

The Natal Chart as a Map of the Psyche

*'The fault, dear Brutus,
is not in our stars but in ourselves.'*

First, the disclaimers

As you know by now, there was a two-and-a-half-year gap between my astrological studies and Jungian studies. But I want to present them here as I wish I had discovered them: as one story. I'm also not going into Jung's whole model of the psyche, which is beyond the scope of this book, but only those concepts that are particularly game-changing in the practice of astrology; and those that I have found both personally transformative as well as consistently useful in my practice as a psychological astrologer.

I'm keeping the astrology itself super simple, sticking with just the basic alphabet—planets, signs, houses and aspects—because this alone can be a lot for the absolute beginner whom this book is intended for.

Volumes have been written (mostly by Liz Greene) on every concept and idea I've only briefly touched on in this book. But unless you are super nerdy about the topic, diving into 500-pagers on *one* planetary archetype may not be your thing. And the way I see it, that shouldn't discourage you from discovering something that can potentially make this whole being human thing profoundly more meaningful, if not any less messy.

For this reason, I must, out of necessity, be reductive both with the astrology and the psychology, which is why I ask you to use this section as a taster. Hopefully, if I get it right, you'd want to disappear into a rabbit hole of your own after reading this book.

1

The Reality of the Unconscious

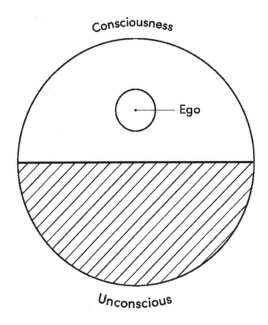

Figure 1. The Reality of the Unconscious

I want to begin with the most basic premise of depth psychology: that there is such a thing as the unconscious, and it holds way more psychic real estate than consciousness. This means that everything you know or think you know about yourself is only a smidgen of the highly complex, richly textured, many layered saga that is you. Look at the circle marked 'ego' in the diagram. That's the part of the story you have access to at any given time. Now compare that to the whole psyche and the part marked unconscious: that's the part you're in the dark about.

Diagrams can be dull and uninspiring when it comes to studying the psyche and this one is only meant to illustrate the conscious-unconscious dichotomy. But it's easy enough to observe the reality of the unconscious in your everyday life:

- When you say 'I don't know what possessed me to do that', 'That was out of character' or 'That was not *me*', you're describing the unconscious at work; when you behave in ways that directly contradict the principles you stand for or the values you identify with, you are behaving unconsciously.

- When people 'push your buttons' or you have a disproportionate emotional reaction to something, it's always a sign that something other than the 'I' (or ego) is in the driver's seat.

- Anything you experience as a compulsion—which implies you have little to no control over it—is the unconscious acting up. Examples include patterns of addiction, from binge-watching-and-eating and impulsive buying, all the way to being 'consumed by' something or someone; this includes neuroses like anxiety disorders and cyclical depression as well as fanaticism of any kind, that swallows you whole and there is little to no room for conscious volition to intervene.

- When you have all the clarity in the world about your self-sabotaging patterns (procrastination, dependency, being disorganised with money etc.) and what you must do to overcome them (become disciplined and cut out distractions, start doing things on your own, make lists and plans to save and invest money wisely etc.) but you somehow can't seem to make any progress or you can't seem to sustain it. It's as if some invisible inner saboteur is calling the shots. And when it seems like you're finally getting it together, something happens in your outer life to disrupt the process and bring you back to square one.

- You find yourself repeatedly attracted to the type of person you know is wrong for you (unavailable, manipulative, emotionally unstable, abusive, Peter Pan etc.) They seem different on the surface each time and yet the pattern mysteriously repeats itself. And even when you know the kind of person you should be attracted to in order to have the kind of relationship you say you want, you find that you're just not attracted to the type at all.

- Interpersonal conflicts can be so revealing of unconscious dynamics; the differences in the way we describe ourselves and the way other people—partners, flatmates, siblings, parents, colleagues, even (and especially) rivals—describe us can, if we're willing to see it, tell us something about what's unconscious in us.

- The symbols in your dreams and nightmares.

- That subtle (or not so subtle) shift in your personality that happens when you're inebriated.

- Any recurring theme or pattern in your life—whether it's relational, an illness, emotional, financial, career-related, spiritual, you name it—that follows you like 'fate' is often the unconscious trying to get your (the ego's) attention.

The unconscious is an ever-present reality—the other half of the 'I'—that trails you like a shadow, informing your decisions from behind-the-scenes and like a magnet, attracting people, situations and patterns that will live out your unlived life for you. Like the dark twin motif in mythology or the wicked step-sister in the fairytale, it'll never tire of tripping you up, till you look into its mirror and recognise yourself.

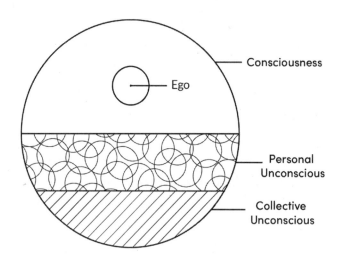

Figure 2. The Personal Unconscious and the Collective Unconscious

In the Jungian model, the unconscious itself has two layers. The first layer or the one immediately below the surface of consciousness, is the personal unconscious or the Freudian layer, if I can put it that way. It is the sum total of all those things from your own history that the ego/'I'—for a number of reasons— decided to repress (with new material being added on a regular basis). This includes:

- Traumas, shocks, fears, shame and other painful experiences and memories that the ego found too intolerable to hold.
- Inner conflicts or pieces of your own nature that don't sit well with your conscious attitudes, values and ethics.

- More pieces of you that got chipped off because they didn't fit in with family, religious or cultural values.

The personal unconscious is the bat cave that Bruce Wayne must someday willingly re-enter; it's the Boggart closet; it's the place emo musicians must visit when they write their song lyrics; and it's the contents of this layer of the psyche that we initially unpack in what we broadly call 'therapy'. This is the part of the unconscious that often shows up in the familiar (if disgusting) dream motif of dirty or overflowing toilets. It's the 'shit you're refusing to deal with'.

The Archetypes and the Collective Unconscious

The collective unconscious is Jung's contribution to depth psychology and as the name suggests, it is about more than just 'what happened to you'. It is the deepest stratum of the psyche that we share with all human beings who ever lived and will ever live; it is the most impersonal layer of the psyche and is the one farthest away from consciousness. It contains every human experience from man's earliest days, and universal patterns and forces called archetypes.* So just as we inherit our big noses and receding hairlines from our parents and ancestors, we inherit archetypes as psychological material from the collective unconscious.†

What Are Archetypes?

To put it in very simple terms, the archetypes are the particular filters through which we see the world, experience life and respond to it. They are formless and cannot be known directly but

---

Jung's Map of the Soul, Murray Stein

†*Psychological Astrology*, Karen Hamaker-Zondag

they have autonomy and possess tremendous energy that Jung called 'numinous'; their essence permeates all the structures of reality and we can experience their effects on us, psychologically. They inform our world views, influence our choices, interests and values and are the basis for why two people respond in completely contradictory ways to the same experience.

They have been described as 'force fields' and 'force centres' and as 'the pattern forming elements of the psyche'* that underpin our existence and our reality. They are the deeply unconscious foundation of the psyche that influence our patterns of behaviour, attitudes and perception of life itself.

Now these archetypes that Jung initially called 'primordial images' are for the most part too vast and unknowable, and exist only in potential, until they reveal themselves as archetypal images.† So, there can be many archetypal images representing one archetype.

The motifs of these archetypal images are universal, appearing and re-appearing through the ages in the religions and mythologies of the world (which Jung understood as springing from the collective unconscious), fairytales, the dreams of lay people, and in the art, music and literature of the modern world. They may change their names and hairdo but their essence remains the same. The Wise Old Man, the Divine Child, the Hero, the Virgin Birth, Dismemberment, the Stealing of Fire are some examples of how these universal patterns and psychic stages and processes are depicted symbolically in myth.‡

> 'In every single individual psyche, they can awake into new life, exert their magic power, and condense into a kind of "individual

---

Psychological Astrology, Karen Hamaker-Zondag
†Ibid
‡*The Psychology of C.G Jung*, Jolande Jacobi

mythology" which presents an impressive parallel to the great traditional mythologies of all peoples and epochs, concretising as it were their origin, essence, and meaning, and throwing new light on them.'

—Jolande Jacobi*

Like the gods and goddesses of mythology that best represent them, archetypes also have a range of expressions—from benign, healing, creative and life-giving, to terrifying, destructive and downright psychopathic. And since they express themselves as 'drives' within us, our task is to understand our unconscious archetypal affinities, and offer conscious outlets for their expression (more on this in the discussion of complexes); so they don't turn against us as they often do in myths when mortals fail to pay them homage.

'Being mindful of the gods is a matter of psychic hygiene, not a matter of piety, social conformity or religiosity.'

—David Tacey†

Archetypes are also intimately related to instincts in Jung's view (though they are not the same thing), which are also universal.‡ We all know what it's like to be in the grip of our instincts. But just as instincts originate in the body, archetypes originate in the psyche. Jung derived his theory of archetypes from Plato's Ideas or Forms but the difference between archetypes and Ideas is that Jung understood the archetypes as embodied, and not as abstractions.‡‡

The Psychology of C.G. Jung, Jolande Jacobi
†*How to Read Jung*, David Tacey
‡*The Psychology of C.G. Jung*, Jolande Jacobi
‡‡Ibid

Now before we go into complexes, which is the primary lens through which we will look at the natal chart in this book, I want to briefly touch on a few more key concepts in Jungian theory.

Ego-Consciousness

Now let's go back to our diagram (Fig. 1). Look at that smaller circle in the centre of consciousness marked 'Ego'/'I'. This is the protagonist of our story, the hero on the quest for wholeness. The ego represents the part of you that is awake and observant. It is everything within your immediate awareness, and is the ground or reality from which you operate. It holds everything you know or think you know about yourself and life.

'I am Harry Potter. I am an orphan who lives with his aunt and uncle, gets bullied by his cousin and sleeps in a cupboard. My parents died in a car accident.' The ego knows what it knows but it's usually not the whole story.

Now the word ego comes with a ton of baggage because we're so accustomed to hearing it in an accusatory context ('ego problems', 'big ego' or spiritual types asking you to 'transcend the ego' and so on) but psychologically, the ego is not a bad word. And a solidly developed ego is essential for navigating both the inner and outer worlds; it isn't possible to become conscious of something without this mirror with which the psyche can see itself.* All the Hogwarts letters in the world would mean nothing if Harry (the ego) cannot actually 'see' it. He is still in the dark and cannot become conscious of who he is.

But how is the ego different from consciousness? Consciousness is a field of awareness, that absorbs and registers information that's constantly streaming in. It's like the dogs barking and the honking of cars outside, the smell of freshly

---

Jung's Map of the Soul, Murray Stein

brewed coffee wafting from the kitchen and the clutter on your desk that you're registering at some level, but not 'holding in your consciousness' because you (the ego) are engrossed in the thesis you have to turn in tomorrow.

So the ego is the wilful, decision-making centre of this field of consciousness that decides what information is worth tuning into, reflecting on and acting on, and what can be dismissed into the unconscious. Until the ego has taken note of something, it's only vaguely conscious.* So again, it's the difference between unread Hogwarts letters and, 'Harry, yer a wizard.' 'I'm a *what?*'

Suddenly, the psyche can see a previously unconscious aspect of itself now that the information has been 'captured and held in place by the ego's reflective surface'.†

Now let's see if we can use the Harry Potter analogy to illustrate all the concepts we've discussed so far.

Harry represents the ego/'I' and 'Wizard' the archetype he has an unconscious affiliation with. We have to look at all the characters in the story as forces within the individual psyche, so Harry's aunt and uncle can be seen as those parts of us that crave control and normalcy. They are those defence mechanisms that repress the intolerably painful, terrifying or embarrassing truths about the past and 'what happened' to him (the personal layer of the unconscious) and his fundamental nature (the archetypal layer or the collective unconscious) and keep it out of reach of ego-consciousness (Harry).

But though Harry has no idea he is a wizard, his unconsciousness doesn't stop 'magic' or the effects of the archetypal realm from erupting in his life. He cannot explain why his hair grows back overnight, why strange things happen

---

Jung's Map of the Soul, Murray Stein
†Ibid

when he's angry or upset or how he manages to set a boa constrictor free by engaging in a conversation with it. He is also punished every time said magic erupts which can be seen as a parallel for how we experience the archetypal layer as 'disturbing the surface of consciousness'.

It feels like a kind of fate—this mysterious 'something' that creates specific patterns in our lives that are often painful, destructive and seem to be in direct opposition to what we (the ego) want.* But once made conscious, Harry has access to Hogwarts where he can learn to relate to the archetypal part of his nature in a balanced way and express it consciously, instead of having it 'erupt'.

The archetype (Wizard) itself is vast and impersonal with a range of expressions from benign (Dumbledore) to psychopathic (Voldemort). We can also see how Harry is connected to both polarities of the archetype (he has as much Voldemort in him as his own parents, and the influence of Dumbledore); and while he may be the Chosen One, he must still choose (this is where the ego's discriminating function becomes crucial). And in so doing, express a unique aspect or version of the god/archetype (Wizard) through the small, finite, individual ego that is Harry Potter.

---

*The Horoscope in Manifestation, Liz Greene

2

Complexes and Fate

The natal chart which we'll get into shortly, can be seen through the lens of any psychological concept but the complex is by far, the most comprehensive. It brings together everything we've looked at so far, and offers multiple levels of insight into the dynamics of a horoscope. The term 'complex' was one of Jung's earliest contributions to psychotherapy though the concept itself had been around much longer. In her brilliant book, *The Horoscope in Manifestation*, Liz Greene presents complexes as a psychological model of fate and how, while the concept itself is relatively modern, understanding of its dynamics go as far back as Greek myth.

> *The Greeks understood that "something"—some compulsive inner pattern which created dramatic repercussions in outer life—had an irrevocable way of passing from father to son, from mother to daughter, and this "something" was usually linked with one or another of the gods. Not only family curses, but also family gifts could be inherited in this way. What is most psychologically relevant about these mythic portrayals is the compulsive nature of this "something" which drives human beings into beliefs, actions and feelings over which they have no conscious control and which are often in violent opposition to their ethics and values. By presenting these compulsive patterns*

as the signature of a dynamic relationship between human and god, myth highlights the numinous nature of complexes.'

—Liz Greene*

Greene traces the history and evolution of the complex as a concept, from Charcot at the end of the 19th century and Janet, to Freud and finally, Jung. But I'm going to jump right to Jung's view of the complex, which is what we're using here.

What Is a Complex?

We've already seen how complexes show up in everyday life when we talked about the reality of the unconscious. But what exactly is the complex? What is it made of? And most importantly, what does it want?

You can think of complexes as fragments of the personality that are split-off from ego-consciousness or the 'I' and lead a separate existence in the unconscious; as sub-personalities, if you will. They have tremendous energy and autonomy. This means they have the power to act on your behalf without your permission.

While in the early stages of research, complexes were understood purely through a pathological lens in severely disturbed patients, by the time we come to Jung, we see that the core of the complex is not pathological.†

The complex in Jung's view, has two levels: an archetypal core that acts as a magnet and is innate; it rests in the deepest layer of the psyche, the collective unconscious, and is a disposition; it's in you long before anyone abandoned you, rejected you or damaged you in any way. This archetypal core contains your developmental

---

***The Horoscope in Manifestation*, Liz Greene
†Ibid

pattern or personal myths in seed form. Remember what we discussed about archetypes having a whole range of expressions? So your archetypal disposition contains both your potential for life, vitality and fulfilment as well as the recipe for your despair and destruction. The archetypal core does not in itself 'cause' anything to happen to you.

But when it collides with outer experience that resonates with its image, a cluster of personal associations—ideas, opinions, convictions, beliefs etc.—are attracted to the magnet, which goes on to form the complex.*

Let's illustrate this with an example.

So let's say you have a victim complex. The victim is archetypal—it's the innate disposition and lies dormant in the psyche until something happens. Perhaps as a child, you had to wear large-framed glasses to school on your first day. The kids teased you and you felt ganged up against. The victim, which is one side of the archetypal core of your particular complex, starts to pulsate and a number of associations with a high emotional charge start to cluster around it. These associations may sound like 'Kids are bullies' or 'I hate school' or 'It's me against everyone'.

Now, another kid who does not have the victim complex may have also been teased or bullied that day but they either seem to be able to shrug off the experience, summon the courage to stand up to it or even fight back. Remember that archetypes are the particular filters through which we perceive and respond to reality.

Now, this is only the first layer of associations. Next, as a six-year-old, you found out that your mother was pregnant. This made you feel resentful because there is already an unconscious

---

Boundaries of the Soul, June Singer

association with kids being mean. As the new baby arrived, much of your mother's attention was directed towards your sibling. Again, the victim complex starts to pulsate and this time, new associations gather around it: 'Nobody loves me', 'I'm always left out' or 'I hate kids'. Now the complex has a lot more emotional or psychic charge than it did at first because now it has two layers of associations. As you got older, you invariably collided with many more experiences that triggered this complex and amplified it. Your friends made plans without you, a partner betrayed you, a promotion you worked for went to someone else, maybe you were even assaulted. All these experiences go on to add more and more layers to this victim complex until it's so highly charged that the mere mention of a name, a smell, or a triggering word, can provoke an emotional reaction or outburst that is beyond your control.

The complex, in this sense, feels like a ticking time bomb and a solidly developed ego is necessary to defuse it by making it conscious, taking responsibility, and finding healthy outlets for its energy. This is where the archetype's range of expression comes into play. The victim may be seen as the polarity of the tyrant, as well as the hero or the savior. They are two sides of the same archetypal principle. So when you're identified with the victim, you experience yourself as powerless and having no agency, while 'they' have all the power. Your own power remains unconscious until the complex pushes you to reclaim it one way or the other. In its extreme manifestations, the same complex could produce a sociopath who decides to gun down school children because 'Kids are bullies' and 'I hate kids', (the tyrant), a Mother Teresa who dedicates their whole life to put an end to the suffering of others (the saviour) or a firefighter who puts his life on the line in order to save others (the hero). And between these manifestations, there is a whole range—therapist, doctor, human rights activist, even the rare politician moved by an inner compulsion to 'make a difference', and equally, the martyr, the person who 'cannot leave' an abusive relationship for whatever reason, the mother who gives up everything for her family but unconsciously exerts an emotional power over them and makes them pay in actions driven by guilt. There are endless ways in which a complex may manifest; a unique combination of factors—archetypal affinity or inherent disposition, environmental triggers, the development of the ego and how conscious the person is—come together to decide how you will express your particular complexes at any given time.

What Does It Want?

When we look at complexes, we're dealing with something in us that is alive, energetic and autonomous. Think about what that means for a second. These pockets of energy or 'drives' within you are going somewhere and they are hungry for something. Depending on how charged they are (which tells us how compulsively they operate), they're not averse to destroying anything on their path to get what they want. And the more unconscious we are of a particular complex within us, the more blind, forceful and autonomous it gets.

Again, we have in myth a language for how complexes operate. When the gods (or the archetypes) feel ignored or crossed by mortals, they afflict them with diseases, meddle with their affairs, cause drama in their relationships or drive them mad. This isn't very different from modern day 'issues'—anxiety, depression, insomnia, self-sabotaging behaviour patterns, relationship struggles, addiction, confusion about sexuality or ideology, problems with money, success and achievement, physical illness, recurring themes that feel 'fated'—that make a person reach out to a therapist or an astrologer.

'The gods have become diseases; Zeus no longer rules Olympus but rather the solar plexus and produces curious specimens for the doctor's consulting room.'

—C.G. Jung

Symbols: The Language of the Unconscious

Plato described two ways of approaching truth: logos and mythos. Logos, from which we get 'logic', is a scientific and empirical way of explaining reality, whereas mythos from which we get 'mystery' and 'mysticism' refers to an intuitive, symbolic approach.* We need both to make sense of life. If you've been diagnosed with a terminal illness, you'd rely on science to make sense of how you got there, guide you on what to expect, on managing pain and keeping you comfortable. But scientific explanation can do nothing for your inner turmoil, which calls for an entirely different approach—one that allows you to make meaning of an impossible situation.

For this, we rely on the symbolic language of mythos—which comes from the Greek word for 'to keep secret', 'to close the mouth' or 'close the eyes' suggesting a sense of darkness and obscurity where meaning is made by pushing one beyond the realm of rational thought.† It is that sense of 'touching the truth' that we have when we enter the world of a great story, a poem, a painting, a musical composition or a dream. You may analyse a dream or your love for a work of art using every rational tool available, but the depth and texture of a meaningful encounter with a symbol is impossible for the intellect to pin down.

To Go Beyond Thought, An Interview with Parabola Magazine, Karen Armstrong
†Ibid

This is because a symbol is not only inexhaustible in meaning, but its meanings are linked by association as opposed to logic.* So, some of the meanings you derive from a symbol may even contradict others—you may associate the moonlight with romance and poetry, as much as madness, terror and foreboding—but the symbol, incredibly, holds together your many oppositions and stitches them into a unified whole. In this sense, the language of mythos is both irrational and true.

This is also the language of the unconscious. We must, therefore, have a basic understanding and appreciation of symbols if we are to make any progress with decoding the messages of the unconscious or 'developing an ear for the psyche'. But first we must distinguish between sign and symbol. A sign is something that means something specific. Road signs, for example, are pictorial representations of traffic rules. They have one absolute meaning with no room for interpretation. The meaning that can be derived from a symbol, on the other hand, is next to limitless.†
'Mother' as a sign means a woman who is a parent. Mother as a symbol may mean 'nurturing' to one person and 'abandoning' to another; it can also mean 'earth' to someone, just as it can mean a country, a home or a particular role one plays in life that is maternal or experienced as life-giving, life-sustaining or nourishing. Symbols, like the unconscious, have two layers of meaning—personal, and universal or archetypal. And because they bring together all our conflicting unconscious associations, they have the capacity to evoke profound feelings, and even temporarily possess us and dictate our actions and behaviours. This is typical of religious and national symbols as well as those that represent social movements. Like the archetypes that

---

Relating: An Astrological Guide to Living with Others, Liz Greene.
†Ibid

underpin them, they invoke a whole range of responses—from love, truth, compassion, justice and sacrifice, to violence, hatred, division, terror and destruction.

But while some symbols (such as the cross, aum, crescent and star, or the swastika or national flags or the rainbow flag) jump out at us and are easy enough to recognise as symbols, we tend to miss the fact that we live in a world surrounded by symbols.*

Archetypes speak through symbols. And since archetypes are the invisible foundational structures of everything that is above, below, inside and outside of us, we can think of symbolism as the oldest of languages—our native tongue in the truest sense.

Everything in nature—the turning of the seasons from the burst of new life at springtime to the ripeness and fruition of summer, the shedding and decay of autumn and the 'barrenness and secret underground germination of winter't—and the heavens—the planetary cycles, the daily cycle of the sun's rising and setting and the phases of the moon, from the fertile void of the new moon to the brightness and culmination of the full moon waning back to the new moon again—and the human body—from birth, to puberty, to middle age, old age and death—and the human psyche—which goes through the same processes at an inner level—everything in reality is engaged in this symbolic dance of correspondences.

Symbols must be felt and experienced as much as (if not more than) analysed and 'interpreted'. If you're struggling with a creative block and you find yourself in the thick of winter in a dream, this could be saying something about the particular season your psyche is in. The barrenness you experience on the surface is not only indicative of the new life that is quietly taking

---

Relating: An Astrological Guide to Living with Others, Liz Greene.
†Ibid

root underground, it is also inviting you (the ego, which has complete faith in its own autonomy) to surrender to this dark half of the seasonal cycle where seemingly, 'nothing happens'. But if you know the myths, then you know that winter solstice time is associated with the birth of the solar gods and it is only a matter of time before you see that spark of new life emerge into consciousness and you're able to create again, not from a superficial place to fulfil purely ego needs (because this, the ego is able to do on its own) but from the depths of the collective unconscious—fishing out as it were—the particular story, painting or piece of music—that *wants* to be born through you.

Archetypes are also eternal and cyclical, having no beginning or end. They appear and re-appear through time, suitably adapted for the particular time and culture in which they re-emerge. If we can keep our eyes and ears open to their symbolic expression in our lives, relationships, dreams, longings, problems, conflicts, terrors and patterns, we're already one step closer to making our complexes conscious.

Our modern world's worship of logos which has disconnected us from the life-giving, meaning-making gifts of mythos, comes with a heavy price tag; not least of which is the widespread sense of 'emptiness and meaninglessness of life' which Jung described as 'the general neurosis of our times'.

Reclaiming our connection to mythos is not about romanticising the world of our ancestors as much as recognising that we are so much more complex and mysterious than our rational faculties would care to admit.

> 'Unlike our forefathers, we no longer worship the sun, but we still respond unconsciously to the symbol.'

> —Liz Greene*

Relating: An Astrological Guide to Living with Others, Liz Greene.

3

Recognising Our Complexes

i) Projection

One of the most common ways a complex makes itself known to us is by projection. Now this is a word that is often used incorrectly and also comes with some of the same baggage as the word 'ego' ('you're *just* projecting' etc.) but it's a perfectly natural psychological mechanism, so let me clarify what I mean here.

When something is unconscious in you, it means there is no room in your 'I' for that particular aspect of your nature. This could be because it clashes with your core values, other more prominent parts of your personality, because your family or religion considers it taboo or simply because it's not ripe enough to emerge into consciousness. But the fact that you have successfully exiled this piece of yourself from your conscious personality doesn't mean it's gone. It is a piece of psyche, so it is alive. And the more unconscious you are of its existence, the more compulsively it operates. Remember when we talked about the complex having a magnetic core? Now this unconscious piece of you, desperately wants to be acknowledged by you and find some room for itself in your life. So, its magnetic properties kick in, and it attracts all kinds of people, situations, events and patterns into your life, that will live out that unlived life *for* you.

Read that again if you need to. It basically means that the

most significant people in your life—those you love, admire and adore as well as those who drive you up the wall, those who repulse you, those you find despicable and particularly those who have the capacity to rile you up and ruin your day—are reflecting back to you a piece of your own unconscious nature. Their essence resembles something in you that exists in potential, and needs to be owned.

'Wait, what? Are you saying I'm unconsciously irresponsible, spoilt, lazy, entitled, commitment-phobic and flakey because those are the qualities that upset me the most in people? What does that even mean since I'm none of those things? And why would I own them?'

It could mean that you're probably too far on the other extreme. You're likely super-structured, organised, responsible, committed and reliable. But the shadow side of those qualities can also show up as rigidity, a hyper-critical nature, intolerance, need for control and perhaps a tendency to be wound up tightly.

'So my unconscious parts are the ones striving for fun and spontaneity and I'm being too controlling, scheduled and uptight for them?'

Quite possibly.

'But what about my brother who can't seem to hold down a job and is always borrowing money from me, my husband who considers being a fun parent more important than being a good one, my colleagues who always leave me to do the heavy-lifting...I could go on and on. Are you saying they are not really like that and I'm just seeing them through my own biased lens?'

Not at all! The people around you do sound like they need to be checked into a rehab for Peter Pans. But the fact that they are all swarming around you, tells us something about an imbalance that is also in you.

Again, remember that archetypes are neither good nor bad,

they just are; and they contain the whole gamut of expressions associated with their essence. The more unconscious we are of our affinity to a particular archetype, the more it's going to turn against us in order to get our attention.

In projection, this happens through what we can broadly call 'others'. In this example, the message is clear. The archetype that's underneath the behaviour you describe is the Child. On the positive side, this is full of potential, creative, individual, spontaneous, with an endless capacity to generate joy and warmth. On the negative side, it's about grandiosity, entitlement, lack of boundaries, chaos, avoiding responsibility, refusal to acknowledge reality, and in extreme manifestations, it can lead to narcissism.

Here's what I would tell you if you came to see me with this specific problem (again, I'm being reductive but trying to illustrate a point): The Child (the archetype) seems to be erupting in your life through others because you've made no room for it in your own personality. This is not necessarily your fault. You are who you are because of a combination of different factors, many of which you had no control over.

But no matter how disciplined, structured and responsible you are, your life is repeatedly flung into chaos because of these individuals. That's how archetypes behave. They have the capacity to affect you in very real ways for what is seemingly, no fault of yours.

'So how do I make this go away?'

Well, you could start by balancing your well-developed 'grown-up' persona, with some of the aforementioned positive qualities of the Child. You could try not to control everything for a start. This is going to be hard for you. But maybe if you let go of your brother instead of feeling the need to step in and clean up his life, he'll learn to take responsibility for himself. He may hate you for it, but that's the price of consciousness.

You, in turn, will have more energy and time available to you to attend to yourself, instead of dealing with your brother's mess. And if you gave yourself permission to have some fun once in a while, maybe you'd even start to develop new interests and curiosities. You may take up a hobby just for the joy of it. And suddenly, your personality is more rounded and you feel just a bit more whole.

Maybe your husband will learn that disciplining children is part of his job profile too if you stopped taking all the responsibility, and focused more on having fun and being spontaneous with your kids. These are just some examples but the bottom-line is that the Child is a big part of what is repressed in you and it's asking for room in your life through these interpersonal conflicts. Once integrated, this Child that was causing so much drama through others, starts to fill you with a sense of vitality; you start to feel lighter, more resilient, develop a sense of humour and radiate joy and warmth. This is what we call 'taking back the projection'. When you do this, the people around you are faced with the choice to take back theirs. The idea is for you both to find balance through the other. But whether the other person does that, or chooses to walk away or develops a neurosis, you'll find that you don't feel so reactive anymore. The compulsion and charge created by the projection dissipates.

Of course, projections don't only show up negatively. We also idealise people, put them on pedestals or worship them as we do celebrities and spiritual figures but also parents, mentors and teachers. But probably the most common example of a positive projection is the experience of falling in love, which is an entirely unconscious process.

There is nothing rational about falling in love—the magnet in you (the archetypal core) is attracted to another who resembles its image. It makes you feel heady, whole, more alive than you've ever been, as one ordinary human being starts to shine like the sun in your eyes. What makes them so special? Why does your heart do a little somersault every time they call? What pulls you so powerfully towards them? Biologically, it is dopamine, norepinephrine and serotonin. Psychologically, it is a projection. So psychologically speaking, you are 'falling into a complex'.

This magical other resembles something in your own nature. Everything in them that you love so much also exists in you in seed form. That's the chemical reaction. They resemble your own unlived life that you unconsciously long for. If it weren't so, there'd be no chemistry or fireworks. The fact that you have attracted them into your life at this time suggests that, that part of your complex is ready to emerge into consciousness. It's really your 'Harry yer a wizard' moment if you want it to be. Except it's not a moment as much as the entire span of the relationship. Which is why the same person who once made you feel alive and whole, eventually makes you want to poison their tea. But if we can step out of the war zones that relationships sometimes morph into, or lower the fortified walls of defence we've built over several years of a marriage, what we're really looking at is someone holding up a mirror for those lost pieces of ourselves that are ready to come home.

So let's say you're always the giving, sacrificing type who cannot say 'no' and you experience your partner as pushy, selfish and getting his own way all the time. Here, the psychological task of the projection is to push your buttons so hard that the only choice you are left with is continuing to be a doormat and dying with your repressed rage still seething in you, or learning to own your unlived life by asserting yourself, drawing boundaries and giving yourself permission to take as much as you give.

Your partner in turn has attracted you so you can teach him the art of compromise, putting other people before himself and learning to take 'no' for an answer. Of course, every complex is like an onion, revealing itself more deeply as we peel off the layers of projection, so we're never really free of projections; but for every layer we peel off, we get to see the human being on the other side a bit more clearly.

But is everything outside of you a projection? How do you tell the difference? By the disproportionate emotional charge whether that's positive or negative. The degree may vary based on the intensity of the complex and how unconsciously it operates, but there is always that sense of being *affected* by something or someone when we're projecting.

ii) Dreams and Nightmares

Another way that the complex tries to break down our defences and get our attention is through the symbols in our dreams and nightmares. Since the complex is essentially unconscious, one of the best ways it can get through to us is when we're asleep and the ego is 'switched off'. This is why dreams often have plot lines that seem bizarre, disturbing or even nonsensical to the rational mind. But if we can recognise the limitations of the intellect when it comes to the unconscious, and make an effort to learn its language—by recording our dreams and paying attention to them, feeling our way through their imagery, listening with the ears of a poet or an artist, tuning into the feelings, impressions and bodily sensations they evoke, the seemingly disjointed memories they bring up, the stories, fairytales and myths they form parallels to, the associations every image throws up—we can begin to develop a relationship with the unconscious, and experience first-hand the fascinating nature of our own psychic life, ever-abundant with mysteries and riches.

Dreamwork is one of the best places to begin inner work. As Jung put it 'the dream is a spontaneous self-portrayal in

symbolic form, of the actual situation in the unconscious'.* So
if you dreamt of a serial killer murdering young children, this is
a symbolic portrayal of something that's actually happening in
you without your awareness. It points to a destructive aspect of
your nature, as health issues in your outer life, or as disturbances
in your inner life that produces neurotic symptoms. The dream
uses this shocking image and plot line to get the ego's attention.
The serial killer here represents the complex—the split-off piece
of psyche that has tremendous power and autonomy. The dream
is telling us that this is an aspect of the dreamer that operates
in a highly unconscious way, killing off new life and potential
(children) in the dreamer. If our dreamer was shocked awake
by the dream, then the dream is screaming, 'Wake up from
your unconsciousness before this complex destroys something
precious in you!'

We'd have to go deeper into the dream to understand the
specific nature of this complex. Is the killer a man or a woman
(which can tell us if this is an aspect of the masculine or feminine
principle)? Are they the same race as the dreamer (a foreigner
may point to shadow aspects, alien to the ego but it's also more
than that)? Does the dreamer know this person in waking life?
Or does the killer resemble or bring to mind someone they
know? Where is the dream taking place? Does our dreamer
recognise the children? How old are the children? Does the
dreamer have children in her waking life? Could this be about
creative 'children'? What else is happening in the dream? What
feelings, memories, sensations or associations does it bring up in
the dreamer? Is there something going on in the dreamer's life
that feels like a parallel to the dream narrative?

Collected Works 8, para 505, Society of Analytical Psychology (www.thesap.
org.uk), C.G. Jung

Listening deeply to dreams can turn our attention inward, to the stories and characters that are both the true source of our pain and discontent, as well as the hope for our redemption. It can bring about the most profound changes in us at an inner level and by extension, alter the expression of our complexes.

This is probably a good time to tell you about a dream I had in early 2017 (which was another memo from the unconscious to descend into the Jungian rabbit hole). I was wrestling with the need to 'come out' about astrology while feeling quite certain that I'd be rejected, isolated and ridiculed by everyone in my life. I felt a great deal of inner pressure that I thought might just make me explode. While I hadn't told anyone in my family about astrology except my mum, I felt convinced that the super-Catholic part of my family would reject it as 'the work of the devil' without even making an effort to find out more. And while I had no problem with the rejection, I felt exhausted by the thought of being the outsider again, and having to explain myself to people who'd never get it. To me, it was perfectly clear that astrology was nothing short of divinely inspired, and I thought I didn't need the church to agree with me. And yet, I felt this rage towards the church that I couldn't shake off, because it became an outer symbol of my own unconscious doubt.

The Dream

28/Feb/2017

I am a white woman, about twenty-seven years old in what appears to be medieval Europe. I'm wearing a hooded dress that seems dirty and made of something that resembles sack cloth, and it's clear I don't want to be seen. I seem to be escaping what looks like an underground prison.

I have been 'captured along with my friends, a group of young men by the authorities of the time, for stealing big secrets'.

The friends however, don't seem to be with me. They are in another room being tortured while I make my escape. I can hear footsteps pursuing me as I navigate the dark, narrow, twisty corridors of this cave or prison. I feel terror because my pursuers are close; I can't see them but I know they are wearing robes like the clergy. But I don't let that stop me from taking a moment to steal what appears to be old rolled parchments, and hide them in my girdle before I move on.

Now the way the prison is built is such that anyone who tries to escape will end up in the wilderness where they will be devoured and killed by wild animals. But in the dream, I have a gift for 'scattering my scent' so the wild animals cannot pursue me.

In the final scene, I am standing in the middle of the road in what seems like a modern city, facing the setting sun. I hold the parchments to my chest feeling the relief of release but it doesn't last because it dawns on me: 'Now that I have made my escape, I must go back in there and save my friends.' But there is this knowing that going back in there is certain death and the friends may not be alive anyway. I'm filled with anguish as I watch the sun go down.

Then I hear a voice from the heavens that in the dream, feels like the voice of 'God': 'This is a past life story that was not resolved. It must be resolved in this lifetime.'

I am not going to analyse this dream but I want to use it to illustrate much of what we've been discussing so far (how complexes show up in dreams) because it's a great example of how dream imagery can reveal the archetypal core of the complex. Now as you know, in my waking life, I was going through a massive inner transformation with the initiation into astrology that left me feeling very confused about where I was headed, among other things. This also meant an 'ego death' because so much of my identity was bound up with writing and comedy but now suddenly, I felt like I had nothing left to say. I cancelled the columns I had been writing, found that I couldn't write or read fiction anymore, and while astrology had turned my world upside down, I definitely couldn't see myself *becoming* an astrologer. So what was I supposed to do with all this knowledge that made me go 'How can I possibly know this?' And what about this radically different worldview? While I felt more connected to the Divine through astrology than I ever had through anything else, how was I supposed to explain this?

In the dream, the person you recognise as yourself, represents the ego. So the dream suggests that the ego here is identified with a medieval heretic. It's taking us to the dark ages with its vivid portrayal of a powerful, corrupt church that captures, tortures and kills anyone who dares to seek divine knowledge (parchments, 'stealing big secrets') beyond what it permits. This is not my personal experience of the church in my waking life by any stretch of the imagination. This is collective unconscious memory of witch burnings; which, by the way, had never been a topic of interest. I had never spent any time reading about this and my entire knowledge of the middle-ages was summed up in a few paragraphs from the history textbooks I had in my Catholic school. So where was I getting this from? One of the first associations the dream brought up for me was Joan D'Arc. I remembered watching the movie as a child and the intense feelings it had stirred up in me. But the scenes that came to mind were exclusively those of Joan challenging the church and standing by the voice she heard as the voice of God. I hadn't thought about Joan D'Arc in all these years. Why had I resonated so much with the movie as a young child? I was nothing like Joan. I'd say whatever I need to, to avoid burning at the stake.

But the dream points to the intensity of my convictions about astrology, which awakens the archetypal core of the complex (the outlaw/witch). I had always been identified with the rebel/outlaw but never to this degree. The dream clearly shows that the rage I felt in my outer life towards the church had nothing to do with my personal experience. The church people in my life were—*at worst*—ignorant, stubborn and incapable of honest inquiry. But the fact that I perceived them as medieval torturers clearly points to a projection. I was projecting my own unconscious doubt, shame and rejection of astrology. The tyrant who shows up as medieval church authorities is an equally powerful archetypal force that is active in my unconscious. And when the tension between opposing psychic forces becomes too much to hold within, we project one and identify with the other. If I was all rebel, I'd have had no problem telling the world about astrology. But the fact that it was such a huge struggle, points to the fact that I had something inside of me that resembled these church folk and I was deeply unconscious of that something. So the church became a symbol and a hook for my own rejection of astrology.

I'm going to stop with the dream now but I remember the impact it had on me. While I didn't understand it in my head (I hadn't yet explored Jungian psychology beyond my studies in astrology), I felt impelled to *do something*. That day, I wrote a long 'coming out' article about astrology and posted it on my social channels. To my surprise, many church folk not only did not react in the way I expected, they even 'liked' it. Of course, there are many who will never get it but that's not the point. What the projection is trying to tell you is that you are giving something or someone way more power than is appropriate because of your own unconsciousness. Once I became aware of my own resistance to astrology and acknowledged it in the piece I wrote, there was a palpable release in the inner pressure I had felt for months. And a little more than a year later, I did become an astrologer.

iii) Symptoms

Another common way in which complexes disturb our outer life is by producing symptoms. These could be physical, mental, emotional or spiritual since archetypes can manifest at any level. While some symptoms may be entirely psychosomatic, there is always a connection between what's happening in the body and what's going on in the psyche. The medical explanation for a symptom and the psychological meaning of it, are not mutually exclusive. For example, you may be throwing up incessantly because of the half-cooked chicken you ate. But psychologically, it's worth asking yourself: 'What can't I stomach?' Or 'What can't I digest?' The answer may not come easily if you habitually push your feelings inside but it's a great place to start.

And even if it sounds silly at first (because you've never worked with the unconscious in this way before), once you open your eyes and ears to the language of the unconscious, it's as if a whole new portal opens up; and you can see everything around you as symbols of the archetypal powers underlying them.

The same goes for neurotic disorders. As Jung said, 'Neurosis is always a substitute for legitimate suffering.' When we're unable to tolerate life's ambiguities and the suffering it sometimes brings us, the neurosis becomes an unconscious way of avoiding your suffering.

For example, if we were to look at early onset Alzheimer's or dementia in general through a symbolic lens, what questions must we ask? This is a condition that is characterised by memory loss and general mental decline. 'What is so unbearable that you wish you could just forget?' 'What about your present reality is beyond your capacity to tolerate that you'd rather just not be "here"?' Or maybe it's something in the past for which there was no closure. Again, I'm being reductive (you cannot take a 'this means that' approach to the psyche) but it's meant to give you a sense of the archetypal basis that is alive and present in everything that surrounds us, and particularly in those things that disturb us.

Now you may look at such a person from the outside and insist they had a normal life and there was nothing so awful that such a symptom should've manifested. But the truth is, we know nothing of the unconscious lives of those around us. We barely even know anything of our own.

Take a self-righteous, religious fanatic whose entire life focus is to avoid the 'sinful' path, for example. Let's say he also takes great pleasure in pointing out other people's sins. One day, he commits one such unspeakable sin (as he is wont to, given his level of unconsciousness about his capacity for it). He can't bear the shame, humiliation and horror of realising he's just like 'all these sinners'. A couple of things could happen at this point: he may discover forgiveness, love and mercy that are central to his faith; and having been tempered by his own failings, accept his humanity and develop a more balanced approach to religion. Or this reality check could produce a disorder. The truth is so shocking and impossible to face, that 'forgetting' may be the only way to continue living.

While these are some of the most common ways in which complexes make themselves known, we may look at anything in our lives—our particular longings, fascinations, gifts, ambitions, needs, fears, behaviour patterns, phobias, addictions, those specific things that leave us feeling *achey* and unfulfilled, anything that affects us emotionally and creates patterns in our lives—through the lens of complexes. And now that we have a basic idea of what complexes are, how they operate and the symbolic language they speak, let's dive right into the astrology.

For more on introductions to Jungian theory, please refer to the bibliography. In order to not be overwhelming, I've kept the list very short.

4

The Natal Chart

Before we get into what a natal chart is and isn't, here's what you will need to access yours:

I'm a western astrologer so I use the tropical zodiac which is based on the seasons, as opposed to Vedic/sidereal astrology which is based on the constellations. In order to keep this simple and pull up your chart quickly, let's not get into the technicalities. You can use any website or app that uses tropical astrology to pull up your chart but at the time of writing, the one most recommended by professional astrologers is Astrodienst (www. astro.com) which is free to use.

You will need:

Your date of birth
- Accurate time of birth (the source is important: a hospital birth record, birth certificate or even the family astrologer's notes if that was a thing in your house; mother's memory is usually unreliable given that mothers were probably otherwise preoccupied at the time, but it's definitely better than nothing)
- City/town and country of birth (if your birth place doesn't show up on Astrodienst, use the nearest big city/town)

No birth time?

If you don't have a birth time, you'll still have half the information—the planets, the signs they are in, and the aspects they make to each other, which can yield a lot of useful information. So just set it for any time and ignore the angles and the houses in your interpretation (we'll get to all this). If you know you were born in the day or night, or if you have a small window, then you can adjust the time accordingly. If you have a small window (within two hours), you can usually get hold of your rising sign (which is extremely important) if not the ascendant (which is a specific degree of the rising sign).

If you were born on a day when the moon changed signs, then see if you can get hold of an approximate window ('within two hours after sunrise' or 'sometime in the afternoon'). While these approximations can be inaccurate, they can still go a long way when it comes to determining the moon's position. Typically, you should be able to tell what your moon sign is if you were given two signs but in some charts, this can be tricky.

The house system I use for Jungian astrology is Placidus. You can use whatever house system makes intuitive sense to you (most traditional western astrologers prefer whole signs which is simpler, but for starters, I do recommend Placidus for the Jungian method). This is also the default setting on Astrodienst, so like I said, just leave the settings as they are. You can, however, use whole signs (select it in the drop down menu under house system) if you have your rising sign, but don't have an accurate birth time (i.e the ascendant).

What is a Natal/Birth Chart?

> *'We are born at a given moment, in a given place, and like vintage years of wine, we have the qualities of the year and of the season in which we are born.'*
>
> —C.G. Jung

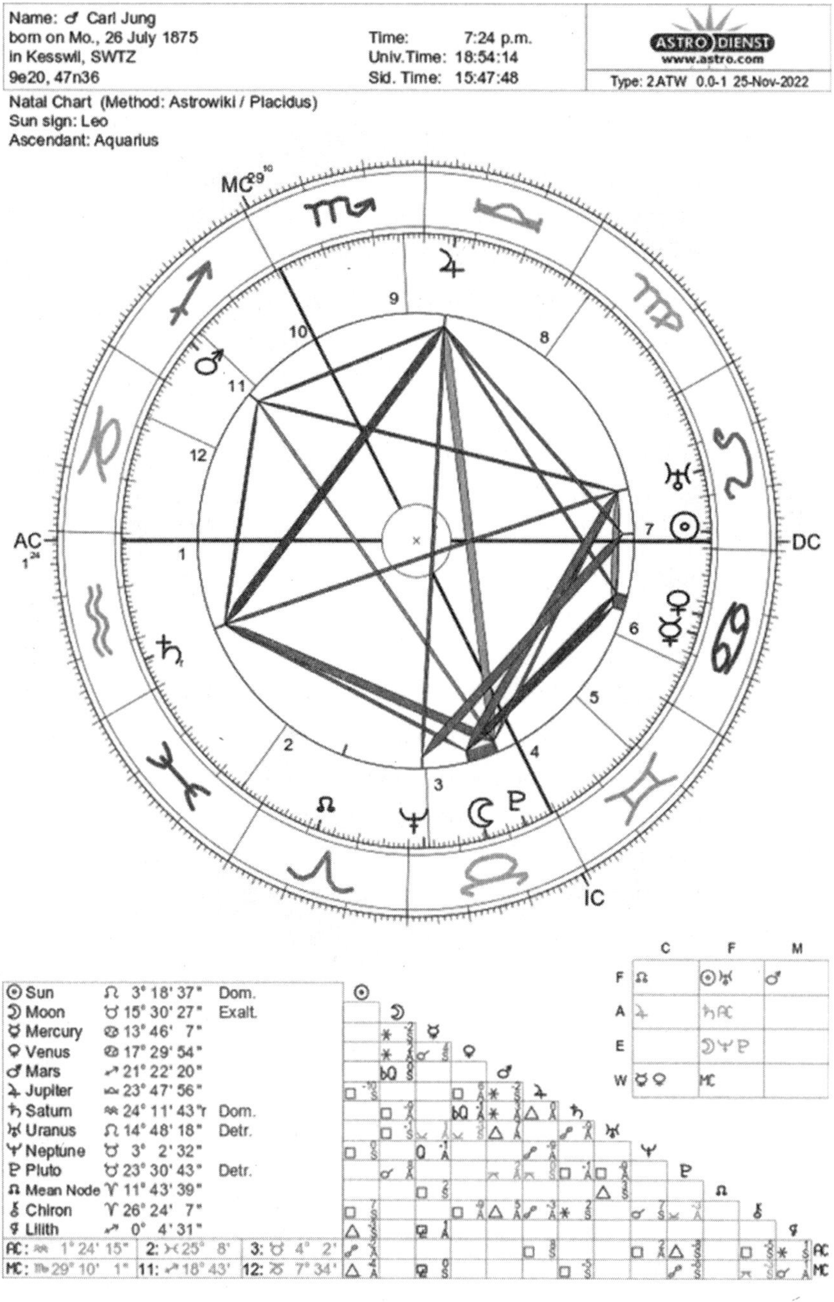

Figure 3. *Source: Astro-Databank wiki*

It is a snapshot of the sky at the moment you took your first breath. Astronomically, it is an accurate map of the sky as it appears at the precise time, from the specific place of your birth. The circle with the twelve zodiac signs that you see around it, is a totality symbol, much like the cosmic egg or the world tree or any other archetypal symbol of wholeness.* Please take a moment to note that we all have *all* the signs in our chart (which is your cue to stop fixating on signs and judging them based on the two people you dislike with the same sun sign).

This zodiacal circle or wheel is known as the ecliptic, and it is the apparent path of the sun as it moves about the heavens. So the position of the sun, moon and the planets on the zodiac and their relationship to each other as well as the earth's horizon at the moment of your birth, is your birth chart. We all have the same planets or drives, as we understand them psychologically, but they form unique patterns in a birth chart, making your chart different from mine.

So symbolically, there is the circle of wholeness on the outside representing what the individual psyche is striving towards, and the planetary combinations that make up your particular psychological patterns on the inside.† Each planetary symbol represents an archetypal principle with its entire range of expression. Each of these planets is also placed in a particular sign, a house, and forms relationships with other planets, and each of these elements is encrusted in a whole body of myth. So exploring the chart is like entering the world of myth, fairytale and story, where the gods are as benign and sympathetic as they are manic and deranged, and it would take free will and a conscious ego to express their hungers in a way that is creative, healing and ultimately, life-affirming.

Relating: An Astrological Guide to Living with Others, Liz Greene.
†Ibid

Astrology, like myth, does not moralise. It simply holds up a mirror. It's a map of the psyche, charting out your archetypal nature with its gifts and challenges, your developmental pattern and your potential pathway to wholeness. So if it is predictive, it is only symbolically or archetypally predictive, and we miss out on its larger meaning and purpose when we literalise it or assign concrete meaning to its imagery.

> *'It is a roadmap in the truest sense, for the object of studying it is not to "overcome" the "influences" of the planets, but rather to allow room in one's life to express all those qualities and drives of which the chart is a symbol.'*

—Liz Greene

The Natal Chart and the Self

In the Jungian sense, the zodiacal wheel comprising all the signs, is also a symbol of the Self. The Self, that I've already briefly touched on, is central to Jung's theory and paradoxically, the Self is not oneself. It is not the 'I'. In normal usage, we refer to the ego or the 'I' as the self. But in Jungian theory, the 'I'/ego, is only the centre of your conscious personality (we've already covered this), whereas the Self is both the centre and totality of the whole psyche, comprising both consciousness and the unconscious. The Self is the archetype of wholeness and the ordering principle of the psyche. It is also transcendent, which means it rests outside the psyche's limits and yet defines it.* It contains the essence of who you are meant to be, and is the goal of individuation—that lifelong process of realising your inherent wholeness.

It's Jung's god word. Except he arrived at it by observing facts as an empirical scientist, not as a mystic.

Jung's Map of the Soul, Murray Stein

The Self being the archetype of wholeness cannot be mapped out in the natal chart because it is bigger than you and is therefore symbolised by the whole zodiac containing all the signs. The particular patterns formed by the planets and their placement in your chart, is a portrayal of all the conflicts, contradictions and mythic themes you're set up to encounter, integrate, reconcile and stitch into the meaningful whole that is your individual life, as guided by the mysterious, transcendent centre that is the Self.

But just as the chart cannot map out the Self, it also cannot factor in free will. So we cannot tell, just from looking at the chart, how one might express the potential it portrays.*

Relating: An Astrological Guide to Living with Others, Liz Greene.

5

The Planets

'Astrology, like the collective unconscious with which psychology is concerned, consists of symbolic configurations: the planets are the gods, the symbols of the powers of the unconscious.'

—C.G. Jung

Pop astrology has reduced the study of astrology to the signs of the zodiac, but it's the planets that tell us about the psychodynamics portrayed in a horoscope. The planets are the symbols of the archetypal forces that lie in the deepest layer of the unconscious and form the core of our complexes.

So we're basically replacing 'archetype' or 'god' with 'planet', and 'planet with 'drive'.* Without the planets, there is nowhere to go. Nothing happens. There is no action, no story. It's like a play with all the settings and costumes in place, but no actors.

Now every planetary symbol represents an archetypal principle, which means it contains within its symbolism, the potential for the whole range of the archetype's expression. This is why prediction in any concrete sense is not only tricky—because literally everything on earth has a planetary correspondence—but from the psychological point of view, kind of pointless. Because

---

The Horoscope in Manifestation, Liz Greene

when seen through a Jungian lens, the question you should be asking is 'Why is this archetypal principle manifesting in this way? What is it trying to say to me and how can I consciously embody its essence?' as opposed to 'What's going to happen?' which suggests you have no agency.

> *'For astrology, according to Tarnas' helpful definition, is not to be understood as literally predictive of future events and therefore indicative of the inescapable workings of a preordained fate; rather, astrology is archetypally predictive in that it gives insight into the background archetypal factors, the general themes and motifs, evident in our experiences and not to the specific form of manifestation of these archetypes.'*

—Keiron Le Grice*

When you're looking at a planet, you're looking at a field of energy (the archetype) that has its own essence, consciousness and volition. It's hungry for something, it's going somewhere, and it expresses itself through the individual as a 'drive'. For example, mars represents the principle of aggression and initiation, among other things. We all have mars in our charts so we all have the potential for aggression within us. When mars is functioning consciously in our psyche, we are able to assert ourselves when necessary, take charge of situations and thrive on healthy competition. But there are a number of factors in the chart that can get in the way of mars' expression. The sign and house it is placed in, and the relationship it has with other planets, may or may not be conducive for the expression of the martian drive within us. If the chart indicates excess, our mars may have developed lopsidedly. In this case, it may go looking for a fight, create patterns of rivalry and so on. On the other hand,

---

*The Archetypal Cosmos, Keiron Le Grice

we could have a mars deficit which can show up as repressed rage with a tendency to bottle up anger and explode without warning, or a proclivity for scheming and manipulation while avoiding direct confrontation. We know by now that anything functioning unconsciously always spells trouble. While knowing your astrological placements alone is not going to change the way they behave, it is an excellent first step in understanding what your unconscious is up to at any given point and learning to work with it creatively, so you experience it as an inner ally rather than a saboteur.

We can now briefly explore each of the ten planets (for the sake of convenience, I'll refer to the sun and the moon as planets) and the basic impulses and archetypal patterns they symbolise in the individual.

> *'In astronomy, these ten heavenly bodies are the components which form the organism of our solar system. Symbolically, they form the organism of the human psyche.'*
>
> —Liz Greene[*]

THE LUMINARIES: THE SUN AND THE MOON

The Sun

As the centre of the solar system, the sun corresponds to the heart of the human anatomy and everything it symbolically represents in the psyche. It is the desire for selfhood, that fundamental urge to become oneself; the potential for individuality within

---

[*]*Relating: An Astrological Guide to Living with Others*, Liz Greene.

every person as well as the unique—read potentially lonesome, uncertain and calling for tremendous courage—path that one must take in order to fulfil it. In this sense, the sun corresponds to the archetypal hero and his eternal quest; with all its attendant challenges, tests and trials, divinely orchestrated to call forth his true nature, his individual essence. So, contrary to the popular understanding of sun signs corresponding to a set of readymade traits we were born with, we might want to look at the sun in the astrological chart as an area where we must consciously strive and as qualities we must deliberately nurture and cultivate, in order to become ourselves; it is a symbol of our particular hero's journey. The sign, house and planetary aspects (which we'll get to) give us clues about the nature of our quest—the treasures we are setting out to find, the dragons, giants, sea-monsters or orcs we are likely to meet on the way, the particular riddles we must solve and curses we must break, as well as the helpful animals who come along to assist us and the gifts and boons bestowed on us by the gods.

So psychologically, the sun represents the ego, that bright light of consciousness, without which we cannot know ourselves. The light of the sun illumines and clarifies, leaving no room for doubt or ambiguity; it is our capacity for consciousness through reflection and discrimination, and the piece of sky that's lit up by the astrological sun in the natal chart symbolically points to a place within us that radiates this sense of piercing solar truth.

It is the truth of who we are. The core of our *I-am-ness*; not in the superficial sense that we know ourselves but those rare glimpses of the gold within, that certain moments afford us. We know when we make contact with this place within us, by the way it makes us come alive, filling us with joy, vitality and a profound sense of freedom to be ourselves, much like a wilting flower in need of direct sunlight. You'd do well to notice what you're engaged in, in these moments, because they reveal something about what it means to express your particular sun. You can begin to see why keywords on the lines of 'identity', 'vocation', 'creative self-expression', 'play' and 'inner child' are attributed to the sun in modern astrology. But keywords, though they have their place, can be a gross injustice to archetypes, which speak to us as symbols; and symbols, as we've already seen, are inexhaustible in meaning.

Mythically, the sun is the creator spirit, the father god, the source of all energy and life; the creator and the fructifier. And because we all come from a father—whether we knew him or not and whether he was loving, cruel, inspiring, betraying or whatever else—father belongs to the universal/archetypal level of the human psyche, taking us back to the sun as father-god, life-giver and creator. So through a Jungian lens, the story of the sun in the astrological chart can tell us something about an individual's father complex.

We've already discussed complexes in detail so the father complex refers to those inner images or filters through which we are predisposed to perceiving the father archetype in all its manifestations (our personal father and father figures, our sense of self, identity and vocation, mentors, leaders and governments, inspiring figures or modern-day heroes etc.) even before we have any personal experience of our own fathers.

And because your personal father or father figure is the very first person through whom you experience the archetypal father, you will first project your inner images of the father archetype on him. If your sun is in aspect to saturn (we'll get to all this later), this might suggest that your inner image of father may be that of a strict disciplinarian who takes pleasure in saying 'no' to you (as one example). If this is the most dominant image of father you carry within you, then this is the one you will most clearly see in the outer father, whoever he may be as an individual. So whether or not your father is objectively strict, you will be far more receptive to him when he says 'no' to you or otherwise disciplines you, because that's the image you carry inside. If the outer father is able to bring enough joy, freedom and love into the equation, this may help neutralise the 'charge' of the negative image inside, though you'd still have a tendency to see him as saturn, who in his destructive aspect, is the devouring father. And because you see the person through a particular filter (in this case, a negative one), you always invoke it in them.

This is a fascinating thing to watch, and it actually wasn't clear to me until I saw my daughter's chart for the very first time when she was still young, about 8-9 years old, and saw everything I had read about, come alive in our dynamic. The moon in her chart (which corresponds to the mother complex) did not describe me as I experience myself or even as others describe me (at least, not for the most part), but it was a stunningly accurate portrayal of how she experienced me—both positively and negatively. I also observed how she, simply by viewing me through these particular filters, repeatedly invoked these sides of my nature. This is the nature of projection and it's true for all relationships. We cast people in roles based on the costumes we already have laid out for them. And we in turn play pre-scripted roles in other people's lives. This is not a bad thing. In fact, it's a necessary thing because it allows us to 'hold' for each other, those facets of self that we're not yet ready to hold for ourselves. And when the time comes when the projection dissolves, we get to choose to take responsibility for those disowned parts of us, as we see it reflected back through the other. And while it's one thing to be aware of these dynamics, it's entirely mind-blowing to see it so clearly portrayed in the natal charts of individuals.

Now coming back to our example of saturn colouring the

father complex, what would be ideal is if your personal father is able to mediate the life-giving qualities of saturn (again, we'll get to this) such as healthy boundaries, protection, responsibility, devotedness to duty and stability, because saturn is always going to colour your inner image of the father principle, and the best way for you to develop its positive side in yourself is by seeing it reflected back to you in your outer world.

Now the reason the sun, which is associated with selfhood and identity, is also related to the father principle may have to do with the fact that the father is the first stranger in the child's world. He does not belong in the enmeshed world of mother and child, so he is typically, the first person who sees you as a separate individual. And how this relationship goes (which, to a large extent depends on your own inner images as we've already seen) will determine your internalised sense of self or I-am-ness.

Jung used the term 'amplification' for using one language (primarily drawing from myths, fairytales, religion, history and culture) to elaborate on a symbol's universal level of meaning. And that's exactly where you'd want to go if you want to explore a symbol in any depth. The stories of the solar gods (Apollo, Helios, Surya, Mithras, Christ, as some examples) and solar heroes (of part human and part divine parentage, suggesting there is something within the individual that partakes of the eternal and the transcendent)—like Herakles and Perseus to Harry Potter—all give us a sense of the essence and meaning of the astrological sun. Where your sun is placed and how it's configured with other planets in your birth chart, clues us in on this divine spark within you.

Of course, we're speaking of potential here and that can go several ways. As life-giving as the sun is, it can also scorch you to death and blind you should you get too close. Stories of 'flying too close to the sun' (from the flight of Icarus) and falling from the heights or being struck down by the gods (as when Hanuman attempts to 'eat the sun') are also recorded in myth, warning us of the perils of solar ambition, often characterised by pride, ego-inflation, self-aggrandisement and in extreme cases, narcissism and mania. When the spark of divinity is confused with one's whole sense of self, the individual becomes inflated, a god in his own eyes. Dazzled by his own brilliance and terrified by ordinariness, the individual may spend his whole life chasing every shiny thing and never actualise the potential he senses. He may refuse to leave the paradise of childhood like Peter Pan or chase fame and celebrity like so many who confuse solar gold with its counterfeit—the glitz and glamour of the spotlight. The sun also symbolises the king, who in ancient times, was considered a descendant of the solar gods; in this sense, the sun symbolises sovereignty, authority, leadership and justice. When we are in the right relationship with our sun, we can trust our own centre—our inner king—and summon the courage to answer its call to adventure.

So the astrological sun is an ancient symbol of the archetypal masculine/yang principle. Particularly those facets of the masculine that have to do with spirit, creation, reflection, illumination, consciousness, vitality, truth, courage, justice, inspiration, self-government, enlightenment, selfhood and individual destiny. The solar path invites us to recognise and embrace our separateness from others—courageously taking on those forces that lure us towards safety and security, rather than our development—without which we'll never be individuals.

The Moon

As the luminary of the night, the moon corresponds to the night world of the unconscious, where dangers lurk at every corner and we rely on the wisdom of instincts and the intelligence of the body, to ensure our survival. Much of what we have always projected on the night—our fear of thieves, murderers, ghosts, demons, witches and sorcerers, the wild unknown of the woods at night time and the dark or forbidden forest that we often meet in children's stories and fairytales—tells us something about the lunar consciousness within us. This knowing of the moon is very different from the bright, daytime clarity of the sun, but it's a knowing nonetheless. In the light of the moon, everything morphs and changes;* what looks like a hooded man in the shadows, could be a tree; a firefly could be a fairy and the reddened face of the moon during a lunar eclipse could be the bloody face of a monster about to devour you whole. The moon itself looks different in its many phases and depending on what's going on in the life of the observer, she may appear romantic (if we could only count the number of love songs and poems inspired by the moon) or sinister (as in horror stories, werewolf and vampire lore, and of course, Hallowe'en) or tender and maternal (as in lullabies and kindergarten rhymes). The moon in this sense, corresponds to the symbol-producing aspect of the unconscious.

If we're feeling lonely and longing for connection on a Sunday evening, gazing at the moon may seem to mysteriously

---

*The Luminaries: Seminars in Psychological Astrology Vol 1, Liz Greene and Howard Sasportas

amplify these feelings, and maybe even make us reach for a drink (or two, or too many), which may then culminate in a drunk text we'll regret the next morning; and when daylight floods our consciousness, we cannot explain the irrational moment the night before. 'I don't know what happened there, I think I'm going a bit mad,' we might joke it away ('lunacy' from 'luna'). This pull in us towards the irrational, the instinctual, the unconscious, is the lunar urge for safety, belonging and fusion, which goes against the solar struggle for consciousness, separateness and a distinct sense of self.

On a practical level, when we lean towards the sun, we are willing to sacrifice security, relationships, belonging and kinship for the sake of identity, vocation, achievement and sense of self; and when we go too close to the moon, we readily relinquish our ego needs for the comfort and nourishment that comes from fusion with others, our individuality and place in the world for the sake of intimacy, connection and the well-being of the family and tribe. Too much sun, and our ego-needs swallow up our capacity for empathy and connection. Too much moon, and we are consumed and overwhelmed by feelings and instincts with little to no volition.

So the moon corresponds to the Great Mother archetype in her many manifestations: as life-sustaining, nourishing, cherishing, protecting, sheltering, the feminine wisdom that transcends reason; as well as devouring, mad, poisoning, seducing, and 'all that is inescapable and terrifying like fate and death'.* Our experience of the moon, therefore, precedes the sun just as our experience of the personal mother and her womb, precedes the father or anyone else in the outer world. When we are born, our needs—to be fed, changed, held, touched and soothed—are entirely lunar; the most basic needs of the body and the instincts.

Four Archetypes, C.G Jung

Studying the astrological moon, then, can tell us something about our instinctual nature, and what constitutes 'safety', 'belonging' and 'sustenance' for us.* Unlike the sun, there is no conscious striving involved when it comes to how we express our moons. It is the part of us that arises most spontaneously when we're not operating by reason and logic. It's who we are when we're most 'at home'. Now you can see why the internet says the moon in the chart means 'mother', 'emotions', 'home and family'. But understanding the chart through a Jungian/archetypal lens makes it easy to see how even your mother is an outer symbol of the archetypal mother, the matrix ('matrix' from 'mater'), the beginning of all life; and since there is no end to an archetype's manifestations, the information you can glean from each planet in the chart is limitless. So the astrological moon can give you deep psychological insights about your emotional hunger, instinctual nature and attachment patterns; while also revealing more superficial things like how you keep your house or what kind of comfort food you prefer.

Since our focus here is on the psychology of the individual, let's look at how the moon expresses itself consciously and unconsciously; what 'lunar malfunctions' look like and what we can do about them. The moon represents our basic need to feel safe in the world (without which we cannot even begin to follow our solar urge to become conscious) so studying the moon by sign, house and aspect, can tell us what this particular person needs at the most fundamental level. If these needs are not adequately met, we start to feel anxious, which is basically a feeling that we cannot trust life to keep us safe.† While feelings of anxiety are

---

The Luminaries: Seminars in Psychological Astrology Vol 1, Liz Greene and Howard Sasportas
†Ibid

normal in themselves, we might want to start paying attention when said anxiety starts to disrupt our normal functioning (or when it qualifies as a disorder). As we've already seen, the Jungian approach to symptoms is to see them as messengers; they come to tell us that something in the unconscious is calling for our attention. So instead of attempting to cure the anxiety, we speak to it, explore it through the chart and through dreams, to examine what specifically makes us anxious; and how, by consciously 'feeding' the moon what it's hungry for, we might get closer to being free of this symptom. The same goes for every other type of lunar malfunction from eating disorders, disrupted sleep patterns and menstrual cycles, to problems with attachment (too needy, too distant, too suffocating, too cold) and intimacy (wanting too much of it or fearing it and running away from it) and relationships (difficulty sustaining long-term relationships of any kind, highly-charged familial relationships, any problematic patterns such as feelings of possessiveness and jealousy, co-dependency, fear of abandonment, fear of rejection, attracting people who are unavailable, people who are manipulative or narcissistic, triangular relationship patterns, and on and on) to mood disorders, cyclical depression and anything else that affects us emotionally or physiologically.

For example, if the chart suggests that one of the fundamental needs of your particular moon is autonomy, freedom and independence (moon in Aries or moon in aspect to mars, for example) but—perhaps due to other chart factors that override this need in favour of intimacy, belonging and connection—you are unconscious of this side of your nature; then you're going to meet those repressed qualities in a partner by projection and most likely to an excessive degree. The more you want to get close, the more they seem to run away. When you've repeated this long enough to notice that it's your pattern, you may want to ask how this person is mirroring your own unlived life. Of course, you can do this without the chart through months and years of talk therapy; or you can get there right away if you have the chart to take you to the archetypal core of your mother complex.

As we've already seen, the complex is an inner image and must not be confused with any person in your outer life.* But since the complex determines the filter through which you experience everyone and everything that falls under the mother archetype, studying the moon can tell us how you subjectively (this cannot be emphasised enough) experienced your personal mother or other caregivers, your early environment and any challenges therein (which could hint at any developmental trauma), and how you continue to project your inner images of the archetypal mother on all her outer symbols.

The moon is an ancient symbol of the goddess and the archetypal feminine/yin principle, and especially those aspects of the feminine that represent the fecundity of nature, and the instincts (which Jung understood as nature *within* us), that pull us towards connection, fusion, intimacy, attachment, belonging, nourishment, security and a sense of rootedness in the emotional and material world.

As much as our solar drive wants to soar and test the limits of our potential, our lunar hunger keeps us grounded, reminding us that we're made of earth ('matter' from 'mater') and to the earth we will return.

There is one last thing I want to mention about the sun and the moon in the chart in relation to the parental complexes and that is the insight it can yield on the unlived life of the parents. The way your sun and moon are configured in your natal chart

---

Jung's Map of the Soul, Murray Stein

can tell you about an aspect of your parents' nature that could not be lived out, and that is now part of a generational story that you must complete. You may experience this as a compulsive part of your own nature or it may be more conscious as in those cases where the mother actually raises her daughter to have the life 'I couldn't have'.

> *'Nothing has a stronger influence psychologically on their environment and especially on their children, as the unlived life of the parent.'*

> —C.G Jung

For more on the luminaries read Liz Greene and Howard Sasportas' The Luminaries, *Liz Greene's* Apollo's Chariot *and Anne Baring and Jules Cashford's* The Myth of the Goddess *(for a Jungian deep-dive into aspects of the moon) and Dane Rudhyar's* The Lunation Cycle.

THE INNER PLANETS: MERCURY, VENUS AND MARS

Mercury

After the luminaries comes mercury, representing our urge to understand, as well as share what we understand. The placement of mercury in the astrological chart is a picture of our go-to mode of perception—how we process experience and information in order to make sense of life. Studying the astrological mercury can give us a window into how we learn, as well as how we gather and evaluate information—through intuition (fire), the senses (earth), thinking (air) or feeling (water).

Mythically, mercury is related to the messenger and Trickster gods (the Greek Hermes, the Norse Loki, the Egyptian Thoth as a few examples) who have access to all the three realms—the upper, middle and lower worlds—and relay messages between the gods and mortals. In Jungian language, this attribute of mercury corresponds to 'the transcendent function' of the psyche which bridges the lower, unconscious world with the upper realm of consciousness. It is through mercury that we become aware of something previously unconscious in us. In this sense, the symptom itself (or crisis or destructive pattern) is seen as Hermes/Mercury because it comes bearing a message: 'Something is wrong in the underworld (unconscious) and needs your attention.' If we approach the symptom with curiosity, trying to understand its symbolism and where it's leading us in the unconscious instead of getting caught up in fixing it, we follow Hermes through the labyrinthine underworld of our own psyche, where integration of the exiled pieces of ourselves with our conscious self, becomes possible.

While there are certainly conditions and symptoms that require medication, depth psychology shows us how the symptom itself comes to help us. If we have become unconsciously stuck and don't know how to get out of our own way; or when we've suffered a trauma and though we think we're past it, the body seems to remember; when we throw ourselves into our life and work, as a way of not dealing with what's going on in the deeper corners of ourselves—the unconscious may produce a symptom. This is the trickster aspect of mercury that trips up the ego. This may take the form of a mid-life crisis, a divorce, death, illness, depression, neurosis, recurring nightmares, making 'a complete fool of ourselves' or any number of other symptoms that come to shake us out of our denial and dissociation, so that, by going through the unavoidable crisis, we can learn to integrate these previously split-off parts of ourselves. The emotionally distant man may develop a relationship with his own inner feminine through the loss of a partner, child or pet on whom he had previously projected his feeling nature; the perfectionist artist who second guesses every stroke of her brush may be freed from the tyranny of her inner critic and learn to embrace her need for play, through a bout of depression or creative block; the workaholic may learn to slow down and direct some of their energy and focus towards their loved ones when an accident confines them to bed or makes them dependent on others; and the high-strung, self-righteous person may learn to laugh at himself and develop a sense of humour after making a public disgrace of himself. In this sense, mercury dons the role of the psychopomp—the mediator between the conscious and the unconscious realms, and like the Mercurius of alchemy, is an agent of transformation. As Sufi wisdom goes: 'the cure for the pain is in the pain'.

All this talk of mercury as psychopomp and catalyst for transformation through consciousness, may feel like a far cry from the common understanding of mercury as the planet that rules communication, buying and selling, and technology (further hyped by pop astrology and its obsession with mercury retrograde). But if we can keep reminding ourselves that the planets are the symbols of archetypal powers, then we're looking at the entire spectrum of the archetype's expression. So yes, communication (of all kinds), buying and selling, gathering of knowledge and information, teaching and writing, the exchange of ideas, concepts and theories, anything that involves a descent to gather information (such as research, but equally, the psychotherapist or astrologer tracking a symptom down to its unconscious roots)—all fall under the domain of the messenger and trickster gods that mercury symbolises.

So in order to really understand the role of mercury in the chart and in the psyche, we must begin with a thorough exploration of the mythic aspect of this planet. Immersing ourselves in the stories and language of mythology can give us a felt sense of how a planet operates—in its light as well as shadow aspects. As always, the chart cannot tell us how we will use the potential it maps out, so we cannot tell if a powerful mercury in the chart will produce a renowned writer, scholar, mathematician or a legendary con artist (Hermes is patron of both thieves and scribes, among other things).

Practically, paying close attention to how mercury is placed in the chart, can help us understand our cognitive processes better. As an example, this can be immensely helpful in understanding certain aspects of neuro-divergence (though you'd have to study the whole chart for the full picture) through an archetypal lens, because it allows us to approach it creatively, from an entirely different perspective, which is mercurial in itself.

Venus

> *There is a very beautiful passage in Plato's Phaedro, where he speaks of seeing mirrored in the face of one's beloved, a glimpse of the god to whom one's soul belongs. This is the most profound meaning of venus—the beloved, be it person, object or intellectual ideal, as the mirror of one's own soul.'*
>
> —Liz Greene

In venus and mars, the cosmic lovers, we meet another facet of the yin-yang/masculine-feminine duo that we already saw in the sun and the moon.

If the moon is the maternal feminine, venus represents the

erotic feminine. I use the term 'erotic' not in the hyper-sexualised way that we understand it today but in the wider, psychological sense as the energy of union and the urge for relatedness that springs from love and desire (from the Greek 'eros' with all its attendant madness), not only with people but with all aspects of life.

Eros is the psychic force that powerfully attracts you to a thing in order to be one with it. But unlike the moon that represents our need for merging and fusion for the sake of emotional security, venus is about the urge to define our own values because what we find beautiful and desirable, is a reflection of what we deeply value.

Whether you're gazing at the night sky because you can't tear your eyes away from its magnificence, staying up all night researching a new field of study or topic of interest that has got you hooked, burying your nose in a loaf of freshly baked bread and having a religious experience, being consumed by a hobby or an artistic pursuit and revelling in the incomparable joy of creation, allowing a piece of music or the rhythmic beating of a drum to move your whole body with ecstasy, cuddling a baby or a furry animal that makes otherwise normal adults say such things as 'I want to eat him up' (to take in, to be one), feeling a profound sense of love and connection with the earth as you tend your garden, enjoying a relaxing massage at the spa and of course, everything that pulls you towards a lover, from initial attraction to passionate consummation—eros is the energy symbolised by Cupid's arrows; it is through the love, longing and idealisation in this act of projection that you become aware of those qualities within you that are 'divine' and of the highest value. Because who and what you love, reveals who you fundamentally are, and what is most desirable about you. In paintings, Venus-Aphrodite is often seen gazing into a mirror. This is because venusian love is not about the other as much as how the other reflects oneself; and the urge to be desired for that which makes us so special. In this way, venus helps us know and draw close to our solar specialness. It is our oomph factor.

The mythic parallels of venus—from the Sumerian Inanna and the Babylonian Ishtar (who presided over sexual rites) to the Greek Aphrodite (whose marriage to Hephaestus means absolutely nothing given that she takes lovers and breaks her marriage vows as and when she pleases)—paint a picture of the archetypal Lover or the free woman who belongs to no one but herself. Everything that Aphrodite does, she does on her terms; because she *wants* to.

> 'Her skin is golden, her hair is golden—in fact she shines like the sun. She also seduces men in daylight...this unashamed solar brightness is the creative face of Aphrodite's vanity and "narcissism".'

> —Liz Greene

In some myths, she also bears children but she is by no means maternal in any lunar sense. Venus as a parent is not the most reliable when it comes to packing her children's lunches, fussing over their sleep schedules or wearing the 'right' outfit to a PTA meeting. But in her positive expression, she can be the fun parent or the one who infuses her children's daily lives with a sense of joy, whimsy and wonderment; and when she lavishes them with love and adoration, it's because she is (at least in that moment) delighted by them and not because she needs them to need her (as is often the case with the moon). Carried to an extreme, the venusian mother is often a child herself, refusing to take adult responsibility and creating an unconscious rivalry with any daughter as she reaches sexual maturity. Such envy is often deeply unconscious and may manifest in any number of ways including a daughter who is unable to kickstart her love life, or one so overshadowed by her mother's beauty and charm that she suffers from severe body-image issues and/or eating disorders. This is typical of the shadow side of the mythical Aphrodite who is known to become jealous, spiteful and treacherous towards anyone, like the mortal Psyche, whose beauty rivalled her own. So the potential for vanity and general cattiness is also very much a part of the venusian story.

Every archetypal power has its own laws and ethics, often in direct contradiction to the values of other archetypal principles. So the complete and wilful abandon in the pursuit of pleasure, which is sacred to venus, is horrifying to the moon who places emotional security above everything else, a weakness or mere nuisance to mars who values self-assertion above all things, and abhorrent to saturn which represents societal norms and social structures among other things. Needless to say, among all the planetary archetypes, venus has been the most repressed and the most demonised in our societies for several hundreds of years. And as anything that is repressed for too long, she 'erupts' and disturbs the surface of collective consciousness through affairs that end presidencies and marriages (saturn and moon), as venereal diseases ('venereal' from 'venus'), sex scandals in religious organisations and institutions (where venus is most repressed) as our culture's obsession with eternal youth and Botox, as the rise of hook-up culture, diet culture, and the sexualisation of everything (from food to Santa Claus to the dirty joke your otherwise conservative uncle told that made you cringe).

But as with all archetypes, venus has a range of expressions from light to shadow; life-giving to destructive or 'amoral'. And how she shows up in our individual lives (as a fertile creative life, as a rich aesthetic sensibility, a stimulating social life, a colourful love life etc. or as issues around self-worth and sexuality, jealousy, catty people, certain addictions) has a lot to say about our relationship with the archetypal Lover. The astrological venus then, is a symbol of everything we value as well as that which is most valuable and desirable in us (the 'gold' of our solar selves) even if we are unconscious of it. Studying this planet in the chart by sign, house and aspects, learning to love what is most loveable in us, and giving ourselves permission to find channels for the conscious expression of our individual venus, is one way to break free of the suffering that stems from her shadow side, and relate to ourselves—first and foremost—as beings worthy of love; not because of anything we do but because of who we are.

Mars

As the masculine counterpart to the venusian urge to understand ourselves in relation to others and discover how we are similar, mars represents the urge to assert ourselves and have our way *despite* others, revealing our differences.* As an aspect of the masculine, mars is a symbol of the archetypal Warrior, just as the sun represents Father, King and aspects of the Hero.

Psychologically, it is the principle of aggression that we all innately possess and rely on, in order to assert and protect our sense of self. Without a healthy relationship to the martian drive within us, we have no fight in us. And fight we must, if we are to be separate individuals in our own right, with the capacity to function independently of others. Without mars, we are impotent; our volition is thwarted and we feel ineffectual

---

The Inner Planets: Seminars in Psychological Astrology Vol 2, Liz Greene and Howard Sasportas

and incapacitated. Unable to take on those forces that challenge our development—whether they show up as outright rivals and oppressors, or overprotective mothers and enmeshed family units that keep us dependent, and relationships that hold us back from asserting our individuality, or our own fears and insecurities, lethargy, overwhelm and inertia that prevent us from taking on daily challenges—we feel defeated by life, and experience ourselves as victims, with little or no agency.

In this sense, mars serves the sun by acting as a vehicle for the expression of our solar essence.* When we have a well-functioning mars, we have a direction to follow; we know what we want and we're willing to do what it takes to get it. A healthy mars does not back down in the face of opposition, challenges or obstacles but is instead oddly roused by the prospect of risk, competition or danger. It is mars that makes the firefighter charge into a burning building when everyone else is fleeing in the opposite direction. And while we may not all be equipped to do that, we will, without a doubt, face a few metaphorical fires in our lives, and it is mars we must rely on in those moments, to take charge of situations and act on instinct.

In myth, Ares-Mars is a warrior and is himself conceived as a result of the longstanding competition and rivalry between Zeus and his wife Hera. Zeus is always violating his marriage vows by sleeping with other women and begetting children; Hera is relentlessly spying on him and plotting ways to exact revenge. But then Zeus takes his Zeus-ness up a notch and produces Athene from his head, without a mother. This insults and outrages Hera who presides over marriage and childbearing. And in classic Hera fashion, conceives Ares-Mars without a man.

The Inner Planets: Seminars in Psychological Astrology Vol 2, Liz Greene and Howard Sasportas

'Ares has no father-principle in him, which I understand to mean that he does not spring from logos, from the spiritual or intellectual dimension of the masculine realm. He is male, but he is pure instinct, without any reflective or symbolising capacity.'

—Liz Greene

Even if you've never actually been in a bar fight or got into trouble with the law, there are plenty of opportunities to brush up against your mars function on a daily basis. If you've ever felt your blood 'boil' or the urge to punch someone in the face, let your competitive side ruin game night (or for that matter, date night); if you've had trouble standing in a queue, felt your foot push the gas pedal harder than you knew you should, bought something on impulse, couldn't take 'no' for an answer, acted territorial or felt so consumed by a desire that you forgot to consider the people you were hurting along the way—you know what it's like to be in the grip of your mars. Depending on the sign and placement of your astrological mars, you may or may not have easy access to this archetypal principle that—despite its tendency to stir trouble for kicks—is so central to your survival and the safeguarding of your boundaries.

A repressed mars for instance (easy enough to spot in a chart), often shows up as a difficult relationship with anger. If your early environment sent you the message that your anger is 'wrong,' 'bad' or 'sinful', then this can react with your not-so-ideally placed mars (your innate disposition). You may live this out in a number of ways including bottling up your anger, only for it to explode out of proportion and without warning, taking the 'turn the other cheek' route without giving yourself permission to process your entirely reasonable anger, becoming compulsively positive or using humour to diffuse tension because you cannot tolerate conflict. Needless to say, this can have a domino effect on your whole personality, making you timid, diffident, passive, unmotivated, lethargic, ineffectual, frustrated and impotent (in every sense of the word).

At a more fundamental level, mars is our survival instinct—it is in charge of protecting us and also acting as our personal first responder. The inflammation that occurs as a result of the body's immune response when it's busy fighting off an infection is as much a mars function, as the adrenaline making your heart race and your brain more alert when you're in 'fight-or-flight' mode.

Whether we're going to war, the sports field, the courtroom or the therapy room, a reliable mars is our greatest psychological ally.

Of course, it is equally possible that your mars tends towards excess. And depending on the degree, you may be more impulsive, needing instant gratification, impatient, perhaps have a bit of a short fuse, all the way to being violent, volatile, sadistic, addicted, combative, selfish and ruthless, a reckless adrenaline junkie— putting yourself and others at risk without any thought and so on. Again, the chart can give us the archetypal picture. But the family and larger cultural background may either amplify it or help neutralise it.

The astrological mars sheds light on this principle of aggression within us; its strengths and weaknesses; its pattern of development; as well as what we might do to help awaken its potential, redirect its destructive urges and make an ally of this planetary archetype that (along with saturn) older astrology textbooks deemed 'malefic'.

For more on the inner planets, read Liz Greene and Howard Sasportas' The Inner Planets, *Liz Greene's* Relating: An Astrological Guide to Living with Others *and Karen Hamaker-Zondag's* Psychological Astrology

THE SOCIAL PLANETS

Jupiter and Saturn

♃ ♄

We now leave the realm of the personal planets (the sun, moon, mercury, venus and mars)—so called, because they symbolise aspects of ego-consciousness; drives that are easily accessible to the ego—and arrive at the threshold of the transpersonal level of consciousness. Orbiting between the personal planets and the transpersonal planets (uranus, neptune and pluto), jupiter and saturn are the threshold guardians; they traverse and bridge the space between our personal experiences and everything else beyond it—the great unknown—inquiring, interpreting, learning, growing, gaining perspective and making meaning until everything is broken down and crystallised into a worldview.

Mythically, Chronos-Saturn and Zeus-Jupiter are a father son-duo and archetypal enemies; Saturn is a Titan, a god of earth, psychologically representing the 'lower world'—the realm of matter, reality, mortality and the limitations of the body; Jupiter is an Olympian, a god of heaven and thunderstorms, representing the 'upper world' of the intuitive mind* and the fertilising capacity of the creative drive.

Zeus, as the god of heaven is grandiose and inflated—an image of vigour, vitality and limitless potential, as well as a parody of the masculine in its bombastic extreme. Kronos, his father, the god of earth and Father Time, is an image of fear, cold calculation and the capacity to bide one's time in order to win the war. Unlike Zeus, we don't see Kronos making a

---

Relating: An Astrological Guide to Living with Others, Liz Greene.

show of his power and potency. Instead he schemes with his mother Gaia, hides in a nook with a sickle and sneaks up on his father Ouranos before castrating him in the throes of the sexual act. Disturbing as the image is, it tells us something important about how we experience the archetypal principle that saturn represents in contrast to jupiter, both within and outside of us.

In the story, Kronos receives a prophecy that he would be dethroned by one of his children, as he himself castrated his father Ouranos (the sky god). Overcome by fear, Kronos swallows each of his children—representing a psychic process we are all quite familiar with by midlife; the sense of the passage of 'time' (Kronos) devouring future potential (as represented by children). By the time Zeus is born, Rhea, Kronos' wife, who has lost too many children and has had enough of her husband's paranoia, tricks him into swallowing a stone, and has Zeus raised in secret, before he returns to imprison Kronos in Tartarus, but only after he has made him regurgitate his siblings one by one.

And while jupiter and saturn represent two opposing forces both within and around us, they are both urging us towards the same psychological goal: our growth and development.

> *'...they are respectively, like the carrot which leads the donkey on by promising him future possibilities of reward, and the stick which drives him to move because it is too painful to stand still.'*

—Liz Greene*

The jupiter impulse within us, shows up as inspired ideas or a vision for the future. When we're in the jupiter zone, we feel expansive and undefeated by adversity and hardship because we 'know' that it all works out in the end. If our relationship with the jupiter principle is overall balanced, then this can

---

Relating: An Astrological Guide to Living with Others, Liz Greene.

offer tremendous resilience and faith in life because jupiter represents our ability to see the big-picture; it takes us out of our small-mindedness and literalism and imbues our experiences with meaning because jupiter is the symbolising as well as the reflective faculty within us. In the Jungian sense, it corresponds to what Jung called the religious function of the psyche—our need to know that there is an intrinsic order, a grand pattern and meaning to life—as well as the part of us that intuits its meaning. When jupiter is well integrated, it infuses the personality with a generosity of spirit that allows one to feel immense gratitude, see the humour in difficult times, to forgive others easily (because one is usually 'above' such pettiness but also because there are far more interesting ways to expend energy than holding a grudge), a visible zest for life, and a gift for generating genuine goodwill. I sometimes wonder if this is what is interpreted as 'Jupiter luck'. After all, if one embodies all the life-giving qualities of jupiter, isn't it only natural that they experience at least some of it in return from those who are touched by their energy? So maybe what we've been thinking of as luck all along is simply a jupiter that is working right in us and therefore attracting the 'abundance' and 'luck' that we're told we all have in one area of the horoscope.

But all archetypes have a shadow side and jupiter is no exception. An excessive or unconscious jupiter is often to blame for a difficult relationship with reality, self-aggrandisement, fanaticism, delusions of grandeur, a tendency to live in the realm of possibilities and potential and not be able to actualise any of it, religious extremism and extremism of any kind because it is the nature of jupiter to magnify and amplify everything that it touches. In its pathological extremes, jupiter, like the sun, is associated with mania, and in combination with certain planets, drive one to the most destructive extremes of behaviour.

The sign, house and aspects of jupiter in the natal chart can tell us where we carry the potential to make something 'big' of jupiter's life-giving qualities, and where we can bring more consciousness into the challenges it poses.

But we needn't worry too much about jupiter's shadow because every chart comes with a saturn, entrusted with the task of keeping our excesses in check. Every time jupiter lures us with optimism and a sense of adventure or abducts us into a flight of fancy, saturn reminds us of all those times when it didn't quite work out as we expected it to or when something blew up in our face, bringing us right back to solid ground. We may experience this as a bout of fear, insecurity or cold feet that takes hold of us when we're about to do something 'big' like walk down the aisle or start a new business. 'Are you really ready to do this?' saturn asks. 'Do you understand the reality of what you're signing up for?' 'Are you willing to make sacrifices and keep your eyes on the long haul when things get tough as they inevitably will?' You better make sure you know what you're doing when you answer 'yes' because saturn may recede into the background for now and let jupiter take charge with a big, noisy celebration. But rest assured, he'll be hiding in the corner with his sickle, biding his time until the next saturn transit when everything you are, will come up for inspection.

Who are you becoming? Did that big adventure you embarked on make you take your commitment seriously, confront reality, take responsibility and grow the hell up? Or did you abandon ship when things got tough, blamed everyone else involved, and decided that you didn't like 'being tied down' by anything (a classic jupiter response)? If you answered 'A' and the commitment you took on is on fairly solid ground, congratulations! Saturn is about to send you some well-earned goodies but only after he tests this house you've built. Will it stand the test of 'time'? Can it survive a rocky season? How solid is it, really? With every saturnine test you pass, you build your endurance as well as your ability to consider the limitations of the realm of earth that saturn rules.

If you're an artist or writer, you know this jupiter-saturn conflict all too well: You're in love with this new idea that's been swirling around in your head. It's so invigorating when you consider the whole breadth of possibilities (the fertilising capacity of jupiter in the creative phase). So you sit down to write the first chapter and suddenly, it's gone. The 'whoosh' you were hearing in your head all this time has mysteriously disappeared now that you've made it 'real'. You've brought Zeus down from heaven and into saturn's realm. The infinite creator spirit is now confined to a file on your computer and it just feels...wrong. Suddenly, no word or phrasing is good enough to capture the magnificence of the idea when you first envisioned it. If you cannot get past this phase, you're never going to have the book written—a consequence that saturn reminds you with much pain, regret and hindsight at the next saturn transit. As the archetypal principle in charge of bringing us to maturity, saturn runs a tight ship. You can either choose growth by breaking free of childish fantasies and illusions, interrupting your infantile patterns and taking responsibility for the unpleasant outcomes in your life, accepting reality and the consequences for your actions; or you can have growth forced upon you through illness, financial crisis, relationship troubles and cyclical struggles with inadequacy, envy and fear of failure.

But as long as you are attached to a mortal body, you participate in the earthy realm that saturn governs, which is why no matter how rich, famous or spiritual you are, you will age, experience pain, rejection, loneliness, the weight of responsibility or the consequence for avoiding it, and one day, in the hopefully distant future, you will die.

There is a finality with saturn that is so hard for jupiter, so in love with his omnipotence, to wrap his head around. But without saturn, we'd never be able to bring anything to form. If we are to actualise anything—the 'divine' potential we sense in ourselves, our creative gifts or our most deeply-felt convictions, we must have a good relationship with saturn, who represents the stern face of the archetypal father who teaches us the value of such things as boundaries, focus, tried-and-tested rules and self-discipline.

In a Freudian sense, saturn represents the super-ego or the ethical aspect of the personality that defines an individual's sense of right and wrong. But the super-ego does not refer to any innate morality but one that is derived from the parents, family, society and time in which one incarnates. This is a key aspect of what makes saturn a social planet because no matter how individual one is, he still belongs to a society and a collective and must, at least to a reasonable extent, adhere to the laws that govern it (both in a strictly legal sense and otherwise). So when we refer to 'well-adjusted individuals', we're talking about their relationship with the saturn principle.

Jupiter and saturn act as complementary forces that help us navigate the outer world; one that helps us understand and appreciate the spirit of the law, and the other that reminds us of the consequences of straying too far from the letter of the law. Jupiter resides in the upper world of possibilities and saturn in the lower world of limitation but they are both concerned with helping us grow beyond our little ego-centric selves. We need saturn to temper jupiter's omnipotent fantasies. We need jupiter, to keep saturn vital and relevant. This is not only an eternal war within ourselves but one that is frequently played out in the outer world as evident in culture wars and generational conflicts. If we can use our jupiter-given gifts for seeing the big-picture or the archetypal dramas playing out in our lives and beyond, and learn to do the difficult saturnine work of withdrawing our projections and taking responsibility for how we respond to a potentially-triggering situation, person or event, we may—at least in the Jungian view—be contributing a lot more to society than we imagine.

For more on Jupiter and Saturn, read Liz Greene and Stephen Arroyo's The Jupiter-Saturn Conference Lectures, *Liz Greene's* Saturn: A New Look at an Old Devil, Barriers and Boundaries: Defences of the Personality *and* Relating: An Astrological Guide to Living with Others

THE OUTER PLANETS:
URANUS, NEPTUNE AND PLUTO

As we move past saturn, we are well and truly outside the boundaries of ego consciousness with all its illusions of separateness; as well as what we call 'objective reality' (though it is entirely subjective) because the ego cannot apprehend the space beyond saturn, who is both the lord of boundaries and the lord of chronological (from Chronos) time. Uranus, neptune and pluto are transpersonal energies that lie in the collective unconscious, symbolising the larger matrix from which the ego emerges. These archetypal energies or drives are not as easily available to the ego because they mark different phases of consciousness and the ego cannot really grasp states of consciousness beyond what it's experiencing at any given time. So the outer planets are usually projected and their transits are often experienced as events or those things that 'happen' to us.*

The transpersonal planets are also related to the collective rather than the individual; their cycles corresponding to

---

*Relating: An Astrological Guide to Living with Others, Liz Greene.

movements and shifts in collective consciousness. When they form aspects to the personal planets in the natal chart, we may understand them as these collective cycles impinging on the individual's story. Since we cannot do justice to the transpersonal planets in a book like this, I'm keeping the focus on how we can understand them in relation to the individual psyche. In order to keep myself from digressing, I'm ordering this section in the following ways: 1.) the teleology of the planet (or its ultimate, big-picture meaning or purpose) 2.) its particular mode of operation or the channels it employs to achieve its purpose and 3) the subjective experience of the individual who has these configurations in the natal chart or who is experiencing them as transits.

For a deep dive into the outer planets and how they affect the collective, read Liz Greene's The Outer Planets and Their Cycles *and Howard Sasportas'* The Gods of Change

Uranus: Awakening and Liberation

Teleology: The goal of uranus is to awaken and liberate the psyche from outworn patterns, structures, relationships, ideologies or anything else that keeps it stagnant or hinders its development; invite it into uncharted territories where it can partake of the divine spark of consciousness, experience true progress, and embrace a new way of perceiving and being.

Mode of operation: While the teleology always looks attractive in principle, an outer planet must go to great lengths in order to get the attention of our limited ego consciousness. For uranus, these lengths often look like shocks, unexpected events, sudden changes, turbulence, disruption, destruction, instability, chaos, radical re-invention. As the planet that rules lightning and electricity, we tend to experience the transits of uranus as a storm that shakes up the foundations of our lives (in the area where it's hitting us), often leaving widespread loss, terror or destruction in its wake. But just as the storm also fertilises the earth, so uranus prepares the psyche's soil for input it couldn't have previously received. In popular astrology, uranus is considered a wildcard, making it extremely hard to predict how it may manifest; the 'shock' it's associated with, is really a shock in consciousness, jolting us awake, as if from a nightmare, to the particular ways in which we've imprisoned ourselves. Given the suddenness with which uranus strikes, I imagine it's the cosmos grabbing us by the shoulders and giving us a good shake because whatever it is that uranus is doing, really cannot wait another second. Even when we're doing a lot of inner work and are familiar with astrology, uranus transits are almost always a surprise at some level. But if we can put on our archetypal glasses and try to understand that the outer situation, person or event—no matter how terrible, unfair or undeserved—is really a catalyst for our freedom and growth, we may not only make the experience easier on ourselves, but begin to open our eyes to what this planetary archetype has to offer us.

In the natal chart, uranus' aspects to the personal planets tell us something about the uranian layer of our own complexes. For example, the moon in aspect to uranus, describes one aspect of our mother complex—the subjective filter through which we experienced our mother or mother figure, how we attach, our emotional hunger, etc.—as well as our particular emotional template. At the most literal level, moon-uranus suggests that the experience of mothering was in some way unstable, severed or even shocking. It may also suggest the experience of a mother who felt deeply fettered. I've seen this aspect in the charts of people who were adopted, separated from the mother soon after birth because they needed some sort of surgical intervention (the shock of surgical trauma), those whose mothers attempted to leave or actually left the family when they were young children or in the very least, felt suffocated. Given the conflicting natures of the two planets involved (in this case, the moon which seeks to nurture and uranus which hungers for freedom), we may project one side and identify with the other. If uranus is projected, the subjective experience of mother may be 'abandoning', 'rejecting', 'unstable', 'volatile' or less negatively, 'unconventional' or 'avant-garde'. This may be as a result of situations that were completely outside the mother's control such as the aforementioned surgery or some other situation where mother is experienced as absent. If it's the moon that is projected, then mother may be experienced as 'suffocating', 'too needy' or even 'selfish' given uranus' urge to go beyond personal needs. Since the aspect to uranus is usually not the only aspect the moon makes in the chart, this is just one layer of the mother complex and must be read along with others as a whole.

In myth, Ouranus is the sky god (ruling the realm of ideals) who is married to Gaia, the earth mother (the realm of reality). When Gaia gives birth to their children, the earthy Titans, Ouranos recoils in horror and shoves them back into her womb because he finds them ugly. This conflict between uranian ideals and earthy reality is archetypal, and one most visible in those individuals who have these planets in aspect to each other. It may also say something about the parental experience when uranus makes a hard aspect to either of the luminaries. 'Nothing I did was good enough for my father,' we may hear someone with sun-uranus complain. But if we can separate the father complex (which in this case is coloured by the inner image of the Sky Father) from the outer human father on whom it is projected, we can learn to recognise sun-uranus as an aspect of the individual's nature that seeks expression and conscious outlets in the person's life.

There is another myth that is closely tied to the astrological uranus and that's the story of Prometheus and the stealing of fire. Prometheus is a Titan, and one of the sons of Ouranos and Gaia. The matter of parentage is important in the psychological analysis of a myth because it tells us something about the nature of the archetypal principle in question. As the son of Ouranos, Prometheus, whose name means 'foresight', possesses a visionary spirit, that strives towards progress and the realisation of potential. But he's also the son of Gaia and a Titan, as opposed to an Olympian, which makes him a god of the earth—the realm of the material world. In some versions of the myth, Prometheus is credited with the creation of the human race whose potential he sees, and with whom his sympathies lie. Now Zeus, the king of Olympus, has denied human beings access to cosmic fire, because he fears it would make them god-like and it is this fire that Prometheus steals and offers to humans against Zeus' wishes. This cosmic fire has been interpreted in a number of ways. Richard Tarnas associates it with the 'creative spark, cultural and technological breakthrough, the enhancement of human autonomy, the liberating gift from the heavens, sudden enlightenment, intellectual and spiritual awakening'.* Liz Greene adds 'Prometheus steals the potential of consciousness from the gods' to this list, which to me, sums up everything else. Without consciousness, human beings are creatures of instinct, governed by nature and with no awareness of their own creative potential. But now with the capacity to become conscious of that something within them that is eternal and god-like, they can partake of the

---

The Art of Stealing Fire, Liz Greene

divine spark of creation (as one example) through which they may live on, much like the immortals of Olympus. Suddenly, they have access to knowledge that is not their own. In the story, Prometheus, who is a culture-bringer, teaches human beings architecture, astrology, astronomy, navigation and everything else that involves an understanding of cosmic systems.

> *'...he is a force within the psyche that has access to knowledge of how the cosmic system works, and how to apply it to the everyday affairs of human beings.'*

> —Liz Greene*

But all this enlightenment and progress comes with a heavy price tag. Prometheus sets himself against the gods when he upsets the natural order (because fire once given to human beings cannot be taken back) and Zeus punishes him for his crime by having him chained on top of a mountain. Here, the noble Titan is deprived of all contact with humans and gods while an eagle (Zeus' bird) visits him every day to peck away at his liver (the part of the human anatomy ruled by Jupiter-Zeus). By night, the liver regenerates and come morning, the eagle is back again for his eat-all-you-can breakfast. This cycle of physical and psychological torment is equally a part of the Promethean story and may be experienced in a number of different ways as a consequence or the cosmic bill for those who get an extra helping of the uranian spirit. Prometheus is a rebel and an outlaw and we may understand one aspect of the uranian/Promethean suffering as a profound sense of isolation or alienation whether this is an inner experience or something that plays out in one's outer life.

In the dream I related earlier, which pushed me to 'come out' about my love for astrology (which I got into under a venus-

---

The Art of Stealing Fire, Liz Greene

uranus progression to begin with), we can see these Promethean themes loud and clear ('captured by the authorities of the time for stealing big secrets', the image of the stealing of parchments, the sense of an awakening, the archetype of the outlaw, the theme of breaking free from a state of imprisonment, the intensely powerful sense of being given a mandate, that the dream ended on, etc.). I had that dream on the 28th of February, 2017 when transiting mars and uranus formed a volatile conjunction in the skies (basically, they occupied the same spot in the skies) and made an exact aspect to pluto (which we'll get to) in my chart. This is just one example of how astrology captures the archetypal essence of the moment. In psychological astrology, astrological transits are not understood as happening 'up there in the skies'. They are a reflection of the currents of time—the movements in the world, in the psyche, in the body and everything else that makes up our reality. This may sound far-fetched or even 'batshit crazy' if you've never experienced it, but whichever side of the uranian experience you stand on, 'batshit crazy' is a good way to sum up the subjective experience of uranus.

We must also remember not to assume that a uranus-inspired ideology is always on the side of what we understand as 'good' or the political left (Hitler had uranus on the ascendant and Donald Trump has both the sun and moon in major aspects to uranus). Uranus is a symbol of the archetypal mind which can be both mind-blowingly ingenious and terrifyingly cold, and devoid of feelings or empathy. Again, archetypes comprise a whole gamut of expressions and only a solidly developed ego is capable of mediating its compulsions and expressing its life-giving side.

The subjective level: While every planet has its own teleology and unique way in which it achieves its purpose, we may experience each one differently based on how we are wired. For someone with a lot of planets in the fixed signs (which we'll get to), uranian energy may be experienced as deeply threatening because the fixed signs are fundamentally averse to change. Similarly, a person who is identified with saturn (boundaries, conformity) may be deeply uncomfortable with the uranian type whom he may describe as 'volatile', 'has no respect for boundaries' or 'a bit of a character'. So when uranus hits the chart of such a person by transit, they're likely to put up a fight and attempt to control the inevitable, making the experience so much harder on themselves. On the contrary, someone who is well related to the uranian principle at an inner level, may feel highly invigorated by the transit despite the shock and the chaos; because they either have a natural tendency to live on the edge, or intuitively know that change is the only constant.

For more on the psychological and archetypal exploration of uranus in astrology, read Liz Greene's The Art of Stealing Fire *and Richard Tarnas'* Cosmos and Psyche.

Neptune: Dissolution and Purification

Teleology: The purpose of neptune—who is Poseidon, the oceanic deity in Greek myth—is to remind us that the ego's sense of separateness and what it understands as reality, is a fiction; and to reconnect and fuse us with the Divine, which in neptune's view, is an 'unconditionally loving maternal source'.* This urge for immersion in the waters of 'collective feeling' and fusion with the Divine that neptune represents, means the sacrifice of individuality and the dissolution of the boundaries of the 'I'.

---

*The Astrological Neptune and the Quest for Redemption, Liz Greene

This necessary act of purification—easy enough to observe in rock shows, cricket matches, movie halls, raves and mobs as much as religious movements and esoteric cults or anything that causes us to lose ourselves in a singular feeling that dominates an entire group—has its roots in Dionysian mystery rituals (the astrological neptune is also connected with Dionysus, the god of ecstasy), where the individual who offered himself up in such immersion was cleansed of his past and born again.*

Mode of operation: With the gradual disappearance of religious containers such as the ancient mystery rituals of Dionysius, we tend to experience the more shadowy face of neptune in unconscious modern-day 'rituals' and 'immersions' such as Netflix, food or shopping binges, gaming marathons and substance abuse or anything that makes us lose sense of time (a construct of the rational mind) or be taken out of the body, reality or the 'I'. The neptunian urge within us is a longing for transcendence and union, and in the absence of appropriate outlets (spirituality and mysticism or artistic pursuits as some examples of relating to a world beyond the 'real' world), it latches on to anything that offers a fleeting sense of touching the divine or escaping the bondage of the material world, but leaves us feeling more lost, vague, confused and disconnected, than purified and born anew. But even when we're neither addicted nor particularly unrelated to the archetype, a neptune transit always indicates a time when something is ready to be dissolved and washed away. This dissolution may come through an experience of loss or bereavement where neptune comes to us as the cleansing waves of grief; but equally in the ecstasy of union with a beloved whom we may experience as a 'soulmate' only to learn by the end of the transit that those rainbows and

---

Relating: An Astrological Guide to Living with Others, Liz Greene.

unicorns we could've sworn we saw and touched, never existed in any 'real' sense. Either way, we cannot—at least temporarily—rely on the 'I' as the centre of the personality; not until we find a larger 'divine' centre or 'unconditionally loving maternal source' to immerse ourselves in.

The dissolution of the 'I' that I talked about in the relationship that preceded my immersion in Jungian studies, happened under the transit of neptune in opposition to my sun (ego). It was quite literally dissolving my sense of self in union with the 'magical other' (a modern-day experience of Dionysian ecstasy) because though I couldn't see it then, I needed a larger source from which to draw life and inspiration from, and the relationship was the catalyst in the process. For me, that larger centre became more accessible through the experiential aspects of astrology and Jungian psychology.

While individual experiences may vary, neptune either takes us out of, or makes us question our perception of time and reality. Clients often describe their neptune transits as 'feeling lost', 'foggy', 'vague and directionless', 'like I'm just floating around', 'losing sense of time', 'confused', 'spaced out', 'unable to have a routine', or 'disenchanted', 'disillusioned' and 'not sure where I'm going or how to carry on'.

So whether you're shooting heroin up your veins, experiencing the paranormal through near-death experience, ESP or seeing an apparition, feeling blissfully fused with a lover or other soulmate, experiencing the reality of the unconscious through dreams and active imagination, a psychotic disorder or anaesthesia, drowning in tears of grief, losing yourself in a song, painting or a fictional world, going through an illness that temporarily dissolves your routines and commitments in the outer world, or feeling a profound sense of connection and relatedness to the whole cosmos, an experience of neptune can warp and distort the boundaries and limitations of ego consciousness.

The subjective level: Neptune is represented by the ocean and its world is by definition boundless, which can be terrifying for the ego. But it's precisely in this boundless world that the ego must immerse itself periodically in order to be renewed and feel a sense of connection to something greater than itself. When the chart indicates a strong drive towards fusion and belonging (such as those with a dominance of water signs or a prominent or heavily aspected neptune), the siren call of neptune may be hard to resist, leading the individual into potentially dangerous waters. In this case, one may need to work on grounding and exercising the rational mind as a much-needed defence against neptune's more destructive face. On the other hand, the transits of neptune may be harder on those who have a difficult relationship with the feeling function, understand themselves as hyper-rational or pragmatic, and tend to derive their sense of safety and security from having control and being fully entrenched in the 'real' world.

For an in-depth look at neptune, read Liz Greene's The Astrological Neptune and the Quest for Redemption *and Richard Tarnas'* Cosmos and Psyche *for the archetypal view.*

Pluto: Annihilation and Transformation

Teleology: The plutonian urge within us seeks transformation through the archetypal process of death and rebirth. And like uranus and neptune, the experience of pluto—who is the god of the dead and the underworld in mythology—is usually projected and experienced as an event or something that 'happens' to us. The idea of death of any kind seems to rattle the ego, which is rather fond of stasis, of being in control and having things just the way they are.

But the process of death and rebirth is a ceaseless cycle echoed in all nature, and the human psyche is no exception. From the pregnant full moon to the fertile void of the new moon, the barrenness and bleakness of autumn and winter giving way to new life at springtime, the decaying smell of kitchen waste that becomes the nutrient-rich compost for your vegetable garden, even our nightly descent into the darkness of sleep is a necessary plutonian ritual in order to be re-born with the dawning of a new day. 'Sleep on it' we're often told when we have trouble working something out with our logical mind. And when we're too exhausted, emotionally depleted or traumatised to fall asleep, medication is often prescribed to induce it because without our nightly death, we cannot sustain life. Something happens in the secret darkness of the plutonian underworld that seems to transform whatever passes through its gates. When we look at this image of night and day, sleep and wakefulness symbolically, we get a sense of the essence of pluto and its ultimate purpose. Everything that is alive, changes. Psychologically, our feelings, thoughts, ideas, attitudes, beliefs and behaviours follow the same process from newness to decay to being reborn in another form. But we instinctively fear this passage into the underworld and do our best to resist it, because it means dying to some cherished part of ourselves. And even when we understand that it's necessary in order to be truly alive, we fear the experience of annihilation that will inevitably come on pluto's orders. But if we submit and surrender (not that we have a choice), we find that by the end of the pluto transit, we are reborn with a massive upgrade in consciousness and a profound sense of empowerment.

Mode of operation: As the god of the underworld, Hades-Pluto tends to do his best work far beneath the surface of consciousness. So the outer event or experience that the pluto transit may reflect, has actually been brewing in your unconscious for a good long time, which can explain the characteristic intensity of the experience.

Whether your pluto transit involves the ending of a long-term relationship or professional path, beginning your new life as a parent (which means the death of your carefree life), uprooting your life from your homeland to live on the other side of the world, a profound emotional, sexual or spiritual experience that changes you beyond recognition, declaring bankruptcy, spending the year in rehab (or prison or psych ward) as you battle your inner demons, the experience of betrayal that changes a relationship or the actual death of a loved one—the encounter with the archetype of death, and the feelings and fears that it evokes in us, are very real.

Plutonian terror has a way of gripping us at a level where the intellect and its rationalising and civilising capacities cannot reach. We operate purely on instinct as we are faced with a profound threat to our survival. Again, this is rarely a literal threat but to the psyche it makes no difference whether you're actually dying or experiencing your partner's betrayal or the ending of a long-cherished dream as a death.

This is why the experience of pluto has a way of bringing out the most primitive aspects of our nature. Faced with annihilation and with little to no access to our civilised selves, we may become consumed with feelings of paranoia, suspicion, jealousy, terror, obsession and passion (of all kinds) that can manifest at any level—from compulsive or obsessive feelings that get in the way of normal functioning, all the way to stalking, blackmailing, getting involved in shady 'underground' activities or anything else that consumes us and affects our ability to think straight.

The subjective level: The more dissociated we are from pluto's subterranean world of instincts and primeval desire, believing ourselves to be decent, civilised human beings, the more terrified we are likely to be when pluto brings this to the surface of our consciousness or when we see these behaviours in others by projection. Does this mean we must regress into less civilised versions of ourselves and freely indulge in everything our instincts demand? Of course not. But when we are forced to take the descent into the plutonian underworld, it is helpful to become aware of those aspects of ourselves that we pretend don't exist, because we've successfully repressed them. Those behaviours or qualities that we most despise in the world and in others, exist in potential within us too, and it is the nature of pluto to confront us with this truth. I often see this kind of shock in the faces of clients who may write in, requesting an urgent consult. 'What is happening to me' they might ask. 'I'm not myself' or 'I have no control over what I'm feeling'. This is usually the case with those who, as in the case of neptune, struggle with the feeling function, tend to be thinking types (as seen in the dominance of the element of air) or prefer to live in the 'upper worlds' of jupiter or uranus. In this case, there is often a tendency within the individual to dismiss or invalidate feelings (that are first of all classified as good and bad) and 'rise above' them. But whatever the individual disposition, an encounter with the lord of death is a profoundly transformative experience that initiates us into our new life.

For a thorough explortion of pluto through a Jungian lens, read Liz Greene's The Astrology of Fate *and Richard Tarnas'* Cosmos and Psyche *for the archetypal view. Also Sylvia Brinton Perera's* Descent to the Goddess *is basically a Jungian exploration of what a pluto transit or progression feels like at an inner level.*

Chiron

Chiron is a minor planet that orbits between saturn and uranus, but as far as interpretation is concerned, we'll give him the same respect we give the outers. Archetypally, chiron is known as the Wounded Healer and where he is placed in a natal chart, usually points to what is often experienced as 'an unhealable wound'.

In myth, Chiron is born of Kronos-Saturn and Philyra, the daughter of Okeanos. Kronos who is married to Rhea, is caught in the act with Philyra, at which point, he transfigures himself into a stallion and gallops away, leaving Philyra to bear the half-man-half-horse Centaur who is Chiron. Philyra, like Ouranos and the Titans, recoils with horror upon seeing the 'child' that she has to suckle, and prays to the gods to be freed and is turned into a linden tree.

We have right here a mythic image of the wound or trauma in the psyche that we call chiron. It is born of rejection, humiliation, terror and abandonment. But contrary to our expectations, the mythical Chiron did not go on to become a serial killer. In fact, he is known as the wisest and most righteous of the Centaurs, who were wild forest-dwellers. His fame as a healer, scholar and prophet spread far and wide, and he became the king of the Centaurs. In his cave beneath Mount Pelion, he mentored the heroes and demi-gods before they went on their quest.

> '...he is a chthonic deity, and belongs to that group of phallic or half-animal tutors of the gods who symbolise the wisdom of nature and of the body itself.'
>
> —Liz Greene

The story goes that one day, while hanging out with his student, the famous Greek hero Herakles before he went on one of his labours, he was accidentally shot by Herakles' arrow, which happened to be dipped in the Lernean hydra's blood (both of whom we'll meet in the signs Leo and Scorpio) which was deadly poison. Since there was no antidote for the hydra's blood, Chiron, who could heal others, could not heal himself, and he retired into his cave, howling in agony. This was made worse by the fact that Chiron was immortal, so he couldn't die; but he couldn't live either because there was no way to free himself of the pain. Later when Herakles freed Prometheus for the stealing of fire, and Zeus demanded that another immortal take his place in Hades, it was the noble Centaur who took his place and became the constellation, Sagittarius.

The astrological chiron, especially when it's strongly configured in the natal chart, can help clarify what we may experience as traumatic. Liz Greene suggests that the 'unhealable wound' refers to suffering that sometimes has no meaning; like the story of Chiron, sometimes, there is no way to frame the experience as anything other than 'unfair'. However, the wound that chiron represents in the chart can also be the very place from which we're able to help and heal others, though we cannot help ourselves. Astrologers often see a pattern of people born with sun-chiron or moon-chiron (we'll get to aspects later) in the healing and therapeutic fields, those that involve mentoring, teaching or coaching others, or in some way tapping into the trauma itself (such as abuse or learning disabilities) as a way of helping others. Chiron transits or progressions on the other hand, have a way of bringing a deep wound (in relation to whatever planetary principle chiron is touching) to the surface. While these periods are definitely no fun subjectively speaking, they offer an opportunity to address a longstanding wound or condition and find healing. For example, I put off dealing with symptoms I knew were PTSD (post-divorce) and ADHD (since childhood) at an intuitive level for the longest time, because a) I absolutely love certain aspects of ADHD such as the hyper-focus which I consider a super-power and wouldn't want it gone, b) I was afraid I might start using the diagnosis as an excuse for bad behaviour and c) I wanted to exhaust all approaches before I turned to a psychiatrist. And while every one of those approaches have yielded insights and helped me cope, the current chiron transit I'm under as I write this, have brought up so many psychosomatic symptoms (chronic debilitating fatigue, body pain, difficulty breathing and persistent insomnia to the point of complete incapacitation) that have given me no choice but to seek out a clinical diagnosis. But while healing is a journey, I am so relieved to finally have an explanation (if not an immediate solution), for all the suffering that I couldn't even give myself permission to call suffering. It's also a classic example of how the body is usually the last place the symptoms go, as a desperate way to get our attention. Somatic healing is a big part of the chiron principle and it's been fascinating to watch myself reconnect with my feelings and body after years of dissociation. Whether one seeks out a psychiatrist, a talk-therapist, a physiotherapist, an alternative healer, a yoga instructer or an astrologer, the chiron transit always brings up themes of wounding and healing.

Psychologically, chiron is also associated with the blacksheep or the scapegoat and stories of being (or feeling) bullied, ridiculed, rejected or victimised are not uncommon when chiron is a key player in the natal chart. But the potential for empathy and natural healing qualities that accompany these placements also stand out because whether one is a therapist or not, chironian individuals have a way of attracting the troubled and the wounded like a magnet. It's almost as if people in pain can sniff out the unconscious healer in them.

For more on the psychological aspect of chiron, read Melanie Reinhart's Chiron and the Healing Journey *and Liz Greene's* Barriers and Boundaries: Defences of the Personality

Planetary Retrogrades

Thanks to pop astrology's obsession with mercury retrograde, most people, astrology enthusiasts or not, are by now familiar with the term retrograde which comes from the Latin retrogradus, which means 'move backwards'. So while the planets aren't actually standing still or changing direction periodically in the sky, it appears that way from the point of view of the earth, which is the only POV that matters in astrology (at least in the astrology of earthlings). Astrologers have noted that the period when a planet appears to be standing still right before the retrograde (known as stationary retrograde) as well as the apparent change in direction itself, brings about changes in the sphere of the planet in question. Usually there's a sense of things being in flux—something may come to the surface that needs assimilation or working on, before it can move forward.

Psychologically, we are invited to withdraw from the extraverted expression of the planet, to a more introverted engagement with what it represents. In the natal chart too, we may experience retrograde planets in a more introverted way. We may feel inhibited, awkward or positively, more measured in how we express these planets.

For example, mars retrograde in Aries may turn its anger inward, toward itself or have the capacity to rein in the recklessness and impulsiveness you'd expect of an Aries mars. Mercury retrograde may not be much of a talker, preferring to spend its energy gathering information, playing with concepts and theories, thinking and analysing. There may be lessons to integrate as it relates to the retrograde planet and if it's a faster moving planet like venus or mercury and one lives long enough, the planet will eventually move direct by progression (which is a predictive technique we won't be going into here); at which point, there is an undeniable sense of changing direction and a whoosh of energy is experienced as the planet is now ready to express everything that's been incubating this entire time.

In March of 2016, my progressed mercury went retrograde and the inner shift I felt was undeniable. I remember panicking, telling everyone 'I have nothing left to say' which is of course a terrifying prospect for a writer. I had cancelled the columns I had been writing just a few months before, and I had no idea how I was going to write the two books I had already signed on. It felt like all inspiration had run dry and I was confronted by the utter meaninglessness of everything I had said or written.

Writing was the one thing I had done consistently since I was a child and not being able to do it meant that I had no way of processing or understanding myself anymore. I told anyone who'd listen how 'emptied out' I felt but everyone thought I was probably being dramatic about something that happens to all writers from time to time. But I knew this was different. I feared I may never write again (except for the two books I *had* to write inspired or not, because I had already signed contracts). This was also the year following my complete immersion in astrology, and the year just before my immersion in Jungian studies began. In 2017, I felt this change in direction so intensely as all my energy went into reading, studying, 'taking in' and recharging my mercurial batteries. The retrograde phase of a planet in the progressed chart goes on for several years (about two decades in this case) and it's already changed so much about my relationship with writing but also opened up whole new wells of inspiration.

The Lunar Nodes: The Head and Tail of the Dragon

The moon's nodes—the north and south node or dragon's head (Rahu) and dragon's tail (Ketu) as they are known in Vedic astrology—are not planets, but two highly sensitive points where the moon's orbit intersects with the ecliptic, which is the apparent path of the sun around the earth. This happens a few times a year, which is when we have eclipses.

Given the relationship of the nodes to the sun, moon and the earth, they are bound up with themes of destiny, fate and all those cosmic forces that urge us forward towards the integration of life lessons and the fulfilment of soul purpose (north node); as well as lure us into the past, the familiar, and all those places we no longer need to go (south node). So there is a solar quality to the north node, which invites us into the future and towards our development, and a regressive, lunar quality to the south node that pulls us towards that which is familiar in a big, cosmic sense. South Node experiences often come with a sense of déjà vu whether they are experienced in a subjectively positive or negative way. Planets conjunct the north node (we'll get into aspects shortly but the orbs used for nodes are quite tight, typically within 5 degrees) may play a big role in one's life—as aspects of the self that need to be developed, challenges that may be encountered, as well as guides that assist in the fulfilment of one's destiny; whereas planets conjunct the south node may represent both gifts or well-developed aspects of the self that may be integrated in one's life, as well as what evolutionary astrologers call 'karmic debts' or what one must release or perhaps experience 'again' in order to release. But whatever one's individual beliefs, there is often a strong subjective sense of fate and destiny that accompanies nodal contacts, and this is best observed in the transits of the nodes over planets in the natal chart as well as in synastry or relationship astrology (when someone else's planet triggers one of your nodes or vice versa).

Sitting directly opposite to each other in the sky, the north and south nodes must be read together as they symbolise two halves of a whole. The glyph for the north node vaguely resembles a horseshoe and its opposite point on the chart by sign, house and degree is where the south node lies (though this isn't marked out in the chart). So if you have your north node at 14 Aries in the 5th house, it goes without saying that your south node is at 14 Libra in the 11th house.

Since I cannot do justice to the symbolism of the nodes in this book and the different ways in which they are viewed in the Western and Vedic traditions (both of which I have found to be useful), I recommend reading Jan Spiller's *Astrology for the Soul* (which takes you through the meaning of the nodes by sign and house), and Melanie *Reinhart's Incarnation: The Four Angles and the Moon's Nodes*, for the Western view.

6

The Signs

Now that we have a basic understanding of the planets and the archetypal energies they symbolise, let's look at the next part of the astrological alphabet: the signs. Just as the planets are the drives that tell us 'what' we're hungry for, the signs tell us 'how' these drives are likely to manifest.

If the planets are the actors, the signs are the costumes that give us a sense of the particular role the actor is playing. And just as actors are naturally cut out for some roles more than others, the planets too tend to have affinities to some signs where their energy flows freely, while they tend to sit more awkwardly in other signs where their expression is inhibited or challenged in some way.

The basic urge that mars represents, for example, will always be the same, but the sign it is placed in, will determine how this is expressed. Mars in Aries (its natural home, which we'll get to) has no problem with conflict and even enjoys the occasional head-butting. But mars in Libra (a sign that values diplomacy and refinement) has a hard time expressing its martian urge to 'bite someone's head off' (even when it's well-deserved) because the sign gets in the way of mars' natural expression.

The mars in Libra person may be seething beneath the surface but they're 'not going to make a scene' because they feel an inner pressure to be civilised and 'rise above' the primitive instinct that mars represents. On the other hand, they may dress up their anger as humour, passive-aggressively leave you out of a dinner party or write a scathing review of your new book, show or restaurant, and convince themselves that they're 'only being objective'. Because while the sign may have the capacity to thwart, neutralise or amplify the expression of a planet, the fundamental hunger of the planet itself remains unchanged.

Let's now look at the twelve signs of the zodiac, ordered into polarities of masculine and feminine or yin/yang and then further categorised into four elements—fire, earth, air and water. Since this is a book intended for beginners, I'm not going to assume everyone knows the natural order of the zodiac so here goes:

Aries, Taurus, Gemini, Cancer, Leo, Virgo, Libra, Scorpio, Sagittarius, Capricorn, Aquarius and Pisces.

Now the odd signs, from the first sign which is Aries, are masculine/yang, while the even signs beginning with Taurus, are feminine/yin. This derives from the Pythagorean tradition where odd numbers were associated with the masculine and even numbers with the feminine.[*]

So we have:

- Masculine: Aries, Gemini, Leo, Libra, Sagittarius and Aquarius
- Feminine: Taurus, Cancer, Virgo, Scorpio, Capricorn, Pisces

I doubt this needs to be said by now, but masculine and feminine in astrology and Jungian psychology, do not refer to gender or our social definitions of these terms but to archetypal

---

[*]*Hellenistic Astrology: The Study of Fate and Fortune*, Chris Brennan

principles—those original pair of polar opposites—and their relationship to each other, from which everything springs. We may call them masculine and feminine, yin and yang, active and passive, light and dark, right brain and left brain and so on.* The masculine is associated with light, extraversion, outer focus, logos, science, rationality, thinking, clarity, separation, spirit, intuition, action, penetration, objectivity, autonomy, movement, control, boundaries, fertilisation and the future, while the feminine relates to darkness, introversion, inner focus, mythos, art, imagination, feeling, ambiguity, union, matter, sensation, receptivity, yielding, subjectivity, relatedness, stasis, relaxation, flow, gestation and the past. So the six masculine and feminine signs, correspond to different facets of the masculine and feminine polarities respectively.†

The Four Elements

These two groups of six are further divided into two each, so we have two groups of masculine signs and two groups of feminine signs. This quaternity or basic structure of four that we see in the astrological elements—fire, earth, air and water—is also an archetypal symbol of wholeness (the four seasons, the four directions, the four horsemen of the apocalypse, the four winds, the four main stages in the alchemical process, the four Hebrew letters in the sacred name of God [YHVH], the four humours of ancient Greek medicine—adding a fourth to a three, completes it; in geometry, 'squares' it out).‡

These four elements also correspond to the four functions

Relating: An Astrological Guide to Living with Others, Liz Greene.
†Ibid.

‡www.carljungdepthpsychologysite.blog: *On the Nature of Four: Jung's Quaternity, Mandalas, the Stone and the Self.*

in Jung's typology: thinking, feeling, sensation and intuition. Sensation and intuition are opposite ways of perceiving, while thinking and feeling are ways of evaluating. Through the information received through the five senses, sensation tells you that something exists, whereas with intuition, you 'just know'. Intuition in this sense is not to be confused with what we understand as psychic phenomena. The intuitive type perceives not by considering what's in front of him or by looking at the facts, but by looking all around, having a sense of the possibilities and 'reading into' the situation. Intuition is an unconscious way of knowing something. Thinking and feeling, on the other hand, are opposite ways of judging or evaluating. Once we know that something exists, thinking helps us differentiate 'this' from 'that' through logic, reasoning, ideas and concepts; whereas the feeling type makes decisions based on how they are emotionally affected by something.

But while we all possess all these functions in potential, there is an imbalance in development. So one function may dominate because it is most accessible to the ego, the second may take longer to develop, while the third may be partially developed and the fourth, mostly unconscious.* The popular Myers-Briggs Type Indicator (MBTI), which is based on Jung's typology, gives us (if done right) this ranking of our four functions based on their strength or how conscious and accessible they are. The most conscious function is called the dominant, the next in line, auxiliary, the somewhat developed, tertiary and the least conscious, inferior. So if your dominant function is thinking, feeling is your inferior function. If your dominant is intuition, sensing is inferior. Please note that 'inferior' in the typological sense means 'unconscious'.

---

*Relating: An Astrological Guide to Living with Others, Liz Greene.

But while typology, like astrology can make us feel seen and understood, the point of studying it is not so we can feel smug about our dominant functions or use it to amplify other people's faults or challenges, as much as work towards making our tertiary and inferior functions more conscious. The psyche always strives towards wholeness, and it will relentlessly confront us with the pieces of ourselves that we are poorly related to. This is why we are compulsively attracted to people who are identified with our inferior function and later find that it's those very qualities that drive us up the wall. But whether it's through relationship to others and the conflicts it generates, or any other pattern or symptom—big or small—our solutions lie in integrating our unconscious functions.

Now that we have a basic understanding of the four functions and how they operate as a pair of opposites, let's look at each of the four astrological elements. Each element consists of three signs and represents a sphere of existence and a particular type of orientation to life. Every element comes with its own urges, fears and defences of the personality, and each sign within an element, expresses the needs of the element in its own unique way. Even a cursory look at the natal chart can tell us what a person's leading function is likely to be, based on the element that the majority of their planets is situated in. We feel most at home in the element where we have the most planets. Sometimes there'd be two elements vying for supremacy and then you'd have to consider other factors. The exceptions tend to be singletons (when you have just one planet in an element). Singletons often have a way of hijacking the whole chart because as Liz Greene suggests, 'like any living thing, it fights for its survival'. In such cases, the singleton expresses the nature of the element compulsively, and it's often the first thing one might notice about the individual. While there are exceptions to every rule in astrology, the themes of the element that the singleton occupies, tend to be central in the life of the person. Missing elements, on the other hand, operate unconsciously. We may become fascinated with the missing element, look to others to show us how to carry it or it may show up in any of the ways that the unconscious manifests in outer life. Now, before I find another digression, let's get to the elements, which I'll touch on briefly here.

For a study of the four elements from a psychological perspective, please read Liz Greene's Barriers and Boundaries: Defences of the Personality, Relating: An Astrological Guide to Living with Others *and Karen Hamaker-Zondag's* Psychological Astrology.

Fire

Symbol: △
Signs: Aries, Leo, Sagittarius
Function: Intuition

Fire corresponds to the realm of spirit and the intuitive function. And just as intuition is concerned with possibilities and potential rather than what is right in front of us, fire is most at home playing with the creative fire of divine inspiration, big visions and grand ideas, where energy is limitless and anything is possible. Operating on the knowing that there is something divine or god-like within human beings, capable of extraordinariness (whatever 'extraordinary' means to the individual) fire is driven by a hunger for immortality,* the quest for greatness, for 'something more'. If the gods were to bestow the typical fiery type (someone with the majority of planets or a singleton in fire) with good looks, a successful career, a bottomless vault of cash, loving family, fabulous friends and a soulmate for a partner, they'd go, 'Yeah,

---

Barriers and Boundaries: Defences of the Personality, Liz Greene

that's all very nice, but shouldn't there be something more to life than all this?' What 'more' is, they may never be able to define, but this preoccupation with 'soaring above' or transcending the world of limitation is a characteristic feature of fire signs whose greatest fear is ordinariness. Any reminder that he is human can trigger this fear and there are a number of ways he protects himself from it:

Refusing to slow down and pushing the body beyond its limits until he falls sick and has to be reminded that while he may be god-like in spirit, he is attached to a mortal body that is capable of feeling pain and slowing down; ignoring his emotional needs for intimacy and belonging because he doesn't want to be 'tied down'; avoiding any sense of structure or routine in his work life, perhaps by being an artist, an entrepreneur or in some other way, 'doing his own thing' or on the other hand, living irresponsibly, unable to hold down a job or pay his own bills because working at a job that is 'not inspiring' like everybody else, would be an admission that he is not so special after all.

While these are just a few examples and there are many creative ways through which an individual can protect himself, the underlying pattern is denial, which seems to be fire's go-to defence mechanism.

Defences are essential, universal and not in themselves bad, but it helps to become aware of how we instinctively and unconsciously respond to these deep-seated fears within us, so we can choose to interrupt the pattern.*

At best, fire types can be positive, creative, courageous, bold and adventurous, natural visionaries, spontaneous, inspiring, generate joy and warmth wherever they go and embody a generosity of spirit that is hard to come by (because they operate from a space of limitlessness).

Barriers and Boundaries: Defences of the Personality, Liz Greene

When unconscious, fire can show up as self-aggrandisement, entitlement, arrogance, ruthlessness, hubris, a difficult relationship with reality, and in extreme cases, narcissism and mania.

In order for fire to make the best of its gifts and actualise its potential, it must be tempered by, and have a healthy relationship with earth, its psychological opposite.

Earth

Symbol: ▽

Signs: Taurus, Virgo, Capricorn

Function: Sensation

Earth corresponds to the material plane and its typological parallel is sensation, which relies on input from the five senses in order to perceive. Earth types are the pragmatists of the zodiac, and unlike fire, they are very good friends with reality, accepting its laws and limits and striving to operate within it, in order to actualise the potential that fire intuits. Earth isn't too impressed by the initial spark of a grand vision because it's all too aware that such sparks come and go; and until the idea can fit within a budget, become attractive to someone with deep pockets and really bad taste, meet a deadline, fit within a word count or whatever other obstacles and tests it's likely to run into, it's not 'real'. And making things real is what gratifies earth.

So it takes the vision from the upper worlds of the intuitive mind and births it by giving it form in the material plane. It does this by relying on methods that are time-tested: becoming clear about the time, energy and other resources that this vision would take, having a plan, having a deadline, making a realistic commitment that it knows it's capable of seeing through, pushing itself through self-discipline, delaying gratification and relying on its own skills, efforts and hard work because for earth, the fundamental urge is to have control by ensuring its security.*

Unlike fire, earth has a natural capacity to see the magic in the ordinary—being in tune with the rhythm of the day by having a routine, the solidity and quiet comfort of a long-term relationship, the simple pleasure of a warm bath, a home-cooked meal or cuddling a baby or an animal, the sense of security that a steady income offers, the rewards of hard work, persistence and taking the long route that may show up as a successful career, a fit and healthy body capable of astounding feats of endurance or a family that stands by each other at all times, experiencing the sacred in communion with nature, learning to be present in the present moment instead of becoming caught up in future possibilities, approaching chores as a meditative act, and everything else that reminds us that we are made of earth.

This sense of connection with manifest reality is what sets earth apart from the other elements, making it grounded, rooted and fully 'here'. The earth type needs this sense of solidity because his biggest fear is chaos (something fire tends to thrive in) and anything that reminds him that he is ultimately not in control. So earth defends itself by making plans, setting goals, increasing effort, having investments, entering commitments, building structures, gathering things in the material world and everything else that assures him that he has fully incarnated; that the Word/Logos (of Fire) has indeed become flesh.

And so at his best, he is consistent, reliable, responsible, dependable, a rock for those around him, self-reliant, self-sufficient, diligent, tenacious, patient, enduring, pragmatic and respectful of boundaries, among other things. But take him out of his comfort zone (which is any situation where he has no control, from tsunamis to spontaneous plans and unannounced

---

Barriers and Boundaries: Defences of the Personality, Liz Greene

visitors which for him, is the same thing) and you're likely to see a very different side. He may become irritable, start to complain or simply refuse to go with the 'fun' plan. He is also particularly difficult to help in times of trouble because he tends to recede into himself or become depressed because the flip side of being such good friends with reality is that he often cannot see beyond it.

This is where earth needs fire to infuse it with life, faith and a sense of what's possible. Without fire, earth can become pessimistic, fearful, controlling even to a tyrannical extreme, rigid and unyielding, lacking in joy, energy, enthusiasm and vitality, small-minded, literal, limited and stuck.

Air

Symbol: △
Signs: Gemini, Libra, Aquarius
Function: Thinking

Air corresponds to the realm of reason and the thinking function, favouring rationality and objectivity over the subjective world of feelings. In other words, the air signs are civilised. Of the twelve signs of the zodiac, the three air signs are the only ones that do not contain any animal symbolism, suggesting a fundamental split from instinctual nature.* Instincts, like feelings (air's psychological opposite), do not behave rationally, which can terrify the airy type who relies on logical thinking in order to make sense of his world. His primary urge is to understand and relate life's experiences through a preconceived framework of ideas, concepts and theories—whether they come from books and systems of study or through his own mental processes which

---

*Relating: An Astrological Guide to Living with Others, Liz Greene.

are rigorous. But he needs to evaluate experiences in this way, by categorising, sorting and comparing them to each other through thinking, so he can find the underlying pattern of logic.*

Air signs are the idealists of the zodiac, always striving to improve themselves, their relationships and the world around them by gathering information, exchanging ideas, engaging in debates and discussions and upholding all those values—fairness, truth, equality, justice, civility, progress, etc.—that differentiate human beings from the animal kingdom. For this reason, the typical airy person (someone with a predominance of air placements in the natal chart), may have a tendency to judge and invalidate their own feelings and instincts because they seem too primitive or petty and they believe they ought to 'do better'. So feeling, which is the air type's inferior function, either appears to be completely non-existent on the surface, or is kept under tight reins for fear that it might behave unreasonably and embarrass them. And like any piece of psyche that's been exiled for too long, feeling does have a way of erupting through the cool, detached surface of the air type's personality, often through relationships. Because as afraid as he is of feelings, it fascinates him—either as a subject of study (like those who'd prefer to learn about their feelings through books, discuss and write about them, rather than feel their feelings) or in people he feels compulsively drawn to. But having attracted such a person, he must then collide with all those aspects of the other that are unconscious in himself. He may complain that his partner is too clingy, needy, moody, manipulative, suffocating, consuming, irrational or just 'too emotional'. Or he may find that the relationship has a way of putting him in touch with his own feeling function, often bringing out the intensity of his

---

Relating: An Astrological Guide to Living with Others, Liz Greene.

previously unconscious feeling nature, until he can make room in his conscious personality for this 'other' within him that longs for connection and intimacy. Encountering such feelings rise up in oneself can be shocking for the airy type who is rather proud of his capacity to keep his cool and remain objective.

Positively, air endows its natives with a sharp, inquiring mind, clear thinking, sparkling wit, objectivity, logic, social graces, communication skills, and refinement that shows up as an appreciation for art, culture and progress. The shadow side of air includes a tendency to dissociate from feeling as a defence mechanism and live in one's head.* While a basic level of dissociation is necessary for our survival, it may become excessive in the airy person whose detached nature can come across as cold, insensitive and hurtful to others. Comedians are often accused of making a joke 'too soon' because of this very tendency to dissociate from the intensity of feeling. Because of his idealistic nature, the air type also struggles with reality as fire does, unable to reconcile his idea of a thing with the thing itself. His need to live by the ideals that he so values can make him say and do all the right things, but his clumsy relationship with feelings and the constant devaluing of his own feelings, can make him appear superficial and inauthentic to the feeling type who can often see right through such behaviour.

Probably the first discovery I made when I learned to read my chart was that I had five planets out of ten in the element of air, all concentrated in one sign (Libra, unsurprisingly, the one that rules partnership and relationships). I had always felt unrelated to my sun sign and its element (earth) and this alone, put so many things in perspective the first time I peeked into my chart. My desperate need to process my experiences through

---

Barriers and Boundaries: Defences of the Personality, Liz Greene

a rational framework since I was a child, my love of ideas and theories, my difficult relationship with feelings as well as the tendency to get completely consumed by them in relationships, and the overwhelming shame I felt when I behaved emotionally. But the point of astrology or any other system of self-knowledge is to make the unconscious, conscious, and by understanding 'my element' through a Jungian lens, I could begin the long, hard work of integrating my inferior function.

Water

Symbol: ∇
Signs: Cancer, Scorpio, Pisces
Function: Feeling

And finally, we come to the water signs, the astrological equivalent of what Jung described as the feeling type. Water is concerned with the world of feeling, without which the world feels dry, barren and inspid. The typical water type (someone with most of their natal placements in the element of water) has a highly textured emotional life, and unlike air, does not feel the need to distinguish between 'good' and 'bad' feelings. Instead, he allows room for the whole spectrum because he understands that like water, feelings are ever-changing and need to be in a state of flow. Being a judging function, the watery type makes decisions based on whether something 'feels right' to him. And while this is entirely subjective, he is rarely wrong when it comes to personal relationships and situations. So if a couple—one, a thinking type and the other, a feeling type—had to come to a decision about buying a house, the conversation may go something like this:

Thinking: *It's exactly what we wanted! The neighbourhood, the security, the space, the water, the people, the view, even the interiors aren't too shabby. But most of all, it fits our budget! What do you think?*

Feeling: *I don't know, but I just don't have a good feeling about it.*

Thinking: *Come again?*

Feeling: *Yeah, I can't explain it but it just doesn't feel like our house. Something is off. I think we should give this one up and keep looking.*

Thinking: *Did we just visit the same house? I don't get it. It has everything on our list! And we've been on this hunt forever now and you expect me to just abandon all logic and go with your completely irrational feeling? At least give me two things that are wrong with it and I'll be more open to having a conversation.*

Feeling: *I can't! I don't have reasons but it just doesn't feel like the right decision.*

Baffling (and frustrating) as this may be to the thinking type, in this situation, the water type's feeling is rarely inaccurate because it involves a decision about a personal situation, and that is his forté. Since feelings are his basic source of sustenance, the world of human relationships and values play a central role in his life.

His fundamental urge is for constant emotional connection, belonging, intimacy and fusion and he'll do anything, even unconsciously create a crisis, in order to evoke a feeling response from those around him.* But given his hunger for emotional satiation, the water type often feels short-changed in relationships and he feels the most pain in the sphere of personal relationships which is his Achilles' heel. When the pain gets intolerable, our defences are mobilised and for the water type, this is often a pattern of addiction that Liz Greene likens to what Freud called a fixation in the oral stage of development, when the infant is at the breast. When the water type is terrified, he unconsciously starts looking for a surrogate breast which can be anything from

---

Relating: An Astrological Guide to Living with Others, Liz Greene.

a literal oral defence such as food, alcohol, cigarettes, drugs or other substance, as well as any other pattern of addiction from shopping and sex (for the instant gratification) to a job, religion or relationship that he cannot seem to leave because it keeps him—much like the infant with his mother—in a state of fusion. Again, defences are normal and necessary but without a proper understanding of his own patterns and the unconscious dynamics at play in any relationship, the feeling type may end up destroying the very thing he wants the most.

Often accused of emotional blackmail and manipulation, clinging, dependency, irrationality and a tendency to consume and suffocate his partner with his own needs which he often mistakes for love, the feeling type must learn to integrate thinking (his inferior function).

Developing his inferior function which is often projected on thinking types that he is compulsively drawn to, can offer him the balance he desperately needs when it comes to separating his feelings and needs from those around him. And as is the case with all the types, the feeling type is also fascinated with his inferior function, which in this case, can show up as un-reflected opinions and a tendency to be small minded, judgmental and even fanatical. Since his strengths lie in the subjective world, he is out of his depth when it comes to matters that require emotional distance, objectivity, discrimination, logical thinking and analysis but it's also what he most needs so as to not become inundated by his feelings which, left unchecked, can swallow him whole like the ocean itself.

At his best, the feeling type is emotionally intelligent, empathetic, sensitive and attuned to everything around him with a gift for subtlety, and the capacity to feel what others are feeling. His ability to read between the lines, pierce through the veil of what's unsaid and his receptivity to the subtler aspects of life, makes him particularly gifted at the healing arts and care-giving professions, just as his vivid imagination, willingness to explore the depth of his feelings and his need to be in a state of emotional fusion, makes him a natural artist and mystic.

The Three Modalities

The signs are further divided into three groups, called modalities or quadruplicities with each group containing one sign from the four elements. The three modalities are cardinal, fixed and mutable and align with different stages of the four seasons.

When the sun enters a cardinal sign, we are at the beginning of a season, when everything is new and the whole atmosphere has shifted. The cardinal signs are therefore associated with the urge for change, newness, initiation and beginnings. By the time the sun enters a fixed sign, we are in the middle of the season when everything is stable and there is a sense of 'this is how it is'. The fixed signs are therefore concerned with permanence, stability and the urge to put down roots. They operate from a place of certainty and are famously averse to change. And finally, when the sun enters a mutable sign, we are in a state of transition, navigating our way from one season to the next. We are not quite in the new season yet, but there is a sense that major change is afoot. The mutable signs are therefore associated with flexibility, adaptation, preparation for change, and known for their inherent duality.

Since every modality contains one sign from each element, understanding a sign through the aforementioned filters alone—masculine-feminine, element and modality—can go a long way in interpretation. Since the sign tells us how a planet is likely to behave, understanding it by element and modality is a big part of grasping its essential nature. So we have:

The Cardinal Signs: Aries, Cancer, Libra, Capricorn.

When the sun enters 0° of Aries, we have the spring equinox in the northern hemisphere. At 0° Cancer, we have the summer solstice, at 0° Libra, the autumnal equinox and at 0° Capricorn, the winter solstice.

The Fixed Signs: Taurus, Leo, Scorpio, Aquarius

These represent the middle of spring, summer, autumn and winter respectively.

The Mutable Signs: Gemini, Virgo, Sagittarius, Pisces

The last four signs represent the end of a season going into the next, beginning with spring-summer, going into summer-autumn, autumn-winter and back to winter-spring.

Every sign is also associated with a constellation and ruled by a planet, each steeped in its own mythologies. In Jungian terms, this can help us 'amplify' the meaning of the sign imaginally, as we would a dream. But as rich as the signs are in symbolism and imagery, I must emphasise yet again that they do not tell us the 'what' of the story. They tell us the 'how'. The planets determine the action of the story. The signs tell us how they go about achieving their ends. For example, I often find that the signs—especially when they're hosting planets that are completely contradictory in nature—operate like defence mechanisms, acting as a barrier to the natural expression of the planet. While the planet (or the archetype) will ultimately have the last word, our subjective experience of that can be painful or in some way embarrassing or difficult when the planet is in a sign that isn't 'friendly'. Which brings me to:

Essential Dignity: Domicile, Detriment, Exaltation and Fall

The planets, just like people, consider some places home (domicile), some places uncomfortable or foreign (detriment), some special, such as a luxury hotel or anywhere one is treated as an honoured guest, but not home nonetheless (exaltation), and some that make them feel stifled or imprisoned (fall).

Domicile: When a planet is in its home sign, it has complete access to its resources and is able to behave as it is supposed to. Psychologically, the person feels well-related to this drive within them (though there are always exceptions which we'll get to when we discuss aspects) and unless there are other contradictory chart factors, they're able to express it in a healthy, balanced way.

Detriment: This is when a planet is in alien territory—the polarity of the sign it rules. Here, it's forced to behave in ways that don't come naturally and its expression is thwarted, inhibited and awkward.

Exaltation: The exalted planet is like a revered guest and though it's powerful here, this isn't its home. Psychologically, an exalted planet has obvious gifts but it can still feel excessive in its behaviour and prone to extremes.

Fall: This is when a planet feels so imprisoned that it's forced to bottle up its nature until it gets to a point where it just snaps and explodes, and the person has a way of going to the opposite extreme. This happens in a cyclical way until we do some serious inner work in making the issues we face in relation to that planet's expression, conscious.

Now let's look at each planet through the lens of essential dignity. Useful hint: Detriment is always the sign that falls exactly opposite the domicile, and fall is always the sign that opposes exaltation on the zodiacal wheel.

Sun

Domicile: Leo
Detriment: Aquarius
Exaltation: Aries
Fall: Libra

Moon

Domicile: Cancer
Detriment: Capricorn
Exaltation: Taurus
Fall: Scorpio

Mercury

Domicile: Gemini and Virgo
Detriment: Sagittarius
Exaltation: Virgo
Fall: Pisces

Venus

Domicile: Taurus and Libra
Detriment: Scorpio and Aries
Exaltation: Pisces
Fall: Virgo

Mars

Domicile: Aries and Scorpio
Detriment: Libra and Taurus
Exaltation: Capricorn
Fall: Cancer

Jupiter

Domicile: Sagittarius and Pisces
Detriment: Gemini and Virgo
Exaltation: Cancer
Fall: Capricorn

Saturn

Domicile: Capricorn and Aquarius
Detriment: Cancer and Leo
Exaltation: Libra
Fall: Aries

In modern astrology, uranus is considered the ruler of Aquarius, neptune, the ruler of Pisces and pluto, the ruler of Scorpio. While there is obvious affinity between these planets and the signs, many modern astrologers now agree that the matter of rulership cannot go beyond the seven visible planets. I'm not going into rulerships in this book in terms of interpreting the chart but I will be using both traditional and modern rulers to amplify the signs. So without further ado:

The Twelve Signs of the Zodiac

One thing to keep in mind while reading the signs is that they refer to archetypal patterns of development as opposed to any individual who may be born under the sign in question. When I refer to someone who is typical of a sign or use such terms as 'Taurean' or 'Libran', I don't only refer to sun signs. This may include the ascendant/rising sign, moon sign, those with three or more planets in a particular sign (or what's called a stellium), the sign that hosts the chart ruler aka the ruler of the ascendant etc. If you have a stellium in Aries and the sun in Pisces, and have always felt more Arien, than Piscean, this may offer one obvious explanation. But the fact that your sun is in Pisces cannot be ignored and it's extremely important to understand how Piscean themes seem to repeatedly play out in your life, how you even unconsciously invoke them, and how by making this conscious, you can strive to integrate and express this fundamental aspect of who you are.

Aries ♈

Symbol: The Ram
Modality: Cardinal
Element: Fire
Ruler: Mars

Also read: Planets: Mars; Elements: Fire; Modality: Cardinal; Houses: First

Aries, the first sign of the zodiac, represents the psyche's urge for separation from the waters of the unconscious from which we all spring, to become an 'I'—an individual ego with its own consciousness and volition. This sense of an 'I' is a defining feature of Aries whose primary impulse is to forge a path that is entirely his own.

The feverish enthusiasm of the fire element combined with the initiatory impulse of its cardinal nature* and the thrust of mars as its ruler, is often the drive behind Aries' compulsive need for conquest and forward momentum. Whoever said 'Go out there and do something' probably had Aries emphasised in their chart. It doesn't seem to matter where one is going or what one is doing as long as there is the promise of new discovery, and opportunities to find and prove oneself. As mythologist

---

*Psychological Astrology, Karen Hamaker-Zondag

Joseph Campbell (who had the sun, mercury, mars and jupiter in Aries) put it, 'If the path before you is clear, you're probably on someone else's.'

In nature, this sense of awakening and bursting into new life is most observable at the spring equinox which is marked by the beginning of Aries season (when the sun enters 0° Aries) in the northern hemisphere. So the Aries phase is about life endlessly renewing itself. This is the time of the year when 'Christ is crucified and resurrected, Attis is castrated, dies and is reborn, Tammuz and Adonis die and are reborn—the spirit of nature, the beautiful *puer aeternus* dies and is reborn.'* And with that, the spring equinox marks the death of the old season and the beginning of the new one.

So it's probably not hard to understand why someone who is typical of the sign, embodies this instinctive faith in life ultimately working out. It's almost as if they 'know' even in the face of extreme adversity, that spring will come and the god will rise.

Of course, we cannot talk about Aries without an understanding of mars, its planetary ruler, whom we're already acquainted with, from the chapter on planets. So we're well aware of its propensity for impulsive action, hunger for conquest and the urge to prove itself as the first, the best, the one and only. You can see why pioneers, entrepreneurs, those most eager to jump off airplanes for the adrenaline rush, fall under the domain of mars. It's also easy to see why someone with Aries emphasis may unconsciously go looking for a fight or create a pattern of rivalry in their life—if you're driven by the need to win, it automatically implies that you're going to get yourself a rival.† I know people with prominent Aries placements who

---

The Horoscope in Manifestation, Liz Greene

†*Barriers and Boundaries: Defences of the Personality*, Liz Greene

are well in touch with their Arien nature and are therefore instinctively drawn to entrepreneurship, sports, activism, some kind of pioneering role, or any other external container for their competitive, combative, adventure-and-challenge-seeking spirit. I also occasionally see charts with the sun in Aries or mars in the first house but the person sitting across the video call seems to have made little to no contact with the potency of their own life force. In this case, the shadow face of Aries tends to be more evident, and often in projection—'Why am I always surrounded by these pushy, aggressive people who can never take no for an answer?' or 'I'm an easy-going person but I always attract temperamental types and also find myself in triangular relationships' or 'I'm a pretty chill person but my blood pressure is off the charts.'

While these are just a few examples and there are endlessly creative ways in which an archetypal pattern may manifest, I hope by now it's easy to see why this may be the case. A person with a dominant mars or Aries emphasised, is already set up to encounter archetypal themes that are distinctly Arien. If it's the sun in Aries—which implies a struggle and a conscious striving—then the individual may find herself born into a culture or family whose values feel restrictive or oppressive, invoking the Arien's innate need to rise up, fight and set herself up as her own authority. This theme of having to wrestle against the Father principle as negative authority figures or collective values that are outworn and toxic, and establishing one's autonomy, is typical of hero myths in general and bears particular allusion to the story of Jason, the Greek hero of Golden Fleece fame, who is closely related to the Aries story. In the story, Jason is the rightful heir to the throne of Iolkos in Thessaly, but his uncle usurps it, and puts Jason's life in danger. Jason is secretly mentored by Chiron the wise Centaur who teaches him the art of war and prepares him for his quest. When Jason returns to claim his inheritance, his uncle, the archetypal Terrible Father who sends the son away into danger in the hope that it might undo him, sends Jason on the quest to retrieve the Golden Fleece, which Jason happily takes on. He rallies his crew of Argonauts, meets with many dangers on his voyage but is helped by gods and goddesses, as well as Medea, the daughter of the king, who is a priestess and sorceress. So Jason slays the dragon, steals the fleece and returns home to rid himself of his wicked uncle and becomes king.*

> *The impulse to launch oneself into dangerous situations in order to prove one's manhood is characteristic of Aries.' (irrespective of gender)*
>
> —Liz Greene†

Hopefully, the Aries type learns, eventually, to direct his aggression and fiery, adventure-seeking spirit into appropriate outlets, failing which he 'creates a disruptive atmosphere in class', is unreasonably competitive, runs away with someone else's fiancé and abandons her the instant the thrill subsides—like Jason, who, after abandoning Medea, must suffer the powerful sorceress' wrath. Whether we see Medea as the inner feminine aspect of the Arien or projected on another, this theme of hubris and greed (Jason abandons Medea for the daughter of the King of Corinth so he could have more power and recognition—ironically, the very collective power he began his quest fighting against), abandonment, betrayal and revenge (Medea not only slaughters the new bride, but also her own children with Jason) is a big part of the Arien's developmental pattern.‡ This capacity

---

The Astrology of Fate, Liz Greene

†Ibid

‡Ibid

to bring out the worst in others as a result of one's own blind ambition, selfishness, ruthlessness or greed, is as much a part of the Arien story as the triumphant return with the Golden Fleece.

I suppose the ideal parent would be able to temper the Aries child's tendency towards impatience, aggression, lack of self-reflection and impulsive action, without thwarting his self-confidence and trust in his intuitive function; in which case, we have someone whose spontaneity is delightful as opposed to disruptive, whose courage is inspiring and whose intuitive sense of timing is a hard-earned gift for years of lessons in humility. But since there is no such thing as the ideal parent, the Arien is set up to learn these lessons through a lifetime of collision with authority in all its forms; through relationships and experiences that seem to thwart his will, frustrate his desires and create inner conflicts with his compulsive attachment to his autonomy.

If Aries can learn to wrap his head around the concept of 'consequences' and take responsibility for his own actions—if he can rein in his urge to say 'yes' to every opportunity before he's had the chance to reflect on his motives, take stock of the energy he has at his disposal or his ability to see something through to the finish line—then he's able to direct the rush of energy he feels in the most useful ways.

The gift of this first phase of the zodiac is the ability to find a way where none exists. In the Hero's Journey, Aries marks the emergence of the hero into the world and his call to adventure. As the first sign, there is no baggage here—the hero is yet to set out, fight dragons and monsters, die and be reborn—which explains Aries' fearless, risk-taking nature.

Often, the Arien's fearlessness is not a conscious act of bravery as much as an inability to see the danger. He's only able to see the many possibilities.* As a fire sign who operates

---

*Psychological Astrology, Karen Hamaker-Zondag

in the realm of possibilities and potential, it's hard for Aries to see where his limits lie. This is a lesson that all fire signs must ultimately come to terms with, but particularly emphasised in this first stage, where the element of fire is at its most heroic and most infantile.

In the Aries stage, we are sent on a quest for our sense of self and identity which we learn to guard fiercely, while particular challenges and lessons invite us to recognise and honour our limits. If we can come to terms with the lessons, we are able to embrace our instinctive faith in life, develop a healthy level of self-assurance and set out to do exactly what we're here to do, without an exaggerated sense of self-importance.

Taurus ♉

Symbol: The Bull
Modality: Fixed
Element: Earth
Ruler: Venus

Also read: Planets: Venus; Elements: Earth; Modality: Fixed; Houses: Second

The compelling rush of energy and appetite for life that took over us during the Aries phase, enters the next stage of development. In Taurus, a fixed, earth sign, the scattered creative impulses of Aries get slowed down and brought into sharp, sensory focus. We realise that we're not just spirit, we also have a body. One by one, our senses awaken as we notice we're well and truly in the middle of spring, which aligns with the beginning of Taurus season. There is so much to take in during this phase—the sights, the sounds, the scents, the textures—all of nature seems to be inviting us to slow down and savour the moment. What we experienced as possibility and a surge of optimism in Aries, is now concretised in the world of form.

Aries marked the end of a cold and dry winter, ushering us into the glory of spring, but it was all so new, we couldn't be sure it was going to last. But by the time the sun enters Taurus, there is a quiet stability in the air and we find ourselves getting used to life in full bloom—we're settled in, and in no hurry for change. This drive to 'settle in' and create permanence is a key part of the Taurus phase of the psyche's development, and is often what's behind Taurus' somewhat compulsive attachment to the material world and concrete plans. The micro anxieties that Taurus displays when you change their environment or plans in some way, stem from this combination of its fixed nature with the earth element—'You said 3 o' clock, now you're saying 2:45! I can't work with that!' But it's only fifteen minutes, you may argue but it's not the fifteen minutes that's a problem, as much as the unforeseen change which triggers a deep-seated insecurity about the future—an understandable reaction to the chaos-driven Aries stage.

After the roller-coaster of the first phase, predictability feels comforting. 'I can only poop in my toilet' is another famous Taurean quote in a long compilation of quotes that have 'my' in italics. Which brings me to another well-known Taurean quality—its need to ground itself through the material world, which often shows up as a need to own things. Taurus loves its creature comforts and as a venus-ruled sign, has a refined appreciation for every fine thing that the sensory world has to offer, be it decadent food, stunning art, high quality sound or sex on sheets made from the finest fabric with a specific thread count (great sex sans fine sheets is acceptable too but they'll notice the lack of quality sheets and who knows, they just might get lost in thread count thoughts midway and decide to stop and give you a lesson on fabric appreciation—you've been warned).

But let's go back to the middle of spring for a second because it's the imprint of this part of the season that anyone with Taurus emphasis carries within them. And it is here that we can begin to appreciate the essence of this sign. What is the mood like in the middle of spring? A quiet sense of contentment with things as they are? Yes. A refined appreciation for the beauty that surrounds you? Sure. A deep trust in natural cycles, knowing that what you sow, you will reap because the evidence is all around you? Totally. It is impossible to capture every sign in its entirety but these three, I believe, form the essence of Taurus. Ruled by the earthy aspect of venus, Taurus possesses a rare gift to be fully present to the present moment, even in this digital age where our collective attention span has been severely compromised.

Whoever said 'Stop and smell the roses' probably had Taurus emphasis. Like Jerry Seinfeld who has both the sun and the ascendant in Taurus. So telling for a man famous for 'The Show About Nothing'. Do you know who the other famous Taurus comedian is? Tina Fey. It's not about comedy as much as the particular brand of comedy. These are two people who excelled at writing and performing situational comedy which centres around ordinary, everyday matters—the domain of Taurus. Seinfeld is also famously wealthy—another Taurus topic. Which brings us to: Why is Taurus associated with money and banks and material security? Again, the answer lies in the middle of spring when all of life is thriving. And should you carry the imprint of this season within you as Taurus does, you'd deeply value the security that comes from knowing that your material world is not only intact, but beautiful and thriving too. And you'd do everything in your power to ensure it never changes. But money is only a symbol of that inner state of contentment that the middle of spring seems to inspire.

This brings us to the fact that the moon is exalted in Taurus.

The moon, while it's ever-changing, does so in a reliable manner—you can set your clock by lunar cycles. And Taurus, with its high level of attunement to natural cycles, can be similarly relied upon—if Taurus loves and values you, that is—to work steadily and patiently to ensure that your life too is filled with the quiet contentment of the middle of spring. The textbook Taurean is often accused of cheesy displays of romance such as roses, cruises and candlelit dinners but if you know what the present moment means to Taurus, and how the bull isn't one to invest in you unless he thought you were worth your weight in gold, you just might get past your hang-ups and develop a taste for the small joys too.

Mythically, the bull that represents the constellation of Taurus is most associated with the story of Theseus and the Minotaur. It begins with Minos, the Cretan King, asking the god Poseidon to send him a white bull as a special sign that he was favoured by him. The god duly sent a magnificent white bull that arose from the sea which is Poseidon's realm, with the understanding that Minos would immediately sacrifice the bull to the god. But Minos couldn't bear to kill such a magnificent creature and so kept the white bull for himself and sacrificed the best bull from his herd instead. This angered the god, who in collaboration with the ever-mischievous Aphrodite, caused Pasiphae, the wife of King Minos, to be overcome with lust for the bull. Pasiphae then mated with the bull and gave birth to a half-bull-half-human monster called the minotaur, who devoured human flesh and ravaged the kingdom. Minos trapped the minotaur in a labyrinth at the centre of his abundant kingdom, but he couldn't get rid of it. And because Athens owed the Cretan King, it was decreed that every nine years, Athens must supply seven youths and seven maidens to be fed to the minotaur.

Psychologically, the bull is 'the primordial unregenerate energy of the masculine archetype that is destructive to consciousness and to the ego when it identifies with it'.* So, Minos taking the bull for himself, ultimately breeds a monster that starts to devour human beings, that is, civilised aspects of the self being taken over by primitive, untamed instincts. This monster that represents instinctual power—greed, lust, power, covetousness, sensuality, control—that is trapped in the labyrinth of the unconscious and demands to be fed, is a central theme in Taurus' pattern of development. If it is not faced, it leads to stagnation and destruction, like Minos' kingdom, which despite its abundance has no way of dealing with the monster that wreaks havoc right from its centre.

Now our hero Theseus, who was himself the son of Poseidon, arrived on the scene just as a new batch of humans from Athens were about to set sail to Crete to be offered to the minotaur. Theseus volunteered himself as one of the youth with the intention of slaying the minotaur. Upon arrival in Crete, Theseus, with the help of Ariadne (the daughter of Minos) and her magic ball of thread (representing the guidance and insights that come from being related to the feeling function),† was able to navigate the labyrinth, find and overcome the minotaur, and make his way out.

Now we have three aspects of the archetype that is central to the Taurus story—Minos, who represents the ego overcome by instincts, the minotaur which is the bestial aspect of the bull or the destructive side of the instincts, and Theseus, the conscious, heroic aspect of the ego who must confront and overcome the bull at the heart of the labyrinth.‡

The Eternal Drama: The Inner Meaning of Greek Mythology, Edward Edinger

†Ibid

‡*The Astrology of Fate*, Liz Greene

In the Taurus phase, we become focused on our relationship with the realm of earth. In other words, we already know that we are separate individuals, but the urge is to define and ground this sense of an 'I' in the material world—I am an 'I' because 'I have'. I have values, tastes, skills, talents, time, relationships, plans, energy, resources, money. The challenges we encounter in the Taurus phase have to do with the wrestling and overcoming of the bull, which represents both the fecundity of the earth as well as its power to keep the Taurus type trapped in his senses. The bull must not be killed (or repressed) but like most mythical monsters, it can be transformed so that it serves the expansion of consciousness rather than feed off of human values.

If we can accept the lessons and work with them, we are able to bring a reliable, stabilising energy to whatever environment we may find ourselves in, while embodying the earthy sensuality of venus, the goddess who presides over Taurus.

Gemini ♊

Symbol: The Twins
Modality: Mutable
Element: Air
Ruler: Mercury

Also read: Planets: Mercury; Elements: Air; Modality: Mutable; Houses: Third

The preoccupations of the Taurus phase around material security, give way to an unfettered, unstoppable curiosity as the sun enters Gemini and we're officially in the end of spring, going into summer. In the northern latitudes where our zodiacal myths come from, it isn't quite summer yet, but there is a noticeable shift in the atmosphere all around—the days are getting brighter and warmer, trees start showing the earliest signs of fruit that will become the pick of the next season, children restlessly await the end of a school year as spring begins to morph into summer and there is a palpable sense of being 'in-between'. While this in-between-ness is common to all the mutable signs, in Gemini, we meet this energy for the first time. And combined with the element of air which corresponds to the mental plane and the thinking function, our primary urge during this phase of our development is 'to know'.

We see ourselves for the first time beyond the body needs highlighted in the Taurus phase, and realise that there is a larger world outside and we know very little about it. So we gather information as we flit about inquisitively between topics, poke, pry and make connections between ideas and concepts in an attempt to make rational sense of the outer world—qualities that the Gemini type displays in his avid interest in everything (and deep engagement with nothing), and the constant need for social and intellectual stimulation. As a mercury-ruled sign, he loves language and as the first of the air signs, he plays with it, with the gleeful spontaneity of a young child. Whether its limericks, puns and good old-fashioned banter or fiction, journalism (Hermes as news-bearer) and advertising, Geminis often love words, and words tend to love them back. This is a handy quality to have in one's possession given how quickly Gemini's brain whizzes between spotting a new idea, trend or news clip, having a clever take on said idea, trend or news clip, and sharing his commentary with anyone who'd listen, all the while finishing up an actual work project, googling something completely pointless, and sending a flirty text to someone and forgetting to check the phone when they actually respond. Gemini is interested in everything all the time. A close relative who has the moon and venus in Gemini (and shall remain anonymous) once confessed to me that he has a separate hard drive just for the footnotes he compulsively collects from the articles and books he compulsively reads.

Your typical Gemini always has too many tabs open in his head at any given time, and while this makes him an engaging conversationalist, it's also his least attractive quality when it comes to any kind of emotional exchange. For starters, he is easily distracted; his eyes always darting across the room, his ears perennially perked for any new and interesting information that he might otherwise miss; not because he's not interested in you or what you're saying, as much as he's also interested in a million other things that vie for his attention all at once. As an air sign, he is also averse to the emotional realm, and any outpouring of feelings usually embarrasses him or makes him deeply uncomfortable. So he'll quickly switch tabs and make a joke to distract you from the torrent of feelings headed his way, which might upset a feeling type who might then accuse him of being superficial or shallow, neither of which he necessarily is. In fact, he may even appear sensitive, moody or outright emo depending on when you catch him, but try pinning him down and that'll be the last you see of him. He is mercury's child, so shapeshifting is in his archetypal 'genes', and boredom and predictability are his kryptonite. If you'd prefer someone who can be relied upon to stay the same every day, or simply someone 'more focused', get yourself a Taurean.

In this third stage of the zodiac, lack of focus is not a neurodevelopmental disorder. Gemini is the quintessential master of none and this is as it should be, because the focus at this stage is on new intellectual discovery, an open and spontaneous engagement with the environment and knowledge for its own sake. While this means that the Gemini type often comes with the attention span of a gold fish, it is also what makes them your go-to person in almost any situation because they always seem to know a guy who knows a guy, whatever your inquiry. Or if you find yourself in a sticky situation, guess who always has a trick up his sleeve to bail you out? You may not be able to rely on his discretion but you can sure as hell count on his charm, gift for deal-making, shrewdly curated contact list and should all else fail, his sense of humour, to navigate life's challenges.

We have to remember that mercury is Gemini's presiding deity and his Greek parallel, Hermes, is patron of both travellers and thieves; and many facets of the archetypal Trickster are most evident in this phase of the zodiacal story, not least of which is his inherent duality.

> *Jung was fascinated by the sometimes brilliant, sometimes murky figure of the Trickster, and in particular by the Mercurius of the alchemists. To him, this figure represented the mysterious momentum of the unconscious, sometimes destructive, sometimes humourous, sometimes terrifying; but always ambiguous and always fertile.'*
>
> —Liz Greene

The Trickster often shows up as the unconscious aspect of ourselves that has a banana peel waiting for us to trip on when we get too cocky, attached to our sense of certainty and to tired ideas of propriety. He is fond of questioning authority (be it outer or inner), norms and breaking rules, sometimes for no other reason than 'because it's fun'. While many aspects of the Trickster are readily observable in Geminis, sometimes the Gemini type will start to strongly identify with one aspect of his inherent duality, to the exclusion of the other. He may fear his own ambiguity, and try to pin himself down so that he is always social, upbeat and fun, as one example. This is when the twin motif, one of the most widely recycled archetypal motifs—

where one twin is divine while the other is mortal or where one is good and the other, evil—which is closely bound up with the constellation of Gemini, takes on a literal meaning in the life of the Gemini native who, as if by fate, keeps colliding with his dark twin in the outer world. This could be a sibling, friend, partner, rival and sometimes, a literal twin, cosmically assigned to confront Gemini with his or her inner opposite.

While the collision and confrontation with the shadow aspects of oneself is by no means exclusive to any one zodiac sign, it does occupy a central place in the Gemini phase of our development. From Zethus and Amphion, Romulus and Remus, to the Biblical Esau and Jacob, the story of the twins—one light and one dark—occurs throughout the epics of the world* and seem to mirror this inherent oppositeness that we're called to reconcile in the Gemini stage.

But the story most widely associated with Gemini is that of the twins Castor and Pollux. And unlike the aforementioned good and evil opposites, here the twins are in fact bound by love and inseparable, except for the fact that one is mortal and the other, immortal. When Castor, the mortal twin dies, Zeus offers Pollux a choice. He may spend the rest of his eternity in Olympus with the gods, or share half of his immortality with his brother so that they can split their time between Olympus (heaven) and Hades (hell). Pollux who loves his twin, picks the latter, except here's the catch: they may not both be in the same place at once. This darker aspect of Gemini in its ceaseless alternation between heaven (the upper regions of the conscious mind) and hell (the lower world of the unconscious) is just as central to Gemini's duality as the lighter facets of the Trickster. And it may present itself as anything from an innocuous albeit consistent fluctuation

---

**The Astrology of Fate*, Liz Greene

between high extraversion and reclusiveness, feverish enthusiasm and ennui, all the way to sudden and extreme swings between elation and downright black moods.

The Gemini phase invites us into the ever-changing landscape that is Hermes' true home (being the only god with access to all three realms) as we navigate our inner and outer worlds; it urges us to not only accept and tolerate duality but to celebrate it; to approach everything with a spirit of curiosity and cautions against taking anything—especially ourselves—too seriously. If we can remain flexible and open as we navigate Gemini's ups and downs and the many spaces in between, then we can meet anything life throws at us with the most surprising and creative aspects of the Trickster.

Cancer

Symbol: The Crab
Modality: Cardinal
Element: Water
Ruler: The Moon

Also read: Planets: Moon; Elements: Water; Modality: Cardinal; Houses: Fourth

The frenzied cross-pollination of ideas and the excessive involvement with the outer world that characterised the Gemini phase, begins to recede into the background as the outer world makes an impact on the inner via feelings and impressions.* In the first water sign, we become acquainted with the feeling function and its capacity to tug us inward, back and forth and roundabout in the same way that the moon which rules Cancer,

---

*Psychological Astrology, Karen Hamaker-Zondag

pulls the tides. If we let ourselves be pulled by this lunar force within, we may get to dip in the richness and fertility of the inner world with its endless capacity to bring forth life and nourish it. Or we may get sucked into the past, feeling our way through the permanent imprints it's left on the psyche—some so sweet and seductive that we temporarily lose sense of time and get swept up in nostalgia; and others, so painful and undigested, that we experience them as if they were taking place in the here and now. Either way, this changeability that goes with the lunar type, along with the sensitivity to the outer world, and the sense of vulnerability it entails for the crab, is followed by an instinctive retreat into the safety of his shell.

This shell, which is the home that the crab carries on its back, is a central theme in the life of the Cancer type, whose cardinal nature directs the flow of feeling and the quest for the archetypal Home, into the outer world. So the inner need to be intimately engaged with the world of feelings, may express itself as the urge to create emotional security in the outside world through intimate relationships of all kinds—parenting, home, family, roots, ancestry, culture, country and so on. We have to remember that the moon which rules Cancer, is one of the most ancient symbols of the archetypal mother, who draws us towards safety, security, belonging, attachment and nourishment through connection to the tribe, clan and community. But while the mother nurtures the child and loves him unconditionally, she is also equally nourished by his dependence on her as his central source of sustenance.* This can tell us a lot about the Cancerian's need to be needed, and his tendency to become insecure, manipulative, create emotional scenes or fall into despair when someone—whether partner, child, friend or pet— has outgrown their dependence on him as their font of love and

Barriers and Boundaries: Defences of the Personality, Liz Greene

strength. But whether the Cancerian is dealing with a loved one separating from him, or he is the one struggling to separate from bonds that seem to keep him infantile, the issue of psychological separation for the sake of ego development (the solar drive) is central to the Cancerian journey.

Too much Cancer or a problematic moon in the chart may point to a hunger drive where the person confuses love with what is simply a deep need for emotional satiation.* So the presenting symptoms may be 'I just want a relationship' or 'I just want a child' but the psychological subtext is often 'I am perpetually hungry'. This can get projected on actual food, with the Cancer type looking for comfort in a jar of Nutella or using food as emotional currency in fostering connection and sometimes, dependency. I've noticed that many Cancer types do love to cook as per textbook descriptions. They'll also invest considerable emotional energy in intuiting your needs, caring for and even coddling you because it's their nature to be the emotional container for those around them, which is why any sign of independence on your part may be perceived as a threat to their own sustenance.

What the Cancerian is really seeking, however, is the need to be contained from within (like mother once contained him) by a larger source of nourishment that will never run out.

> '...it is both a regressive longing for the womb, and a mystical longing for God.'

> —Liz Greene†

This longing is of course first projected on the personal mother, who looms large in the Cancerian's psyche, whether or not she was actually powerful in any objective sense. Whether the

---

Barriers and Boundaries: Defences of the Personality, Liz Greene
† *The Astrology of Fate*, Liz Greene

mother died young, was mentally ill, had to give up her child for adoption, was extremely ambivalent about being a mother and therefore couldn't adequately nurture the child, had to focus on a younger sibling who had special needs, or whatever other way the Cancer myth may have manifested at an individual level, there is a pattern of the mother principle being either inadequate or denied in the life of Cancer, who initially sets out to find her in maternal people, or in taking on a mothering role herself. But this search is only the first step in a gradual unfolding that leads to the Goddess—the fertile and life-giving source within, from which arise those feelings, impressions and images that the Cancerian must birth either in the form of an actual child or an artistic creation. Sometimes, this is projected on a 'creative type' that the Cancerian decides to love, cherish and empower from behind the scenes.*

But whatever path the Cancer/lunar type chooses, the containers set up in the external world must be cyclically broken as they are outgrown. This is similar to the molting process in crabs whose hard exoskeleton cannot expand as they grow, so the crab's protective shell must periodically break as a new one grows in its place. This can be extremely painful for the Cancerian who, without an understanding of his archetypal pattern of development, may assume that the one thing he had poured his whole self into, is now destroyed. But this is as it should be because it only means that the Cancerian has outgrown his shell and is in the cyclical process of renewal, when a new, upgraded one will take its place.

As the sun enters Cancer, it is summer solstice in the northern hemisphere, and all of nature seems to reflect the essence of the sign—fruiting season begins, the birds build their nests and

---

The Astrology of Fate, Liz Greene

animals, their shelters and families are out picnicking in the sun and there is an emphasis on nurture, safety, emotional security, family and tribe. In the Cancer phase of our development, we come to an understanding of our own feelings through the external forms they take in our lives and we learn to accept them as an essential part of our wholeness. After which, we are ready for the second cycle of the elements beginning again with fire.

Leo ♌

Symbol: The Lion
Modality: Fixed
Element: Fire
Ruler: The Sun

Also read: Planets: Sun; Elements: Fire; Modality: Fixed; Houses: Fifth

In the first four phases of the zodiac known as the personal signs, we are introduced to the four functions that make up the wholeness of the personality. Now as we enter Leo, the cycle begins all over again with the element of fire, in the second stage of its development. In Leo, we already have 'an individual personality that is conscious of itself'.* So unlike the Aries stage, the goal is not to separate the ego from the unconscious or the individual from enmeshment in the family psyche, but to understand and define the 'I' at the centre of the personality.

The intuitive nature of fire combined with the certainty that is characteristic of the fixed signs, can make the Leo type extremely self-willed even as a young child. But this intuitive awareness of his own potential and the fiery tendency to self-

---

*Psychological Astrology, Karen Hamaker-Zondag

Why Am I Like This?

mythologise,* can make him so preoccupied with himself and all that he can potentially be, that he must often be reminded by some long-suffering earth type (whom he compulsively attracts), to go to the dentist, pay the phone bill or pick up the kids from school. To the young Leo (and by young, I do not refer to age but the development of consciousness), such dreary tasks are for the ordinary and uninspired. He, on the other hand, is here to be nothing less than a god and for the world to recognise him as such, thank you very much.

We can begin to get a sense of this inner space that Leo operates from, if we paused to observe the natural world during Leo season which falls in the middle of summer in the northern hemisphere. The sun, Leo's ruler, shines brightly in the sky, the fruits that emerged during the summer solstice are now ripe and luscious, the heat and brightness of the season is stable, and all of nature seems to reflect the fullness, flamboyance and grandiosity we associate with Leo. Imagine carrying the imprint of this season within you. Wouldn't you approach life as if it's full of promise too?

But while Leo's intuition about his inner divinity and natural gifts is not wrong, there is a tendency to identify with the archetypal realm or the extraordinary spirit within, to the point that it consumes him and he becomes more and more disconnected with his ordinary human self. Typically, this plays out as the individual scratching the surface of his inherent solar specialness through some outer accomplishment and acknowledgment of his gifts and charisma; which then causes the Leo type to become inflated, larger than life, and seemingly possessed by his own 'divinity'; at which point his story seems to plug right into the myth of Herakles (or Hercules), the legendary

---

Barriers and Boundaries: Defences of the Personality, Liz Greene

Greek hero—son of Zeus, the king of Olympus and the mortal Alcmene—whose battle with the Nemean Lion is probably one of the most famous myths associated with the solar/Leo pattern of development.

In the story, Herakles being a demi-god, is born with super-human strength. Hera, Zeus' wife is outraged (as she often is) because her philandering husband has had yet another affair and birthed yet another illegitimate son. Hera, who never seems to tire of spying on Zeus, his women and his children and exacting revenge, hates Herakles with a vengeance and wishes to destroy him. This is made worse by the fact that she was once tricked into breastfeeding him, when she inadvertently imbued him with the physical strength of a god. So she sends snakes up to his crib to have the child—whose name, to add insult to injury, means 'the glory of Hera'—killed before the situation gets out of hand. But this super-human baby chokes the life out of the snakes, the first sign confirming Hera's suspicions about his strength.

Fast forward to a day in the life of the adult Herakles, who is now married with sons: Hera sends a madness upon Herakles that possesses him and makes him slaughter his wife and children while they're asleep (which is Hera's intention to begin with). When Herakles comes out of this madness and blind rage that possessed him, he is completely overcome with grief and asks the Oracle of Delphi to help him find a way to atone for his sins. The Oracle asks him to serve Eurystheus, King of Mycenae, who would devise labours (the famous twelve labours of Hercules) for him to expiate his sins.

In the Leo stage, we are concerned primarily with the first labour of Herakles, where his task involves the killing of the Nemean Lion, a vicious monster three times the size of an actual lion, that continues to terrorise and destroy man and beast. Herakles is warned that the lion's hide is invulnerable and cannot be taken down with arrows but that doesn't stop our hero from trying. He pulls the arrow back with all his super-human might but nothing. The arrows break and the lion barely even notices. Now the lion is in a cave with two entrances, so Herakles closes one of the entrances, trapping the beast inside. He then gets closer, this time hitting it with a club, and finally with his bare hands, strangles it to death. Once destroyed, he carries the body of the animal back to the king who hilariously hides in a jar and asks Herakles to please stop bringing these monstrous beasts to his court. So Herakles then skins the animal with its own claws, and cloaks himself in its impenetrable hide, which is now a mantle of heroic courage and one that he becomes wholly identified with ever after.

I am obviously doing the myth no justice here but there are many parallels between this story and the Leo/solar pattern of development. Like Herakles, someone with Leo or the sun emphasised in the chart is likely to have an early sense of their inherent divinity or specialness, causing them to identify with the extraordinary aspects of their nature while disowning or rejecting the ordinary human side of life.* When said intuitions of one's specialness are further validated by the outer world, the person may then become seemingly 'possessed' by their own solar brightness and potency, until the hubris eventually leads to utter destruction and devastation—whether this is experienced externally or internally. This is then followed by a 'coming out of madness' phase or low point, when the individual must consciously submit himself to the hard inner work or 'labours' (or he may just have them thrust upon him by his own unconscious) that will ultimately refine his distorted relationship with his solar self. The struggle with the lion is really the Leo/

Leo in Myth and Psyche (webinar from Astrology University), Jason Holley solar type's struggle with the feral aspects of himself that are as destructive as they are powerful and ultimately, noble and life-giving. In the end, the lion in its tamed form (that Herakles wears as his mantle) becomes the symbol of the numinous he was chasing all along—the search for his wholeness (or Self, in Jungian terms) that he is now one with.

In the Leo stage of our development, we become aware of ourselves with a narcissistic intensity (I don't mean this in any pathological sense as much as a natural process of development)* that, while it's proud and self-involved, is also insecure about its place in the social arena. But the lesson of the Leo phase is to recognise that those things we hanker after, in the process of getting others to recognise our specialness, are the very things that separate us from the Self within.†

Virgo

Symbol: The Virgin
Modality: Mutable
Element: Earth
Ruler: Mercury

Also read: Planets: Mercury; Elements: Earth; Modality: Mutable; Houses: Sixth

And now we come to the last sign of the first half of the zodiac with its emphasis on the development of the individual. Virgo marks a turning point, where the focus begins to shift from the personal world of individual consciousness, to the larger sphere of social and universal consciousness, starting with Libra.

---

*Leo in Myth and Psyche (webinar from Astrology University), Jason Holley
†*Psychological Astrology,* Karen Hamaker-Zondag

In nature, this shift is mirrored in the movement from light, increase, growth, ripening and harvest that we experience in the first six signs, to the darkness, shedding, decay and death beginning with the autumnal equinox that marks Libra season.

This is the circle of life itself, and Virgo sits right in the middle of this seasonal round, with all the introspection, self-examination and self-criticism you would expect of any sign that must follow the excesses of Leo season. I think this is where Virgo gets its reputation for being the housekeeper of the zodiac. Every sign is a reaction to the one that precedes it and in Virgo, there is this distinct sense of coming back home to find that your teenager has thrown a party in your absence, and not only is your house wrecked, but there is a medical emergency and the police is involved. Oh, and the neighbours despise you. So sure, there is major cleaning up to do but it's usually a lot more than the kind we're led to imagine.

Virgo's mutability and feminine orientation combined with the element of earth, makes it about the preparation for change through introspection and self-analysis with a focus on the intelligent use of matter—time, energy, money and other resources. The broader possibilities and ideas we are preoccupied with in the Leo stage come into sharp scrutiny and critical focus. It's no longer about what is possible but about what is useful, and the most efficient way to achieve it.

As the last of the signs that focus on the individual, Virgo is about the purification that is needed in order to reorient ourselves to social and collective concerns. Virgo's need to be of service comes from here. 'Now that I'm a fully formed individual, how can I use my knowledge, skills and resources to be useful to others and the world?'

So the textbook descriptions of Virgo's need to dust every surface and set your bookshelf in order is both a metaphor for the psychic housekeeping it's associated with, as well as its connection to ritual and order which arises from its mythic background.

Now the planetary ruler of Virgo is mercury and much of mercury's gifts to Gemini apply to Virgo as well. But in Gemini, the focus is scattered—his interests are many and he pursues knowledge for its own sake; whereas Virgo is extremely picky about what he chooses to invest himself in and whether the Virgo in question is conscious of it or not, this springs from a need to manage the resources of the material world in a responsible manner, in preparation for the constricting phase of nature's cycle. Unlike the Leo phase, when everything was available in abundance and summer looked like it would last forever, in Virgo, the mood is much like the period before the onset of midlife—when you're not quite old, but you're acutely aware of the fact that you're no longer young. So the urge is to differentiate what is true to the Self discovered in Leo—what is pure, useful, and in line with one's true values—and offer it up as a service to others and the cosmos.

In other words, Virgo is concerned with discrimination (and often accused of carrying it to a nit-picky extreme) and specialisation. The element of earth slows mercury down so he becomes focused, precise, dextrous, devoted to his craft, service or field of study. Contrary to popular belief, the goal is not perfection as much as devotion and precision (which is often confused with perfection). Being an earth sign, Virgo is good friends with reality and knows too well that perfection belongs to the gods. Besides, as the sign that is a reaction to Leo, Virgo is decidedly unimpressed with any display of grandiosity or self-mythologising, preferring quality, substance and the quiet sense of gratification that comes from pouring oneself into one's work. Virgo's modesty acts as a shield against the inflation of the Leo stage, which often gets in the way of the Work.

This is not only mercury's second home but also the sign of his exaltation, where all his distractions are minimised, his focus sharpened, and his gifts finally have the chance to develop and express themselves in tangible form. But despite mercury's many connections to Virgo, astrologers have never been entirely convinced of the planet's rulership of the sign. So until the real ruler reveals itself, there is much to be found in the image of the Maiden or Kore who makes up the constellation of Virgo, and her mythic background for which I shall as always, turn to Liz Greene.

The Greeks associated the constellation of Virgo with the Goddess Astraea (who also goes by Dike) who is the principle of Justice. But not justice in the sense of law courts or even the handing out of fate. Astraea has to do with nature's laws. She is the goddess manifest in the rhythm of nature, the cycle of the seasons, the life and death of vegetation, the phases of the moon and the daily and annual movement of the sun through the zodiac. The story goes that Astraea, who was a daughter of Zeus, lived on the earth in the Golden Age when there was no war, bloodshed or strife. She would sit with the ordinary folk in the market place, gather all the elders around and teach them to obey nature's laws. As men got more and more corrupt, Astraea started to despise the human race for its crimes and eventually flew up to heaven to be with her father Zeus, becoming the constellation of Virgo.*

Astraea may be seen as this sense of cosmic order that is part of the essence of Virgo, whose most fundamental fear is chaos. So Virgo's need to keep everything organised and in its place (whether at an inner or outer level) is merely an extension of this archetypal image as well as a defence against the terror of

---

The Astrology of Fate, Liz Greene

chaos. Many Virgo types also have a natural affinity for astrology, arguably for the same reasons. Because it reinforces the image of a well-ordered cosmos and acts as a defence against the seeming randomness of life.*

> *'She seems to be an image of the intrinsic orderliness of nature, and her disgust at humanity is a mythic image of the traditional Virgoan disgust at disorder, chaos and the wastage of time and substance.'*
>
> —Liz Greene

But there is another aspect to Virgo and this one concerns our understanding of the word virgin which did not originally refer to chastity at all. The Greek 'parthenos' and the Hebrew 'almah' usually translated to 'virgin' originally meant an unmarried woman or an unmarried mother irrespective of sexual intactness. In fact, the early virgin goddesses such as Artemis and Atargatis were both harlots and their temples served by prostitutes. But 'virgin' and 'whore' in this sense are both expressions of the archetypal image of the Free Woman. And as we search the myths and our own lives, we are inevitably brought to an important question central to Virgo's development: who is the real whore?†

So the paradox inherent in Virgo's mutability is this conflict of the inner opposites—the virgin, who represents a trust in nature's laws operating as a strong sense of inner morality, receptivity to life and the willingness to be transformed by it; and the whore who really is anyone who sells themselves short to fulfil collective expectations or live by a morality that is not their own, while violating the demands of their inner moral compass. This may show up as a conflict between marriage and singlehood,

---

Barriers and Boundaries: Defences of the Personality, Liz Greene
†*The Astrology of Fate*, Liz Greene

an ambitious professional life and domesticity, a spouse and a lover, being unattached and having children, mysticism and science, and on and on. Virgo must then separate, sort out and discriminate, in order to creatively express the conflicting need to have order, while following the dictates of one's own nature.

Libra ♎

Symbol: The Scales
Modality: Cardinal
Element: Air
Ruler: Venus

Also read: Planets: Venus; Elements: Air; Modality: Cardinal; Houses: Seventh

We are now in the second half of the zodiacal wheel beginning with the autumnal equinox when day and night are equal all over the world, capturing the essence of Libra. After this, the light of the sun starts to decrease, symbolising the decrease in focus on individual consciousness, and a growing awareness that we're related to a larger collective. In Libra, this begins as an awareness of the differences between self and other; and the urge to find equilibrium both within and without, by considering and holding multiple points of view for the sake of harmony, fairness, objectivity and the vision of a civilised world that is good, true, beautiful, symmetrical, equal, harmonious, refined and ultimately, perfect.

Such idealism can make most earth types want to roll their eyes all the way to the back of their heads but Libra is a reaction to Virgo's deathly practicality and tendency to approach life as if it were one long to-do list.

As the first sign in the second half of the zodiac, Libra faces

Aries on the zodiacal wheel, and the two make up the polarity of self and other, known as the axis of relationship. Aries represents the relationship to self, and Libra, the relationship to others. They are two halves of a whole, where one is the shadow of the other. When we go too far into the Aries extreme, we can become self-centred and ruthless, losing our connection to the whole; while too far into the Libran end can make us lose our sense of identity in the pursuit of relational harmony.

So as the polarity of Aries, Libra puts others and the goals of relationship front and centre. But this isn't the same as the water type's need for fusion, belonging and intimacy. As an air sign and the only sign represented by an inanimate object, the scales, Libra is far removed from the world of feeling. It deals with principles and ideas. It *thinks* about relationships, which is quite the opposite of the depth of feeling and vulnerability experienced by water signs in relational dynamics. Libra would much rather attend a workshop or read about working with its feelings, than actually feel such things as anger, jealousy, envy or spite because they make him uncomfortable and go against his fundamental need to be civilised and rise above such pettiness. So the Libra type will unconsciously invalidate and censor his own feelings because in his head, there is such a thing as good feelings and bad feelings (the bad ones are any he considers irrational, primitive or uncivilised) and there is nothing he finds more distasteful than emotional excess of any kind. So if the Libra type doesn't like you, he may have a hard time admitting this to himself unless you've given him a very good reason. But those instinctual whiffs that water types go by when dealing with others, is absolutely foreign to him and he simply will not be less friendly to you because he's getting a bad vibe from you. In fact he might just compensate by being extra nice to you because it's 'the fair thing to do.'

This matter of fairness is a recurring theme with Libra whose symbol associates it with the mythic image of Justice as represented by the Greek Athene and the Egyptian Maat. But unlike Astraea who governs natural law, Maat's law is concerned with ethics, morality, propriety and everything else that goes into holding together a civilised society. In the Egyptian ritual, Osiris judges the souls of the dead on the scales of Maat, the goddess of Truth. The heart of the deceased is placed on one side of the scales and the feather of truth which is Maat's symbol on the other side. At this point, the deceased must make his 'negative confession', which is basically a list of sins he didn't commit, after which the heart is weighed against the feather. If the two sides of the scales are in equilibrium, it means the man's sin's didn't outweigh the feather, in which case, the verdict is favourable. If not, a mythical monster which is part lion, part hippopotamus and part crocodile devours the guilty heart. This mythic image is a vision that is very close to Libra's heart: the idea that the cosmos is ultimately just, and good prevails over evil.*

But coming back to Libra's reputation for being 'fake and superficial' when he doesn't like you: The reason he doesn't bite your head off like Aries or orchestrate an emotional scene like Cancer, is not because he needs everyone to like him (though sometimes it is). It's usually because he's just trying to be logical, open and fair. And if he's dishonest about his feelings with you, it's usually because he's being dishonest with himself. He can be clumsy with feelings. It is after all, his inferior function. But he's fascinated with them for the same reason, so he attempts to pin them down intellectually by approaching them theoretically, as well as exploring them through art and culture. This endows

---

*The Astrology of Fate, Liz Greene

him with considerable social grace and makes him particularly tactful in navigating interpersonal conflicts. But because he's so well trained in the relational arts (a venusian gift) and thinks his way through life, he may end up saying all the right things that stack up to the grand idea of love he has in his head, but his feelings may never really catch up.

The subject of relating also extends far beyond the sphere of human relationships, into the principles that make two things related. What kind of rug goes best with these floors? What colour palette would bring the best out of this space? What makes a work of art 'out of balance'? What kind of music creates the right atmosphere for a particular event? What type of lighting creates the mood for a particular photograph?

This involves both the art of comparison and differentiation as well as a natural sense of aesthetics, and a venus-endowed capacity to elevate the ordinary world of human existence, into the realm of Platonic ideals.*

The pruning of dry and decaying leaves in autumn when Libra season begins, is a pretty accurate picture of Libra's tendency to constantly edit, tweak, improve and adjust everything, including itself against the energy of the other (and at times, consciously play the contrarian), in order to achieve the balance and harmony it craves. In the Libra phase, we are learning to off-set the self-focus of Aries by developing the necessary tact and skills to work with others and relate to the larger whole of which we are a part.

Astrology for Lovers, Liz Greene

Scorpio ♏

Symbol: Scorpion
Modality: Fixed
Element: Water
Ruler: Mars
Modern ruler: Pluto

Also read: Planets: Pluto; Elements: Water; Modality: Fixed; Houses: Eighth

As we enter the eighth sign of the zodiac, the focus shifts from the bright surface of airy idealism, the urge to civilise and create outer relational harmony, to the deep emotional undercurrents that get inevitably stirred up in the process of relating to another. As the second water sign, Scorpio takes us further into the development of the feeling function. But unlike Cancer, which aligned with the beginning of a bright and abundant summer, Scorpio falls in the middle of autumn, when the light of the sun is growing dimmer, shedding season is in full swing and we're surrounded by colours that create an atmosphere of melancholy. To me, this image captures the imprint of this season that Scorpio carries within himself; and a certainty he knowingly or unknowingly operates from: that everything alive must ultimately die. But just as the decaying leaves fertilise the earth so nature can re-emerge in new form, Scorpio also knows that death—whether literal or symbolic—is not so much an ending as a rite of passage; a stage in the transformation of consciousness. Intense? Absolutely.

So if you're looking for something breezy and casual take your business elsewhere. Scorpio doesn't do casual. Except as a smokescreen. In the Scorpio phase of our development, we are pulled deeper into the waters of feeling and our sensitivity to the emotional undercurrents both in the inner and outer world runs high. This profound capacity to feel, makes the Scorpio type extremely vulnerable and often lonely, driving him from within to seek out relationship above everything else. But he's not looking for security in the Taurean sense, nor is he looking to be anyone's emotional container like Cancer is.

What Scorpio wants is an intense, emotional connection that is impervious to change.*

The problem is, such a union would demand a complete relinquishing of control (over himself, others and life in general) and this does not come easily to Scorpio, whose general mistrust of what he sees on the surface is almost as famous as his 'mysterious' and 'passionate' nature. If you can go back to that image of the profuse shedding of leaves in autumn for a second, you'd see where this mistrust of the surface comes from. It's as if the unconscious question is always 'This is all very impressive but what are you not showing me?' So no, he cannot trust easily. At least not until he's been introduced to all your demons and become intimately acquainted with their respective routines. Unlike Libra who'd probably find any emotional excess—be it a bout of jealousy, a fit of rage or even a meltdown that stems from insecurity, clinginess and a constant need for reassurance—on your part distasteful or dramatic, Scorpio is under no illusions about the dark side of human nature (yours or his own). And he cannot let his guard down until his wolf-like instincts tell him that you've shown him all there is to see. This is not easy to accomplish given that he can often sniff out something in you that even you're not aware of. But once trust is established, and Scorpio can rely on your loyalty (another charged word for this sign), he is as devoted as they come. And because he's

---

Barriers and Boundaries: Defences of the Personality, Liz Greene

a feeling-driven sign, everything he does, stems from intense, personal conviction and there are no half measures (this is why popular astrology is full of cautionary tales about incurring a Scorpio's wrath). As a fixed water sign, Scorpio craves certainty in the emotional realm but as an autumnal sign, life never tires of reminding him that the only thing he can be certain of, is change and transformation.

In ancient astrology, the sign that is now Scorpio was originally represented by the serpent whose cyclical skin-shedding symbolised a process of constant self-renewal. This is a pattern that the Scorpio type is intimately acquainted with; where his life seems to fall into different cycles, separated by dramatic inner or outer events that culminate in an ending or some kind of destruction, that makes him have to start all over again.* But no two experiences of skin-shedding can be compared because the transformation of the inner substance during these periods is so remarkable that the individual often cannot recognise himself from the 'before'. The symbol of the Scorpion is also interesting and relevant. Beginning with the fact that deadly as the scorpion is, it isn't aggressive in itself. But try treading on one and it won't be afraid to sting back, whatever your size. This is pretty typical of Scorpio who has a reputation for not only giving as good as he gets, but thanks to his perceptive nature, being skilled at the art of sticking the knife in, just where it hurts the most.

But the most interesting thing about the scorpion is probably its tendency to sting itself to death when it knows it's fully surrounded and there is no way out. This is Scorpio's famous Luciferian pride. He'd rather destroy himself literally or psychologically than submit to another's control.†

Astrology for Lovers, Liz Greene
†Ibid

When Scorpio shows outer signs of resignation, submission or apathy, it's because he's repressed his own nature and while no kind of repression happens without a price being paid, in Scorpio, it can get particularly ugly. Given the emotional intensity and depth of feeling that go with the sign, any lack of consciousness can prove to be poisonous and ultimately destructive. One of Herakles' labours is reflective of this pattern in Scorpio, and while I cannot go into it in any depth here (please read Liz Greene for the long version), I do want to touch on it before we end. In the story, Herakles (whom we have already met in Leo) must now take on the Lernean Hydra—a large beast with nine snake-like heads and venomous fangs, that resides in a dark, swampy cave, feasting on the folks in the countryside. Herakles at first uses his club to cut off one of its heads but a curious thing happens—new heads spring in its place. Suddenly, our hero remembers a piece of advice from his teacher: the hydra cannot tolerate the light. So Herakles goes down on his knees and lifts the beast out of the dark cave and into the sunlight, where it shrivels and dies. One head remains because this one head is immortal and contains a precious jewel within it. But since one head is not a problem for Herakles, he simply buries it under a rock.

The hydra represents the primitive side of instinctual nature and its many venomous heads could mean anything—resentment, envy, jealousy, rage, violence, sexual frustration, vengeance—that is uncivilised within a person. Left unattended, it can turn poisonous and destructive but repression is not the answer since it always leads to 'more heads' springing in its place, just as the more unconscious we are of a complex operating in us, the more powerful and autonomous it becomes. As Jung said, 'What you resist not only persists, but grows in size.'

As the story goes, dealing with the hydra first of all

involves dropping to one's knees—an act of humility before the unconscious. After which, it must be raised into the light of consciousness. Until we can see, reflect and take ownership of the hydra that lurks in our own unconscious, we will continue to project it on others and the outer world in general. And even when we've succeeded in facing our monsters, it's good to be reminded of the immortal head.

In the Scorpio stage, we come face to face with our monsters and we're reminded that every human being carries the potential for evil within him; that evil is not 'out there' and while, as in the myth, it cannot be destroyed, it may be transformed. And the responsibility, ultimately falls on each individual.*

Sagittarius ♐

Symbol: The Archer
Modality: Mutable
Element: Fire
Ruler: Jupiter

Also read: Planets: Jupiter and Chiron; Elements: Fire; Modality: Mutable; Houses: Ninth

There is a palpable shift in the energy as we emerge out of the underground hydra chamber in Scorpio, apparently in one piece after coming so close to being the serpentine monster's breakfast. As we enter Sagittarius, there is a sense of coming back to life as if from a near-death experience, and we start coming to terms with the fact that somehow, incredibly, we are still here. We are well and truly alive. What could this mean? Where do we go from here? And how do we make the best of the rest of this

---

*Astrology for Lovers, Liz Greene

fascinating adventure? To me, this is the premise of Sagittarius and most of what we've come to associate with the sign, has its roots in this reaction to Scorpio.

Let's begin with the optimism that Sagittarius is now almost synonymous with. This is not the same as the general sense of positivity you'll see in the other fire signs. This is not, for instance, the same as Aries charging blindly into battle without counting the cost. As the first sign of the zodiac and the first expression of fire, Aries can only see the possibilities. In Sagittarius, this optimism is hard won. By now, we've been through eight signs in the zodiacal wheel and we've seen our fair share of life's horrors. And yet somehow, we're still standing so we might as well have hope. Because there's clearly something much bigger at work here that infuses life with meaning and purpose. And it is this urge to intuit life's meaning that is at the heart of the Sagittarian quest.

In the more extraverted expressions of the sign, this may show up as the need to broaden one's horizons by traveling far and wide, collecting experiences, sampling everything—from the new club that's opened up on the other side of town, and that weird new sub-sub-sub genre of alternative rock that feels like it might catch on, to that weekend paragliding class, that art expo and that film that's coming out next week that no one's heard about yet.

Fire corresponds to the intuitive function and in this last fire sign, we see it almost bordering on prophecy. Somehow Sag seems to have a sixth sense about what's going to click. In the introverted types of the sign, this gift of intuition works in a more interior way, directed towards a new idea, a new philosophy, or a new cultural phenomenon that Sag is able to pick up on from miles away and run with, long before anyone else has seen it coming.*

Astrology for Lovers, Liz Greene

But it's not just the capacity to spot something before others can because what good is intuition if you're unwilling to take risks with it? Fortunately for Sagittarius, there is a fair bit of the gambler in his archetypal nature and if there's anything that the encounter with the hydra has taught him, it's that he must live what remains of his life to the fullest (whatever that means, usually even he doesn't know). It's kind of like the symbol of the archer whose arrow is aimed upwards, always shooting for something bigger, something more. And it doesn't really matter whether he is able to reach it, because to Sagittarius, the destination isn't nearly as appealing as the possibilities for adventure, excitement, growth and meaning, on the way to getting there. In fact, the minute Sag gets what he wants—whether this is a person, a career success, a house or funding for a creative project—he's going to start seeing it as a trap. Committing to anything automatically implies that you are, at least temporarily, turning away from other possibilities and this is Sagittarius' fundamental conflict: the urge to earth his powerful intuition and vision for the future, while keeping his sense of freedom intact.

This brings us to Zeus-Jupiter, the ruler of Sagittarius, who embodies many of these aforementioned qualities to a caricatural extreme. But what's relevant here is his inviolable marriage contract to Hera, who is his polar opposite. Hera presides over marriage and childbirth—two things that frighten most Sagittarians because of the demands on their freedom and the sense of being trapped—and Zeus is the daimon of lightning and thunder, and the god of heaven—the upper realms that lie far beyond the world of everyday reality. In the stories, Zeus is always chasing after a woman (who is not Hera) and he's quite theatrical too, shapeshifting each time—into a bull, a swan or a shower of gold (he may be a lot of things but he's never boring)—as he pursues them. This urge to chase after every shining thing is a Sagittarian pattern as it is Gemini's but the shapeshifting tells us something more about the underlying reason. In each of these encounters, Zeus takes a different form; and with every possibility that Sagittarius chases, whether this is a person, idea or whatever else, he too gets to experience many lives in one lifetime. This is not your usual social FOMO. This is about a Zeus-like appetite for life's experiences and the fear of missing out on *being* one of the many potential versions of oneself.

But while Zeus may be the king of heaven, his marriage to Hera, keeps him bound to the world of form and mortal commitments. So Hera never tires of spying on her husband and plotting revenge on his mistresses and illegitimate children; Zeus on the other hand, only seems to pursue these women because they are forbidden to him. And when Hera finally leaves him, he pursues her with the same passion and enthusiasm as he would an unsuspecting nymph.*

This brings us to an important aspect in Sagittarius' pattern of development. Zeus and Hera are ultimately aspects of his own nature, though the Hera part may typically be projected on a person, institution, situation, event or obligation in the outer world. If Sagittarius is to actualise the enormous creative potential he intuits both within himself and in the outer world, he must find a way to reconcile these warring inner opposites. Hera is, after all, the goddess of childbirth and if Sagittarius is to make any realistic contribution with his gifts, he must accept and integrate the world of form and limitation that Hera represents.

In the Sagittarius phase, we enter the last four signs of the zodiac known as the universal signs. After the personal and

---

*Astrology of Fate, Liz Greene

social signs, the focus now shifts to transcending the boundaries of family, relationships and community, to finding our place in the greater whole.

Capricorn ♑

Symbol: Goat-fish
Modality: Cardinal
Element: Earth
Ruler: Saturn

Also read: Planets: Saturn; Elements: Earth; Modality: Cardinal; Houses: Tenth

The Sagittarian impulse to go everywhere, sign up for everything and aspire for the grandest, noblest heights, meets the unimpressed, forbidding face of Saturn-Kronos who presides over Capricorn, the last cardinal sign, marking winter solstice in the northern hemisphere. This is the time of the year when the sun is at its weakest; the days get colder and darker, the trees are stripped bare, and animals go into hibernation, as nature enters her cycle of sleep and rest. The focus is now on conserving and preserving resources in order to survive the long, dark winter ahead.

This is an image of the inner reality from which Capricorn operates and can tell us a great deal about the typical Capricorn's preoccupation with security. But this isn't quite like Taurus valuing material security for its own sake. In the Capricorn phase—the last stage in the development of the element of earth— the need for security has to do with the fear of dependency*, and the urge to clearly define and secure one's position in the larger whole, which began in Sagittarius as a vision (scattered in

---

Psychological Astrology, Karen Hamaker-Zondag

several directions). This often expresses itself as a gnawing need for societal status through some form of outer achievement, be it the acquisition of a title, property, accolade, mastery of a skill, or even a marriage (though it better move him at least a couple of rungs up the social ladder). It doesn't matter how long it takes, what kind of obstacles he must face, how many responsibilities he must shoulder along the way or even if his prospects are too bleak or it's just a case of rotten luck, and whatever it is he's striving for, is going to someone else who didn't have to work half as hard (likely someone born under jupiter).

None of this is fair but Capricorn already knows that life isn't fair. It's where he gets that lovably dry sense of humour from. As a saturn-ruled sign, this pattern of delay, lack, limitation and failure seems to mysteriously play out in the life of Capricorn over and over, and especially so till his thirties. And while most others would pack their bags, quit the game and yell expletives at whoever is running the show, Capricorn plods along, keeping his eyes firmly on his goal. The child of winter solstice, he has more self-reliance, patience, discipline, tenacity and strength of will than any sign of the zodiac and you can rest assured he'll get there. Eventually. And when he does, he'll stay there, unlike that mercurial fellow who took a short cut or that solar type who got so inflated from his own specialness and blew his chances. But being under saturn's tutelage since birth can make the Capricorn type older than he is, whether this shows up as experience, maturity, responsibility and wisdom grounded in reality, or less attractive qualities like cynicism, world-weariness and a mistrust of others. He is also more susceptible to status anxiety and a glass-half-empty outlook than any other sign, for which he constantly compensates by being focused, disciplined, strategic and ambitious, all of which can make him come across as cold and unfeeling. But the goat-fish that symbolises Capricorn is a complex creature and there is often a lot going on beneath the surface of his unflappable, self-contained exterior.

Let's look at the symbol in myth for a second. Remember when Saturn-Kronos was busy swallowing his children after receiving a prophecy that one of them would dethrone him? At this time, the infant Zeus was suckled by a goat-nymph named Amaltheia on Mount Dicte when his mother Rhea hid him and kept him safe from the paranoid psychopath he had for a father.

Kronos is himself the Old Goat and the Terrible Father who devours his young. Amaltheia may be seen as the life-giving aspect of the same goat—the mother who saves the helpless son. This is a paradox that runs through the archetypal pattern of Capricorn's development.*

> *'The Terrible Father, who seeks to destroy his son secretly and unconsciously, also offers him salvation through the feminine aspect of the same emblem which he himself wears.'*

—Liz Greene

It would seem that the tests, trials, restrictions, limitations, fears and deprivation that the Capricorn type is well acquainted with in one form or another, serve a secret purpose. In a mysterious way, he seems to need these very experiences to build the kind of psychological muscle he'd need to attain a greater wholeness and fulfil his particular destiny. The story of Capricorn is also intimately related to the myth and symbol of the Father. But this isn't the solar father who is the life-giving creator spirit. In Capricorn, Father is the law giver. He is associated with control, protection, will, boundaries, stability and strength. These are qualities that Capricorn is called to build in himself, though he may initially go looking for it in the outside world through a job

---

*The Astrology of Fate, Liz Greene

or a partner who embodies these qualities. The relationship with the personal father is also a complicated one. On the destructive end of the spectrum, the father may have been experienced as a controlling tyrant, as unfeeling, uninvolved, aloof, a strict disciplinarian, or perhaps the early loss of the father led to the Capricorn child having to take on fatherly responsibilities from a young age. On the other hand, father may be on a pedestal as an overidealised figure whose approval the young Capricorn desperately craves or the father's societal stature looms so large in the child's psyche that he feels inadequate and defeated. Whatever the individual story, Capricorn must at some point let go of his need to please or rebel against the outer father(s) and turn his attention towards the inner figure who acts as a guide on his pathway to wholeness.

In the Capricorn phase, the focus is on minimising the many aspirations of the Sagittarius stage, by turning them into a realistic number of practical goals that fit in with the larger ambition of finding one's place in the structures of the collective; after which all inner and outer resources are directed steadfastly and resolutely towards achieving them.

Aquarius

Symbol: The Water Bearer
Modality: Fixed
Element: Air
Ruler: Saturn
Modern ruler: Uranus

Also read: Planets: Uranus and Saturn; Elements: Air; Modality: Fixed; Houses: Eleventh

The symbolism that Aquarius is encrusted in is paradoxical, not least of which is the shared rulership (or affinity) with both uranus and saturn, who are mythical enemies and another father-son duo like saturn and jupiter. In myth, Ouranos is Father Sky; he is 'up there' concerned with the realm of ideals that we've already seen in Gemini and Libra. The element of air is about the civilising instinct and the urge to improve, correct, reform and elevate us from being merely human to the most conscious, and idealised versions of ourselves.

While in Gemini, this compulsion to civilise was focused on the personal world, and in Libra, on the relational or social sphere, in Aquarius we are concerned with the human race as a whole.

Now the story goes that when Ouranos' wife-mother Gaia, the earth goddess bore their children, the earthy Titans, Ouranos was disgusted by the sight of them. They were too crude and ugly and failed to meet his aesthetic expectations. Revolted, he shoved them back in Gaia's womb in Tartaros, where they were imprisoned and kept hidden from his view. This is a mythic image of Aquarius' difficult relationship with the 'real' world or the realm of Gaia/matter/instincts/feelings. He is concerned with humanity and the welfare of society as a whole because that's a lofty ideal and he can get behind that. But dealing with actual people and their subjective feelings and small, everyday concerns? Gross. Why do they have to be so self-involved anyway?

So no, he's not going to get your 'irrational' meltdown over him not being more vocal about his feelings when there are far more pressing matters to direct your energy towards. Also, he doesn't know what he's feeling and doesn't wish to know, because he's deeply afraid of anything he cannot rationalise, so can you please leave that stuff alone in the underworld of Tartaros where it belongs?

It is no wonder that Aquarius is known as the most emotionally distant of all the signs; with his constant need to censor and repress his own feelings and instinctual needs, because they're too unrefined (like those earth-borne Titans) and have no place in the kind of progressive society he envisions. Air types can be buffoons when it comes to handling feelings (both in themselves and in others) and this gets carried to an extreme in Aquarius who generally considers them to be a bit of a nuisance. Needless to say, this gets him into a world of trouble in his personal relationships which is a constant thorn in his side. He can be awkward when it comes to any expression of romance which he dismisses as silly; brusque and impatient when you most need to be held, soothed and understood; when someone has been hurtful to you and you just need him to take your side, he's more likely to objectively (and obtusely) analyse what was said, when a hug and 'I've got you' could sort you out; and when, having had enough, you just want to end things, he'll not only deny you the emotional response you're looking for, but tactlessly ask if you could still be friends.

He's not setting out to rile you up (though this can be hard to sell to anyone on the other end of this exchange). He just needs to know that you are both capable of rising above your personal feelings and relating to each other without having to tear down everything you've built together. This means that you're going to have to love each other. Not as individuals (because that's too messy and besides, you've already tried that), but as human beings. This is probably why so many Aquarians value friendship over romantic love. From the abstract heights of uranian skies, romantic feelings seem too regressive and self-indulgent. And any focus on the self makes Aquarius uncomfortable. His identity is in the group; in the collective. This is after all, the sign where the sun is in detriment. All that prioritising of the group's needs over individual needs, makes it hard for the Aquarian type to be in touch with his own solar centre.

Aquarius falls in the middle of winter when the sun is at its weakest and there is still no sign of life above ground. But the focus on survival and preservation in the Capricorn phase now changes, as nature is busy shedding all those forms that no longer serve. And just as the dead branches fall off of trees in Aquarius season, so the psyche too undergoes a crisis, as in the Scorpio phase. But this isn't a crisis over the emotional depths of one's individual nature, as much as a crisis over the human condition itself.*

In its connection to uranus, Aquarius is closely related to the myth of Prometheus. And the isolation and suffering that Prometheus endures for the stealing of fire (or consciousness, enlightenment, culture and progress) belongs to the archetypal pattern of Aquarius who is always the outsider looking in. Prometheus steals fire for humanity, not for himself. And Aquarius, being a universal sign, is similarly concerned with the elevation of consciousness—whether through social reform, scientific discovery, technological advancement or making some form of cultural contribution—and the urge to 'push the human race forward' as the 1997 Apple campaign 'Think Different' goes. This is of course, the more life-giving face of the archetype.

In all this discussion of the uranian aspect of Aquarius, we must not forget its traditional ruler, saturn. There is a part of Aquarius that is extremely saturnian in its love of law, order, structure, respect for tradition and a clear set of principles and ethics to live by. And as a fixed air sign ruled by saturn, its ideological fixity can also manifest as intellectual rigidity.† So on the one hand, this is the iconoclastic uranian who is driven to rebel against the structures of the past so he can create the

---

Psychological Astrology, Karen Hamaker-Zondag
†*Astrology for Lovers*, Liz Greene

perfect society. But according to Liz Greene, the saturnian aspect of the sign can make him suffer guilt as a consequence for all that fire-stealing.

'...the punishment which Prometheus calls down on himself is from within himself. In other words, the price the Aquarian pays for his search for truth is a deep and ingrained sense of guilt.'

—Liz Greene.

Pisces)(

Symbol: The Fish
Modality: Mutable
Element: Water
Ruler: Jupiter
Modern Ruler: Neptune

Also read: Planets: Neptune; Elements: Water; Modality: Mutable; Houses: Twelfth

As we enter the last sign of the zodiac, there is a profound sense of coming full circle, to the primordial unity from which the individual consciousness (or the 'I') was separated in the Aries stage. The crisis over the universal human condition and the subsequent shedding of old forms that took place in Aquarius, is now experienced at an inner, feeling level within the individual.* As the last of the water signs, the feeling function works overtime, making the Pisces type more sensitive and receptive to everything in the atmosphere, which he tends to absorb like a psychic sponge. I've repeatedly noticed that people with Pisces or neptune emphasised in the chart (particularly when it involves

---

*Psychological Astrology, Karen Hamaker-Zondag

the moon) often cannot tell if what they're feeling at any given time, is theirs or someone else's.

Everything that was built and developed in the previous stages, dissolves and disintegrates to make way for a brand-new cycle that will start at the spring equinox; making it exceedingly hard to differentiate 'this' from 'that' and 'I' from 'us' in the Piscean phase, where the focus is on one single unity and the interconnectedness of all life.

What might the inner reality of someone who carries an imprint of this stage of the zodiacal cycle be like? Chaotic? Yes. Confusing? For sure. For starters, there is the blurring and dissolving of all boundaries that makes discrimination next to impossible. For this mutable water sign, everything is related to everything else, which means there is no such thing as one right answer or one way to go, and the possibilities are endless. This isn't, however, the same as the Sagittarian's need to keep his options open. For Pisces, this isn't about freedom or the fear of missing out as much as his tendency to identify deeply with the feelings of others, which always makes him 'get where they're coming from'. Even when the 'they' in question is someone who treats him poorly and walks all over him or takes no responsibility for their self-destructive behaviour. You can see how this can quickly go from highly empathic to highly problematic; especially in the sphere of relationships where Pisceans have a reputation for confusing pity with love.* Of course, this brand of love where Pisces plays either the saviour or the victim (which are basically two sides of the same coin) and his depth and range of feeling, has inspired some of the best works in the world of fiction, music, art and poetry, where the Piscean gift is truly at home.

Barriers and Boundaries: Defences of the Personality, Liz Greene

But all this business of merging, fusing and identifying with the fears, dreams, aches and longings of the collective psyche can be overwhelming, if not downright maddening; and there is a long list of Piscean types who, having no way of containing the waters of the unconscious, become completely inundated. The result is often psychosis, addictions that end in overdose, suicide or some other form of self-undoing (another Piscean keyword). The fact is, the fish is a creature of the depths and like everything in astrology, this is a double-edged sword. On the one hand, this gives him easy access to the unconscious from where he brings forth his gifts in an act of psychic midwifery. On the other hand, he has neither a map nor a lighthouse to help him find his way back.

This sense of holding two realities as symbolised by the two fishes swimming in opposite directions, is most evident in the typical Piscean's struggle to keep up with the demands of the material world where everything operates on facts, systems, logic and deadlines. This is extremely hard on Pisces whose natural home is the imaginal realm of magic, mystery, dreams and fantasy. And so he tends to experience reality as a bondage to be released from, resisting incarnation every step of the way. Needless to say, this can affect his work life, his relationships, his finances and everything else on a practical level because he always seems to forget his appointments, show up late (or at the wrong venue) when meeting friends, have trouble managing his money, doing the chores or meeting deadlines. If the people in his life are thinking types (as they tend to be) who prefer structure and logic, they may find his behaviour infuriating, leading to major interpersonal conflicts. If the Piscean can recognise this difficulty and make a sincere effort at working on his challenges, he'll find that the 'real' world he so despises, offers him the necessary grounding, structure and sense of safety he so desperately needs.

On the one hand, this intimacy with the depths infuses the Piscean type with the wisdom of an old soul who can see the futility of materialistic pursuits from a young age. He may then dedicate his life to a selfless cause or take to one of the helping professions. He may also decide to accept and embrace the imaginal world—with all its gifts and magic as well as its threat of inundation and destruction—as his true home, and find a way to integrate it into his 'real' life through artistic pursuits, mysticism or some form of service to the collective—all of which can help him contain the deep waters without drowning. But whatever the Piscean chooses to do with his hunger for the imaginal or alternative reality, he's going to need conscious outlets or containers, if he is to be a conduit for the mysteries of the depths rather than its victim. Because left unattended, this longing for transcendence can swallow him whole—from seemingly innocuous acts of escapism (such as bingeing on a fictional or fantasy world or losing oneself in a gaming world) to drugs, alcohol, a sense of victimhood and anything else that promises a respite from the exacting demands of the material world.

This is the part of the seasonal cycle when everything dissolves and the outer world is seemingly dead. But in the silence and darkness underground, the seeds germinate, awaiting their emergence into life at spring. The winter solstice has also always been imagined as the death of the old year or the 'old king' because the sun—which is at its weakest at this time—is conceived of as dying. But this is a pregnant darkness, a fertile void, and there is much going on underground that we cannot see. The spark of new life that will become the new cycle is already 'born' as mirrored in the winter solstice birth of the solar gods—Mithras, Horus, Apollo and even Christ, as the 'light of the world'.

So the zodiacal story is the story of the sun on its annual cycle; mythically, it's the hero's journey and psychologically, it's the unfolding narrative of the individual ego on the quest for wholeness.

For more on the archetypal perspective on the signs, read Liz Greene's The Astrology of Fate *(the section on Myth and the Zodiac), Liz Greene's* Astrology for Lovers, *Karen Hamaker-Zondag's* Psychological Astrology, *Jason Holley's* The Signs in Myth and Psyche *available as webinars from Astrology University.*

For a very readable introduction to a Jungian exploration of mythology, read Edward Edinger's Eternal Drama: The Inner Meaning of Greek Mythology *(though it's hard to come across a Jungian book that does not go into myth).*

7

The Houses

The natal chart is geocentric—a snapshot of the sky from the point of view of the earth. So when you look at a natal chart, you'll see the ecliptic—the path of the sun, aka our zodiac—forming the outer wheel. The ecliptic is basically the space in the sky where the sun moves from the point of view of the earth, and it is divided into twelve signs of 30 degrees each, which allows us to track the planets in the sky at any given time. But this alone tells us nothing about how the movement of the planets is related to the individual life. For this, the early astrologers found a way to link the celestial (the movement of the planets) with the terrestrial (the daily rotation of the earth on its axis). So they divided the 24-hour rotation of the earth into four sections based on how long it took the sun to go from dawn to noon to sunset and to midnight.*

We get the houses from this basic relationship between the movement of the planets and the rotation of the earth on its own axis. Now from the point of view of the earth, there is always a sign rising in the east—that you may know as the rising sign—while its opposite sign on the zodiacal wheel, is seen to be setting. The degree of the rising sign in the easternmost point of

---

The Twelve Houses, Howard Sasportas

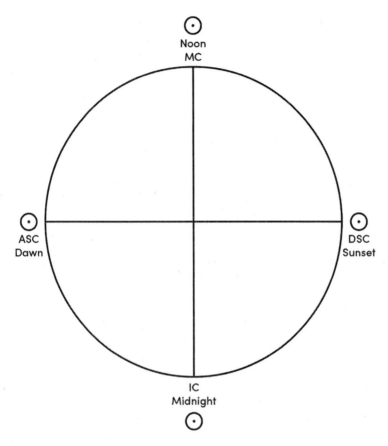

Figure 4. The Sun's Diurnal movement as seen in the chart. The four angles: Ascendant, Midheaven (MC), Descendant and Imum Coeli (IC).

the sky is called the ascendant, while its opposite point in the sign setting in the west, is called the descendant. Astronomically, the ascendant marks the point where the heavens meet the earth—symbolically, the point where spirit enters matter, which is why the ascendant is one of the most important personal points in the natal chart and in traditional astrology, said to represent the native. From an interpretive point of view, we may understand the ascendant-descendant axis as me-versus-we. It's where we balance our personal agenda with the goals and needs of a partnership or 'others'. Psychologically, because the ascendant represents the individual, its opposite point (the descendant) is reflective of what is most often experienced as projected. Opposite points in astrology are two halves of a whole. So whether the descendant represents partners and significant others or rivals and opponents, it contains the essence of what we most tend to disown in ourselves.

The line connecting the ascendant and descendant is known as the axis of the horizon.*

Likewise, the particular degree of the sign that is 'culminating' or at the highest point in the chart at the 12' o clock position is the midheaven or MC (short for the Latin Medium Coeli which means 'middle of the heavens'). While the midheaven is on the top of the chart, it's actually the southernmost point above the horizon in the northern hemisphere. The midheaven symbolically represents the culmination of the individual quest as it may show up in one's outer life—an answer to the question 'Where am I going?' Its opposite point, the nadir of the chart is the IC or the Imum Coeli which means 'the lowest heavens' and tells us something about one's roots (in every sense of the word) and is the answer to 'Where do I come from?'

And so we have the four angles of the chart which at an interpretive level, tell us a lot about an individual's orientation to these fundamental aspects of life. The houses are easy enough to find on the natal chart as they are numbered, dividing the circle into twelve sections.

For more on the four angles, read Melanie Reinhart's Incarnation: The Four Angles and the Moon's Nodes.

---

*The Twelve Houses, Howard Sasportas

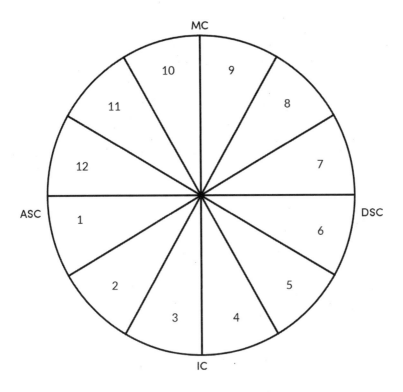

Figure 5. 12 Houses as seen in the chart

Just as the planets represented the 'what' and the signs described the 'how' of the story, the houses tell us 'where' the action is taking place and where these cosmic principles are concentrated in our 3D world.

In ancient astrology as set forth in Manilius' *Astronomica*, the house was described as a *templum*, which is a word for temple, but in Manilius' time, referred to an empty building that only became numinous after the cult statue of the god was placed within.* Seen through this lens, every house in the chart

---

The Astrological Neptune and the Quest for Redemption, Liz Greene

that hosts a planet, is an area of life into which the archetypal powers in question, wish to become embodied through us. The houses anchor us in the physical world, bringing the gods down to earth as it were.

Traditionally, this was understood in a purely concrete sense—the first house represented the body, the second house, livelihood, the third siblings and so on. But in the Jungian view, the archetypes are the foundational principles that connect everything in reality—what is outer and inner and what is above and below. So instead of assigning concrete meanings to the houses and seeing them as existing in isolation, we'll look for the underlying principles that connect the seemingly unrelated meanings of the houses. Also, traditionally, the meaning of the houses was not related to the signs but in the archetypal view, it's easy to see how they are all symbolically bound up together.

So the houses help us understand our lived experiences in an archetypal context. Why do you keep experiencing the plutonian themes of betrayal, ruin, destruction and regeneration in a cyclical way in the sphere of interpersonal relationships? What do you need to understand about pluto pinned to your descendant in order to shift or better relate to these experiences? Could you possibly create a conscious outlet for pluto's urge for transformation in this area? Maybe you have the moon conjunct neptune in Capricorn in your first house and your pattern is that you're a compulsive care-giver, creating dependencies all around you to the point that you cannot separate the suffering of others from your own, and this has now reached a point where it's seriously impacting your health. Understanding the archetypal nature of the moon-neptune conjunction, its particular hunger and offering it healthier outlets can go a long way not only in escaping its destructive side but accessing its creative, life-giving potential.

This does not, however, mean that we can psychologise the planets from manifesting at a concrete level by being clever and doing inner work. At the root of such an assumption is not only hubris, but the delusion that we can, somehow, magically, escape suffering. But suffering is both a part of the human condition and a necessary ingredient in bringing us to growth and maturity as any saturnian knows. The way I understand it is this: there is suffering that is necessary for your individuation that you can do nothing about, and there is suffering that you unconsciously bring upon yourself. And more often than not, it is the latter that makes you go around in circles, rehashing patterns, banging on doors that aren't meant to open and creating endless cycles of anguish and self-sabotage. But without further ado, the houses:

The First House

The ascendant—which is the doorway into the first house— is the most personal piece of the horoscope because it's that specific point in the sky that was rising in the east at the time and place of your birth, when you took your very first breath. It sets the mood, lighting and background score for the precise moment of your emergence into life. Once you've made it past the ascendant, you are truly here; an incarnate being, announcing your entry into the world. In the daily cycle of the sun, the ascendant marks sunrise and the dawning of a new day. In the annual solar cycle, this is the point of the spring equinox.

So the ascendant and the first house are intimately related to initiation and the archetype of birth itself. Since we know by now how archetypes operate, this can shed a ton of light on the outer circumstances of your birth as well as how you handle new beginnings in general. The sign that colours the ascendant as well as any planets in the first house, tell us something about your view of life. And because we tend to call forth that which we expect, it tells us how *life meets you*. If you're an Aries rising, you may approach every beginning as an opportunity to conquer, and prove yourself. If you were born with Capricorn rising on the other hand, you may first experience fear and self-doubt before you proceed to come to terms with the situation by carefully assessing, controlling and planning your strategy. In the end, you may do better than everyone else but your inner experience is not going to be anything like the Aries type who may come charging out into the world, because he can't wait to have new experiences and make a mark on the world.

The sign and the planets in the first house also inform your earliest experiences of life, and the planetary ruler of the ascendant aka the chart ruler, acts as a guide or personal *daimon* who assists in the development and expression of your sun. The sign, house and aspects (which we'll get to) can tell you more about this archetypal guide who helps you navigate the particular quest laid out in your natal chart.

So the first house has everything to do with you and your relationship to the environment and outer world. It hints at your persona (which in Jungian terms, is a bridge between the ego and the outer world). It is often referred to as a social mask but 'mask' can suggest falsehood which the ascendant is not. As the most personal point in the horoscope, this has everything to do with you, the particular filters through which you experience the world, your personal agenda and so on.

The Second House

In the first house, you emerge from the waters of the womb where you were completely enmeshed with your mother, and experience yourself as a separate person. In the second house, you begin to look for ways to define, solidify and ground the separate being that you already know you are. How is the essence of who you are reflected in your tastes, preferences and choices? How does it peek out in the little ways you unconsciously make a statement about yourself? The way you dress, how you decorate your house, the neighbourhood you live in (or dream of living in)—all tell us something about how you anchor your individual spirit in the world. Traditionally, the second house is associated with 'that which I have'—your assets, livelihood and material possessions. But if we can understand this as symbolic of something inner, then money may translate to 'value'. The money you make is a symbol of the value of your contributions. So we're also looking at skills, talents and anything you're able to offer, that allows you to stand on your own feet.

In the first house, you know you are an independent being, separate from others; but in the second house, you find ways to substantiate that statement by developing your own set of values and principles, which go on to determine what you are willing to invest in. Where do your energy, resources, time and money (that which you have) go and why? Why does one person value a luxurious lifestyle with all the creature comforts that life could offer, while for another, all their money and energy go into higher education or buying more books? Because what you do with what you have, says something about what you derive your sense of security from.

The sign on the cusp of the second house and any planets therein, tell us what colours a person's value system, which then goes on to inform their relationship to money and income, how they provide for themselves, what they invest their resources in, and on and on. So someone with Cancer on the second house cusp, may derive their sense of security from the authenticity of their emotional connections. They may choose a job that 'feels right' over a job that pays well. Whereas Leo on the second house cusp may see the job as an extension of his individuality. He may need the job to make a statement about who he is. The sun in the second house can tell us about the need for this particular individual to strive in this area of life in order to express his individual essence. This may play out as someone born into wealth but feels an inner compulsion to step out of it in order to stand on their own feet; just as much as it can be about a person who is set up to go through cycles of material hardship but insists on not taking help and making it on his own, because he knows intuitively that this is where he must struggle and strive to access his solar essence. Planets in the second house may imply a 'money complex' however it manifests. Saturn here may be a statement about the inner sense of lack that a person operates from, which may have latched on to early experiences of financial struggle. He may then go on to compensate for this his whole life and unless made conscious (or there are other 'happy' influences in this house), all the material security in the world may not satisfy the hunger or take away the fear of 'not having enough'.

The Third House

Once you're solidly established in who you are and have the capacity to stand on your own feet, you realise that there is a larger world around you, of which you're a part. In the stages of development, the third house is where a baby recognises itself as separate from mother, and having derived a basic sense of security from the second house, feels safe enough to crawl and explore his environment. There is so much to take in here—so many new sights, sounds, shapes, textures and...language. How utterly stimulating! These curious objects in the environment may now be named, labelled, compared and classified. The mind stretches beyond the here and now of the second house into the realm of abstractions, and starts to play around with ideas, theories and concepts. You start asking questions, making comparisons and learning new ways of seeing the world through interaction with peers.

Siblings, cousins, neighbours, peers at school, aunts and uncles are traditionally assigned the third house for the same reason (they belong to the world just immediately after mother and father). 'But Andy's mom says it's okay to watch TV before homework,' 'Why mustn't I talk to strangers?' 'Where do my thoughts come from?'—the third house is full of questions no matter how old you may be. It tells us something about how we learn, gather and process information, how we communicate and engage with the environment, as well as the lens through which we perceive what's 'out there'.

If Gemini falls on the third house cusp, you may feel a kinship with this house. You may exhibit a hyper curiosity about everything around you—from every new restaurant and bookstore that's opened up in the city, the latest technology, art show, lifestyle and fashion trends to astrophysics, growing fungi and learning Greek all the way to what that mean girl from high-school is up to these days. A lot to keep up with? For sure, but Gemini doesn't care for an in-depth engagement with anything so it fits right in. But what if you had Scorpio on the third house cusp? The energy of the third house is still going to scatter your attention in many different directions but Scorpio might interrupt this process and get you to pick just the few that you feel strongly about: 'They're all interesting but which ones resonate powerfully with who I am? Do I feel a deep sense of conviction and passion for this subject or field of study? What are my deeper, unconscious motives for engaging with this?' On the other hand, the signs and planets as archetypal filters may also say something about how we experience the environment. Is it safe?

For the third house Gemini person, sure. It's curious and

mentally stimulating. For Scorpio, it may feel threatening because he starts to pick up on all those things that are concealed, not said and he may feel the urge to dig deeper because he mistrusts the surface. Venus in the second house may suggest that this is where you're most likely to have an embodied sense of the goddess and her gift of pleasure for its own sake. Learning something 'new and interesting' may not only be the thing that delights you the most, it is also a statement about what you deeply value (venus), as another example. If we look at the third house as the place where you can find your venusian oomph, it may express itself as your ability to fluently toggle many different languages or your easy and personable way of interacting with new people, or it can quite literally describe a sister you always envied because you experienced her as prettier than you and your relationship has been riddled with all the envy, rivalry and cattiness which belongs to Aphrodite's shadow side. As the house of siblings, the third house can give you important feedback on what you may have projected on a sibling (or anyone else in the environment or even your experiences at school).

The third house is associated with writing and communication (of all kinds including computers, advertising, social media) as well as buying and selling, and anything else that falls within the realm of exploring one's environment (like the vehicle you use to get around town). It deals with the mind and expanding us beyond the limits of the material world.

The Fourth House

When you've experienced yourself as an 'I', ensured your footing in the material world and explored and made connections with your immediate environment, you're ready to go deeper. 'But who am I, deep within the chambers of my inmost being?' 'Where do I come from?' 'Where, how and with whom do

I belong?' 'What lies concealed, quietly gestating beneath the surface, awaiting emergence?' These are some of the questions we ask when we encounter the IC, the nadir of the chart.

This is winter solstice in the annual cycle of the sun, and the point of midnight in the daily cycle, which carry a sense of hiddenness, mystery and quiet gestation. Your fourth house is rarely visible to the outer world, even when you don't particularly consider yourself a private person; at least not until someone comes along who 'feels like home'.

In popular astrology, the fourth house is associated with home, family, parents and the domestic sphere. And this is all true but it's also more than that because it's really about the essence or the archetype of Home. If you're a child with Cancer on the IC or the moon in the fourth, the meaning of this house may initially be projected on mother or a mother figure who embodies home; or it may say something about the longing for such a maternal presence. When you're older, this may turn into a nesting urge and home may be projected on your literal house and the partner and children who become your family. If you have Sagittarius on the IC or jupiter in the fourth, your home may be something intangible—the search for meaning through travel, learning, philosophising or telling stories—or it may be about how you always fantasised about getting out of your small town and exploring the great big world outside.

But by relating to the planets and signs in this house as an aspect of your inner world or untapped riches, you may have a more constructive way of finding this elusive home (within or without).

Psychologically, Liz Greene makes an excellent case for the fourth house, as the psychological inheritance from the father, who is usually the 'hidden' or less obvious parent and while this is a point of dispute among astrologers (since the fourth is traditionally associated with the moon and Cancer), in the Jungian approach, this bears out. Planets here as well as the planet that rules the fourth, may give us a sense of what's shared, inherited, projected on the father, the patrilineal line, as well as the unlived life of the father.

Your fourth house is a window into what lies buried in your story—which extends far beyond you into the family psyche, generational conflicts, ancestral patterns and into the very matrix of life itself—the womb of the Goddess—from which all life springs. In other words, this part of your chart describes your origin story. Your ancestors at a physical level, as well as your archetypal parentage. The fourth house describes the tree you're meant to grow into. So if you see an acorn here, you get a sense of the potential you carry, though this may not ripen until the latter part of your life. This is because the fourth is both the point of gestation and therefore 'not ready' for emergence (as suggested by the winter solstice) as well as the point of endings (the last season, the marker of midnight etc). In this way, the fourth house brings the story full circle. It's the spark of life from which you emerge, as well as your endgame.

The Fifth House

In the fourth house, you delved into the depths of yourself and the family stories—the unlived lives, the generational traumas, the buried treasures, the secrets and taboos—from which you spring. And now that you have a more well-rounded sense of self, you're ready to make a statement of your individuality in the world around you. What does it mean to be you in all your you-ness? Have you learnt to revel in and celebrate how you're distinguished from others? How do you embrace those pieces of self, excavated from the fourth house, and allow it to radiate into the world? These are some ways to think about and imagine the fifth house which has traditionally been associated with children, creative self-expression, romance and sex, hobbies and recreation. So from an archetypal point of view, we can say that the fifth house represents the archetype of the Child. There is an innocence and spontaneity to the self-expression associated with the fifth house (much like Leo and the sun) which isn't quite like the ambition we associate with the tenth. This is the creative impulse you see in young children free of inhibition and self-consciousness, and unattached to outcome. There is a pure sense of play for its own sake here. Hence the association with leisure, recreation and hobbies. All those things you do to celebrate the joy of being alive and being an individual, generally belong to the archetypal world of the child and the meaning of the fifth house. This is all well and good but what about romance? And sex?

If you can move out of linear-thinking, and play (like the fifth house type) with the symbol, you'll see that everything you associate with romance—the joy, spontaneity, silliness, feeling special, the sense of being the centre of someone's attention, the sudden surge of energy and enthusiasm you have for life—belong very much to the essence of the child. The fifth house then, refers to the kind of love, romance and sex that has less to do with the seriousness of partnership and marriage, and more to do with the initial sparks, flirtation, dating and courtship. The sex too has a lighter, playful quality and feels more like fun and pleasure than the merging of souls (which psychological astrology attributes to the eighth house and it drives most traditional astrologers absolutely nuts because traditionally, 'sex = fifth house').

So the fifth house can tell us about your relationship with your inner child, which goes on to inform your relationship with creativity—not only in the conventional sense of painting, singing or writing novels but as a way of approaching life—fun, recreation, parenting, children etc. I often see people with

Capricorn or saturn in the fifth house as 'serious creative types'. Or those who feel a compulsion to take their creative side seriously and potentially, make a career out of it. Leo or the sun here may embody the child in a more organic way in their everyday life, whether or not they are creative professionals. Parenting as a role may also be close to their heart and they may even end up projecting the sun or Leo on to a literal child. Meanwhile Scorpio or pluto here can be about a death-rebirth cycle associated with one's self-expression. Perhaps they'd have to shed the superficial layers of self cyclically through an experience of depression or creative block, in order to get in touch with their individuality. Or they may fall passionately in love with a creative type or project their own repressed child on to a lover who is fun, light-hearted and full of life. But understanding your experiences—whether in relation to your expression of individuality, your role as a parent or your capacity to freely engage with the essence of the child—through the lens of psychological astrology, allows you to take responsibility, take back projections and find conscious outlets for your creative nature.

The Sixth House

This is one of the more difficult houses to pin down and like the eighth and the twelfth, has suffered a ton of bad press. Open a traditional textbook and you're told right away that this is the house of 'bad fortune' and that's only the beginning of a long list of examples on the lines of illness, accidents, slavery, enemies, servitude, with the only silver lining—to me, at least—being small animals. But let's file this away for a moment and consider this house symbolically.

Like the sixth sign, Virgo, the sixth house marks the end of the first half of the astrological chart which falls below the horizon. So it acts as a bridge between what is below and what is above. All that you developed in the first five houses is now given form through the work of your hands, acts of service and care of the body. The task of incarnation which began in the first house when you separated from the source of life/God/the waters of the unconscious, is now complete and anchored in the material world. So 'work' or 'service' in the sixth house sense, is a sacred act of bringing the Divine Source into the physical world.*

This is why in monasteries and ashrams, washing dishes and cleaning the toilet are treated with the same sanctity as prayer and meditation. There is no such thing as too menial a task. It's a way of seeing and honouring the Divine in every aspect of ordinary life—eating healthy, exercising, walking the dog, checking off your to-do list, helping an old lady cross the road, babysitting your niece, making a grocery list, caring for the old, the needy, the helpless, and of course, turning your work (whether this involves digging ditches, running a country or making art) into a sacred act of devotion. The routine associated with the sixth house is really a ritual and a way of participating in the cosmic order by bringing order to one's immediate world. As for service, the service of the sixth house isn't to others as much as to the Divine, even when this means serving or 'working for' others. You can see by now that many of the traditional meanings of the sixth house feel like a distortion or an unconscious version of this.

We could say that as the house most concerned with incarnation, the themes of the sixth house, have a way of manifesting when we don't handle its matters with consciousness. For example, I've noticed a pattern of psychosomatic symptoms

---

The Inner Planets: Seminars in Psychological Astrology Vol 2, Liz Greene and Howard Sasportas

in clients with packed sixth houses (more than two or three planets). They seem to have a way of somatising their complexes. I've noticed others with an emphasised sixth house express this as workaholism, which is really a modern spin on being 'enslaved' to one's job. Positively, sixth house planets express themselves as devotion to one's place in the grand order of the cosmos. It's also about the mind-body-spirit connection as the last of the individual houses, and I see this emphasis in the charts of healers, yoga teachers, fitness enthusiasts and so on.

So like everything in astrology and the human psyche, there is a light and shadow side to this house. If you're seeing the more difficult side of this house manifest in your life, check to see if you have any planet here and what sign colours the cusp of the house. This should tell you more about the nature of the archetypal principle that seeks to be anchored in your everyday life. If it's mars in Aries, you may need some kind of physical outlet—a sport or fitness regimen perhaps—or a work environment where there is room for healthy competition, as one example. But if you aren't related to this part of yourself, this mars in Aries may show up as hypertension (so common), migraines or even 'enemies' at the workplace.

The sixth house is a sort of changing room where you make adjustments and ready yourself before you emerge above the horizon and see yourself in relation to others.

The Seventh House

The task of the first six houses is to completely separate from Source for the sake of individual development. So by the time we come to the seventh house, this work of the 'personal houses' is complete and we've come as far away as we can as individuals, from the state of fusion prior to birth. Now at the descendent, which is the point of the chart that lies exactly opposite the ascendant, we recognise that there is more to life than the personal world and we become aware of the need for others. So in the next six houses, the focus is on reconnecting the individual to that original sense of unity with all life.*

This circular path back to the oneness of life, begins in the seventh house as a recognition of 'others'. If the ascendant—the point that rises in the eastern horizon at the time of birth—represents you in the natal chart, the descendant (or the seventh house cusp), which is the point that's setting or becoming invisible, symbolically represents those parts of yourself that you 'cannot see' and therefore comes back to meet you as 'others'. In a psychological sense, we could say that the descendant and the seventh house is what you're most likely to project on others. Since projection is best identified by the emotional or psychic charge it creates, it makes sense that seventh house relationships have been traditionally attributed to 'marriage' as well as 'open enemies'. In modern astrology, the seventh house may include any significant one-on-one relationship that is bound by commitment (and ideally a contract), but either way, it makes total sense from the point of view of projection, because the parts of ourselves that are least accessible to us are almost always embodied by a partner or rival or really, anyone we see as 'other'.

And so the seventh house, like Libra, the seventh sign, invites us to this balancing act that we must learn to do if we are to step anywhere outside our personal worlds. If the chart indicates an excessive self-focus (emphasis in Aries, the first house, or even most planets in the first six signs for example), one of the crucial tasks of individuation would be to balance our needs and agendas against the needs of others and learn cooperation. Because the very act of engaging in this relational

---

The Twelve Houses, Howard Sasportas

dance with others, allows us to see what unconscious material we've projected on them. On the other hand, when the chart indicates too much 'other focus' (a packed seventh house/Libra, the sun or the moon in the seventh/Libra, for example) we may have a tendency to value relationships at the expense of individuality, or focus so excessively on others that we forget to acknowledge our own needs. In this case, the task at hand is to bring the focus back to the self in order to find a balance, which is almost always accomplished through the lessons that 'others'—whether partners or rivals—happily teach us.

Again, the sign on the cusp of the seventh house as well as any planets therein, may tell us more about what we unconsciously seek out in others or have trouble relating to in ourselves. If Pisces colours the seventh house cusp, we may on the one hand, disown the essence of this sign in ourselves as 'too wishy-washy', 'irrational' or 'deceptive' but find ourselves repeatedly attracted to those who embody some aspect of the sign. They may be dreamy and artistic, sensitive, compassionate, whimsical or equally, moody, unreliable, escapist or duplicitous. Planets in the seventh house, particularly the sun or the moon, often show up in charts of those in the helping professions, those that work one-on-one with clients, as well as those whose work involves an audience of some kind.

But if we can look at the seventh house as the process of othering that we do unconsciously all the time, and use the feedback we get from relationships and rivals—and our 'opposites' in every sense—to integrate the exiled parts of ourselves, we may have begun to grasp the deeper meaning of this house.

The Eighth House

Now we come to another of the maligned houses in traditional astrology, thanks to its association with death among other things. But like Scorpio, the eighth sign, and its modern ruler, pluto, this house won't yield its secrets until you've done some digging. Let's begin with the less dismal traditional meanings of the eighth house as 'other people's money' or 'partner's resources'. As the house opposite the second which was concerned with your resources as an autonomous individual, the eighth being the second house from the descendent (partner or 'others') is associated with what the other person brings to the table—whether this is money, assets, time, effort or anything else. As the house that follows partnership and marriage, it has to do with the merging of resources. Your joint property, shared business and bank account, as well as debts (of all kinds), belong to this house.

Psychologically, we may understand this 'merging' that follows a serious commitment as sex, but very different from the fifth house variety of fun or casual sex. In the eighth house, everything is at stake. And when everything is at stake, you either let go completely so you can have passion, or you keep secrets and withhold pieces of yourself so you can have power. Either way, you're never quite the same after eighth house sex, which is a symbol of the willingness to relinquish control for the sake of fusion with another. This is in every sense the 'la petite mort' or 'little death' as the Elizabethans called the sexual act because it means consciousness is no longer calling the shots and you're temporarily overtaken, consumed, possessed and penetrated by instinctual forces* that often put you directly in touch with all those fears, traumas, taboos and everything else you've locked away in the underworld of your unconscious.

When the eighth house is triggered, deeply buried stories rise to the surface and you're often left wondering who you really are.

The Astrological Neptune and the Quest for Redemption, Liz Greene

You've always been the cool and detached one in relationships and yet here you are, feeling a desperation you've never known before. If you have unresolved fears of abandonment or betrayal from childhood, then an encounter with this house can feel a lot like the mythical abduction of Persephone (which in this case could mean the ego's naïveté or lack of consciousness) into Hades (the underworld of the unconscious). I often hear clients describe their eighth house experiences—whether this is the end of a relationship or while someone is still in the throes of the crisis that the eighth house brings to the surface—as 'I can't handle the thought of it. I couldn't bear it. I might just die.'

This is just one example of an activated eighth house and it can be unsettling to look into the mirror it holds up. In the anatomy of the psyche, the eighth house is the personal unconscious or the Freudian layer where your demons take up residence, erupt into your outer life without warning, and do whatever else that demons do in their free time. But from a Jungian point of view, these demons are also potentially your angels and hold essential pieces of yourself, necessary for your wholeness. So an encounter with the eighth house is always profoundly alchemising and you're never the same person (in the best way) when you emerge from it. But it does always involve a death, though it's rarely the literal kind. Have you watched Batman Begins? Do you recall that scene where Bruce re-enters the bat cave for the first time as an adult and faces the bats? To me, that is a powerful image of a conscious eighth house descent.

You can choose to do this of your own volition in psychotherapy or some other form of 'making the unconscious conscious'. Or you can wait for a crisis—the death of a loved one, a divorce, an experience of betrayal in some form, bankruptcy, a terminal illness or anything else (all of which are traditional meanings of this house)—to drag you, screaming and kicking into the underworld. I want to clarify: I'm not suggesting that psychotherapy or Jungian analysis or whatever else is going to spare you the unforeseen crises that the eighth house sometimes brings. But I am saying that a) voluntarily entering this space can help you avoid much of the suffering that stems from your own unconsciousness and b) when life does set you up for the worst, you are in a much better position to face it and integrate its meaning so that the experience empowers you, instead of tearing you down.

But what about that other scenario where you keep secrets for the sake of power? This too ultimately collides with the eighth house's urge for transformation, though the death in question may either be the breaking down of your defences or the death of the relationship itself. Because if there is anyone who can pick up on your fears, secret motivations and those Lernean hydras you keep for pets beneath the surface, it's someone with an emphasised eighth house. Like Scorpio and pluto, planets in the eighth house are intimately acquainted with the dark of the psyche and go through cyclical periods of transmutation and regeneration. The planets placed here as well as the planet that rules the eighth house, are like threshold guardians that bar your way forward and test you through the fires of transformation, before they let you access the dazzling views of the ninth house.

The Ninth House

Surrendering to the metamorphosis of the eighth, means that you're a whole other person as you make your ascent out of the depths, into the ninth house. And the world too, looks radically different, now that you've been through this death and rebirth. It's the same life you're coming back to, and yet it isn't. And now that you've digested and made sense of this experience, you begin to integrate its meaning. You had an encounter with death in one form or the other and you're still here. What does this mean for you going forward? And what does it say about the journey of life?

As the house opposite the third which was concerned with the gathering of information and logical thinking, the ninth house is about the synthesising of that information in order to find the underlying patterns and principles at work in life. This is where you search for meaning and formulate a worldview. Traditionally, the ninth house is associated with philosophy, religion, higher education, foreign places and long-distance travel. But whether you go searching for meaning in organised religion, studying philosophy or astrology or anything else that explains the workings of life and the cosmos, or you travel the world so you can learn from other cultures and traditions about how other people approach life, the ninth house experience is ultimately about finding a philosophical framework to process life's experiences.

As the house associated with jupiter and Sagittarius, it's all about the big picture. We're interested in the laws—whether these are cosmological, psychological or legal—that underpin our existence and give us a sense of a grand design of which we're a part. This is why we write memoirs when we come out of the eighth house. While your eighth house story may be unique to you, it also teaches you something about the shared experience of being human, and navigating a seemingly random and unpredictable cosmos. But the ninth house, like the memoir, isn't only a platform that allows you to share the truth that emerged from your life-altering experiences, but also a way for you to reframe that story in a larger context so it serves as a map for the future. From a Jungian point of view, the ninth house tells us something about your *imago dei* or inner image of God which is then projected on a particular religion, philosophy or whatever your god or religion is.

If you have saturn in the ninth house or Capricorn on the cusp, you may see God as a stern authority figure which may show up as religious conservatism just as much as a non-religious but generally pessimistic, materialistic or bleak view of life. Or it could simply suggest that you need a tried and tested belief system—whether you express this as a hyper-scientific temperament or place your faith in a well-established religious institution. Venus or jupiter here may feel inherently hopeful about life and the future, seeing the beauty and meaning in everything life throws at you. The symbol-making capacity of jupiter may see life as a video game or this grand adventure where every wrong turn and detour offers a clue to the next chapter.

The ninth house describes long journeys whether this involves trekking in the Himalayas or backpacking through Europe, or journeys of the mind. The wisdom distilled from these journeys must be shared so they can serve the broader collective, which is why this house is also associated with teaching, publishing and broadcasting. In the third house, we gather information and in the ninth, we disseminate it. A packed or emphasised ninth house may also indicate an inherent capacity to lean on intuition and see the larger patterns at work at a collective level. Empowered by the perspective we've gained through our eighth house experiences, we begin to have a vision for the future that we're now ready to embark on.

The Midheaven and the Tenth House

And now we reach the zenith of the chart at the midheaven—the doorway of the tenth house—where the journey through the last nine houses reaches a culmination. Traditionally, the tenth house has to do with one's status and reputation in the world and therefore referred to as a 'career house' but it's so much more than that if you look at it through an archetypal lens. This is the point of the chart that aligns with the midday sun (so if you were born at noon, you'd have your sun pinned to the midheaven of your chart), the summer solstice in the annual cycle of the sun and the prime of youth in the stages of human life. So there is a visibility and ripening associated with the midheaven in direct contrast to the dark incubation and seed form of the IC and the fourth house. In the IC, we are concerned with questions of our archetypal roots or parentage because it tells us who we are at a fundamental level, without which we'll never know where we're going, by the time we arrive at the midheaven.

So there is a sense of accomplishment and completion (or disappointment and disillusionment from the lack thereof) when we hit this point in our journey. Everything you've been moving towards, is laid out there in the brightness of daylight. What does it feel like now that you've scaled the heights (whatever 'the heights' means to you)? Was it worth the effort? Does it feel as rewarding as you imagined it would feel? Do you like where you're headed? Do you need to switch routes? These are some of the broader themes and questions that the midheaven poses, and ones that we'll repeatedly encounter through the transits of planets over this point in our chart.

So what's all the fuss about career and the midheaven? While in some charts, planets in the tenth may quite literally describe the person's line of work, literalism robs the symbolic language of its richness and layered meaning. It's like seeing pluto in someone's tenth house and advising them to take up a career as an undertaker (it's a different matter that someone who works in the morgue may actually have pluto pinned to the midheaven but that's not how this works).

The sign on the cusp of the tenth and its ruler may hint at how you are meant to show up in the world, what aspects of the Self—the archetype of wholeness (which is really the entire zodiac)—you've been enlisted to express publicly in your life because it's ripened in your psyche. You may do this quite unconsciously but as always, consciousness allows you to express your placements in the most life-affirming way.

This may be particularly relevant to the MC as planets here are most visible to the outside world (how you show up on Google as one example) which can tell us something about your public image as well as what the public is likely to project on you.

Liz Greene attributes the tenth house to the mother (the 'visible' or 'obvious parent') and the psychological inheritance from mother—be it something shared with mother or an aspect of her unlived life; which is experienced as a compulsive need to express a particular planetary principle. In this case, the inner work of separating one's own ambitions from the unfulfilled longings of the mother can go a long way in dealing with any blind compulsions or frustrations experienced here. With the moon in the tenth, for example, the individual's public life is in some way fused with the longing for mother. If the experience of mother was lacking or inadequate, the career or public image may become a surrogate mother.

In its association with Capricorn the tenth sign, and saturn its ruler, the tenth house has to do with earthing the vision of the ninth in some concrete way. Our contribution to society, our reputation in the world and the status anxiety associated with Capricorn are all aspects of the tenth house experience. Psychologically, the ego has not only solidified but has been recognised by the outer world. This is the peak of the mountain, after which we'll begin our descent once again to be re-united with the Divine Source from which we emerged.

The Eleventh House

From our beginnings as an ego barely aware of its separateness in the first house, we reach a crescendo in the tenth. Everything we aspired for and built steadily towards, reaches a culmination and there is nothing else to prove or hanker after on the individual path. Feelings of gratification (or regret) may be accompanied by a yearning to broaden one's world beyond individual ambitions. It's lonely at the top, even if we only realise it after getting there. Much like the admired, charismatic leader of an organisation whom everyone looks up to but who has no one to eat lunch with, the general tenor of the eleventh house is the need to connect with others and identify with something larger than oneself.

This connection with others, however, is not based on family ties or emotional bonds but by shared ideals.* We are related because we see ourselves as part of the same whole, whether this is about shared interests, tastes or philosophy. We are no longer the lonely 'I' at the top of the mountain. We belong and we're related. As the polarity of the fifth house where the urge was to bask in our individuality in order to distinguish ourselves from others, the eleventh house is about going beyond and even sacrificing ego-needs for the sake of the group or the goals of the greater whole to which one belongs. This is best captured in the famous Star Trek line, 'The needs of the many outweigh the needs of the few.' The eleventh house is about group identity, group goals and a shared collective vision of the future.

Traditionally, the eleventh house is known as the house of friends and also, the house of hopes and wishes. As the house that corresponds to Aquarius, the last of the air signs, these 'hopes and wishes' have to do with collective longings rather than individual ones. It is your urge for a sense of community—to find your people, your tribe, those kindred souls who get you in ways that your family or lover may not. This may be a social circle, a

---

* *The Astrological Neptune and the Quest for Redemption,* Liz Greene

football team, a band or a Reddit forum, just as much as it can be the Pro-Lifers, the Pro-Choicers, the flower children, the BTS ARMY, the climate change activists, LGBTQIA, PETA, the Ku Klux Klan, the anti-vaxxers, you get the drift. The eleventh house is associated with social causes and social reform based on the 'hopes and wishes' for a particular Utopia. The problem—as illustrated by some of these examples—is that these Utopian ideals are starkly varied.

When you're in eleventh house mode, you may feel like an alien at the family dinner table but feel a strong sense of kinship with strangers online who love, believe or care about the same things. The sign on the cusp of the eleventh house as well as any planets here, may tell us something about what you fundamentally need from a community or what you tend to project on groups. The sun here must consciously strive for identification with something greater than itself (this is antithetical to the urge of the sun which is why the sun is said to be in detriment in Aquarius) while saturn or chiron here may point to experiences of isolation, being bullied in groups or even a 'scapegoat complex'. Planets here are also hooks for what draws you into a group and what you're hoping to find in yourself through the hivemind. As with all placements, there is a life-giving aspect to 'difficult' or 'malefic' planets and a shadow side to the 'benefics'. Bringing consciousness into how you experience a planet in this house is the first step to changing its expression.

In the eleventh house, there is no hierarchy as we begin to go beyond ourselves and give up ego needs for the sake of group ideals.

The Twelfth House

The last house in astrology is also the most complex, especially if you have planets here and you happened to open a traditional textbook. Suffering, loss, misfortune, imprisonment, isolation, dangers, secret enemies, and just in case you weren't feeling entirely doomed, Hellenistic astrology calls this 'the place of Bad Spirit'.* What is a twelfth houser supposed to do with such a prognosis? Some go for 'remedies' to offset the expression of these 'malefic placements'. Others roll their eyes and conclude astrology is a load of crap. Many never find out that they have twelfth house placements and unconsciously act them out positively or destructively or both. But whatever you choose to do with your twelfth house, considering it from a Jungian point of view may not only help alleviate some of your anxieties but help you frame your own experiences of the twelfth and allow you to access its gifts (which are many) in a more conscious way.

As the last of the twelve houses, the focus here is on returning to a state of unity with Source/God/the uroboric waters of the womb from which we emerged as an individual ego. In a concrete sense, this refers to pre-birth and the memory of the womb† where you were in a perfect state of fusion with mother, you were kept safe and all your needs were intuited and met, without you having to ask for anything. As a mythic image, this is a longing for Eden, Paradise, God or eternity that exists in all of us. Except such a fusion would mean that you relinquish your sense of separateness, which is a terrifying prospect for the ego. Besides, without the ego, you couldn't possibly navigate these primordial waters which in a Jungian sense, corresponds to the collective unconscious and archaic memory.

This is essentially the dilemma of the twelfth house. On the one hand, there is a very real need for dissolution and sacrifice of individual needs for the sake of fusion with the whole. Twelfth

---

Hellenistic Astrology: The Study of Fate and Fortune, Chris Brennan
†*The Twelve Houses*, Howard Sasportas

house planets don't really belong to oneself as much as the past of all human experience. This is the realm of the ancestors though not in a fourth house sense. The twelfth travels way back into the collective past, into your connection with the myths, stories, traditions, dreams, gifts and rituals* from hundreds and thousands of years ago. But there are some true horrors in the collective past—memories of genocides, witch burnings, wars, medieval tortures and killings, slavery, the list is endless.

Twelfth house planets at one level, may be seen as carriers of the longings and unlived lives of these ancestors who now demand to be lived through the individual. Positively, this may show up as compulsive creative urges and a capacity to spontaneously 'download' stories, images, musical compositions (in a flash or through dreams) that 'must be expressed'. Twelfth housers also often go down the spiritual path where they seem to have easy access to realms that are far beyond the borders of the material world. This is the world of the mystic.

But even when the experience is basically positive, there may be a sense of being haunted. My client, Priyanka, who is a writer of fiction, has the sun, mercury and mars in Leo in the twelfth house, and almost always 'receives' her stories 'in a flash'. She also spends much of her time traveling and in hotel rooms, and a story she related very much captures the essence of the twelfth house. She was staying at the Taj Hotel in Bombay—a place she happens to frequent, and is about a hundred and twenty years old—and on this particular night when she entered the room, felt a strong 'presence' that she couldn't shake off. Creeped out, she switched on the lights and within seconds, a whole story involving a woman who used to work here a very long time ago 'downloaded' in her head with all the details fully fleshed

---

The Astrological Neptune and the Quest for Redemption, Liz Greene

out. After the story was captured in her notes, the presence faded almost as if its job was done, now that the story had been transmitted to this human carrier who must give it a voice.

While having stories, images or ideas come to you in a flash or in a dream is a fairly common experience for artistic individuals, in the twelfth house, there is a palpable connection with the realm from which it emerges, and there is a very thin line here between receiving gifts and being haunted.

We could ask what might have happened if my client did not have a creative container ready and waiting to 'carry' this gift. What if she had not found her calling and had not been in touch with her creative or mystical side? How would she have framed this experience (as well as other similar ones that fall in the realm of parapsychology) in her head? She may have felt haunted (I wonder if the presence would have left at all if she hadn't had the capacity to receive and write the story). Or if she were too rational to accept such a possibility, she may have ended up in the psychiatrist's office asking to medicate the ghost away.

And while twelfth house ghosts are not exactly Casper, like anything else in the chart, they never really 'go away' and continue to demand expression. Only this time, they may show up as longings that threaten to swallow up the ego. Unable to find anything in the 'real world' to satisfy these longings, the individual may turn to drugs or some other form of escape or addiction, and in extreme cases, suicide. And so we come back full circle to the traditional meaning of 'bad spirit', 'asylums', 'suffering', 'imprisonment', 'secret enemies' and the modern 'self-undoing', though these may refer to inner realities as much as outer ones.

We could surmise that twelfth house planets are forgotten stories of the past that demand to be lived out and expressed through the individual in question. Whether this means you become the prime minister, a famous musician, poet, mystic, priest or criminal, addict, cult leader, con artist or choose to die at your own hands, would depend on the solidity of the ego and the level of consciousness you're able to bring into your experiences. In the end, as Joseph Campbell suggests, the trick may be learning how to swim in these waters as opposed to letting yourself drown or attempting to escape.

For more on the twelve houses from a psychological perspective, read Howard Sasportas' The Twelve Houses: Exploring the Houses of the Horoscope

8

The Aspects

We've been looking at the natal chart as the unfolding story of the individual psyche. The planets are the actors (or the drives), each with their particular strengths, weaknesses and motivations. The signs clue us in on the roles these actors have been assigned and the themes they're going to encounter in the drama (or sitcom) of your life. In other words, how good is the casting for this particular show? Does it elevate the story? The houses tell us where the action is taking place and what areas of life assume prime significance. But it's the aspects that decide the script—they create the drama, deliver the plot twists and get the story moving.

Aspects refer to the angular relationship between the planets and the angles on the natal chart. There are five aspects known as the major aspects as well as many minor aspects that we won't be going into here. Each of these major aspects is a symbolic portrayal of the nature of the relationship between the planets in question. They determine the tension, friction, conflict, flow and harmony in the chart.

Psychologically, you can understand these aspect patterns as complexes. To refresh your memory, complexes are those pockets of energy clustered around specific areas of the psyche. Since the core of a complex is archetypal, tracking the patterns the planets form in a chart through aspects, can reveal the nature of these complexes and the particular archetypal dramas that are most likely to unfold in your own journey.

But let's look at the five major aspects before I digress.

The Conjunction: 0°

The conjunction is technically not an 'aspect' and refers to planets that are huddled up together in the same sign within 10 degrees of each other (this is the generally accepted orb—or distance—for conjunctions though the question of orbs varies from one astrologer to the next). The closer the orb, the stronger the effect or 'charge' of the complex.

Given how closely the planets are placed in a conjunction, their energies blend or clash with each other and in terms of interpretation, they are like conjoined twins at a psychological level, and must always be read together as a whole. Conjunctions typically operate as drives within us that we're well aware of, though they may or may not feel comfortable.

Example: Venus at 5 degrees of Virgo and mercury at 10 degrees of Virgo is a conjunction. When you interpret mercury in this chart, you'll always interpret it as mercury conjunct venus and vice versa, as they are fused together.

The Opposition: 180°

When two planets fall on opposite sides of the zodiacal wheel at a 180-degree angle, we have what is called an opposition. In this case, we have two planets falling in a polarity of signs, pulling us in opposite directions. They represent opposing psychic forces that cannot be reconciled; they make us feel torn, conflicted and dramatically increase tension, often by enlisting people in our outer life to 'carry' one side of this polarity for us while we 'hold' the other side—aka projection. Planets in opposition in the natal chart tell us what needs to be reconciled. Jung's prescription for these situations was to tolerate the suffering that ensues from holding the 'tension of the opposites' until a 'third' emerges that is neither 'this' nor 'that' but a combination of the two. We most encounter oppositions in the outer world—both in interpersonal conflicts, as well as in those relationships where the chemistry is off the charts. Either way, the opposition demands integration, and we're never quite whole if we haven't made room for both archetypal principles involved in the opposition.

The standard orb used for oppositions is also 10°.

Example: The moon at 16° of Aries and neptune at 20° of Libra is an opposition and a tight one at that, given that the planets are within a 4° orb of each other. Here the emotional hunger of the moon for a sense of autonomy and freedom (in Aries) collides with neptune's urge for fusion, most likely in significant partnerships (Libra).

The Square: 90°

When a planet forms a 90-degree angle to another planet on the chart on either side of the zodiacal wheel, we say that they are 'squaring' each other. Symbolically, this is a confrontation and creates so much irritation and friction between the two (or more) planetary principles in question, that it demands some kind of action. Psychologically, we may once again tend to identify with one side of the conflict and experience the other planet through others in projection, as well as in recurring themes and situations that seem to follow us like a kind of fate. Alternatively, we may also swing between the two until we find a way to carry both in our lives.

Example: Mercury at 28° Virgo squares neptune at 22° Sagittarius. This is a square from my own chart as illustrated by the compulsive swings I experienced from mysticism and hyper religiosity (neptune in Sagittarius; exacerbated by additional factors involving neptune that I'll touch on later) to hyper-rationalism and the need for facts and evidence to back up everything (mercury in Virgo). The study of astrology and depth psychology has been an excellent container for me since it reconciles the neptunian urge for the transpersonal, with the mercury-in-Virgo urge for systems, structure and empirical evidence.

Orbs used for squares vary typically between 8 and 10 degrees.

Of the five major aspects, the conjunction, opposition and square are referred to as the hard aspects. They are dynamic and demand resolution. They are like the irritant in the oyster that produces the pearl, though in my experience, you may have to produce rocks and gravel for years before you get to the pearl.

The Trine: 120° △

The trine and the sextile are harmonious aspects and refer to energies that flow with ease.

Planets that are 120° away from each other are in a trine aspect to each other. There is so much ease, flow and harmony between the planetary principles, that they have a way of just landing in one's lap. Psychologically, this refers to qualities and creative gifts that come so easily and naturally, that one assumes 'it must be like this for everyone'. Concretely, it may refer to situations or opportunities that just find you without you having to move a finger. Trines may refer to qualities that help the ego such as resilience, the ability to see the humour in adversity or a strong will that one takes for granted, as well as talents, opportunities or even good fortune that come so effortlessly that there is often a lack of motivation to do anything with it.

Example: Mars at 3° Aries and the sun at 5° Leo are in a trine. And since the two planets are in their own signs, it's a trine on steroids. This may confer the individual with any number of the positive expressions of this trine. A strong sense of self, confidence, charisma, creative flair, enthusiasm and motivation, energy in abundance, capacity for self-assertion may come naturally even before one has any accomplishments or achievements in the outer world to validate these qualities. On the potentially negative side, they may operate on the assumption that everyone has access to the same level of energy, good fortune and optimism, which can be particularly aggravating to those with an abundance of earth or water placements.

Orbs for trines are typically between 6-8 degrees.

The Sextile: 60°

When two planets are within 60° of each other, they are sextile each other. The sextile is similar to the trine in the sense that it's an aspect of flow and harmony but it suggests potential that needs a little push from the ego in order to be made into something. It's the mildest of all the aspects and requires some 'tapping into' in order to uncover its gifts. Unlike the hard aspects, there is no tension, irritation or friction to force action or some form of manifestation, but it's not a trine either, so it doesn't really land in one's lap without a little effort and leaning into.

Liz Greene allows a maximum orb of 6° for sextiles but as always, any aspect is going to be a lot stronger when the orbs are tight.

Example: Jupiter at 8° Capricorn is sextile the midheaven at 11° Pisces. Jupiter here can potentially help how the individual shows up in the world at large. Jupiter's natural attributes—positivity, expansion, seeing the big picture and a capacity to generate good will and good luck—may help the person's place in the world but it would require him to consciously tap into the jupiter aspect of his nature. This may be more difficult than usual because jupiter is placed in the sign of its fall where its natural expression is severely impaired or inhibited. This particular jupiter answers to saturn (the ruler of Capricorn) so one may need to balance jupiter's urge for enthusiasm and expansion with saturn's need to be cautious and realistic.

Aspects are usually marked by lines in astrology programs and websites. If you're using Astrodienst, the hard aspects are marked by red lines (which can look like dots or very tiny horizontal lines in the case of the conjunction) and the harmonious aspects by blue lines. Ideally, we want an equal balance of red and blue lines but the chart, like life, is rarely ideal. The one thing you can be certain of is that there is no such thing as a perfect moment in the skies, which implies that there is no such thing as a perfect chart. Likewise, no matter how heavy or challenging a chart may seem, it is never without support and its fair share of life-giving potential. I want to stop here before I wander into territories that might elicit questions best answered by philosophers and theologians. But with this, we come to the end of the basic astrological alphabet: planets, signs, houses and aspects (another quaternity). As you go deeper into the rabbit hole, it gets more layered and nuanced but at least from a psychological point of view, there is so much work to be done with the insights you glean from just the basic alphabet, that anything else is best set aside for later.

Unaspected Planets: Unconscious and Unhinged

When a planet makes no major aspect to any other planet in the birth chart (allowing the orbs suggested here), it is considered unaspected. An unaspected planet is a feral piece of psyche and often has a way of running away with the script. Having no input from any other archetypal principle, it operates like an island with its own laws, carrying its own qualities to an extreme. This may be experienced as an excessive preoccupation with the planetary principle in question, because at an inner level, the individual feels unrelated to the planet, always searching for it in some way, even though it's quite loud and even jarring to those around.

Astrologer and Jungian analyst Karen Hamaker-Zondag has written an immensely useful book on the psychology of unaspected planets and yods, which is beyond the scope of this book but has much in common with unaspected planets. Yods, also referred to as 'the finger of God' or 'finger of fate' are formed by a minimum of three planets that form an isosceles triangle in the chart. The two planets at the base are connected by a sextile and they are both connected to the planet on the apex by a minor aspect known as the quincunx or inconjunct (150 degrees). The orbs for yods are extremely tight (Hamaker-Zondag uses a maximum of 3 degrees) and their appearance in a natal chart is fairly uncommon. I highly recommend Karen Hamaker-Zondag's *The Yod Book: Including a Complete Discussion of Unaspected Planets* for anyone with an unaspected planet, duet (two planets that exclusively form an aspect to each other but nothing else in the chart) and/or a yod.*

Based on her research, there is unfinished business in the

The Yod Book: Including a Complete Discussion of Unaspected Planets and Duets, Karen Hamaker-Zondag

family psyche in both cases and it's almost as if the unlived lives of the ancestors take over the life of the individual destined to carry a yod, an unaspected planet or a duet.

While there are differences in the way yods and unaspected planets are interpreted, both may be experienced in their positive as well as negative extremes, and there is an underlying sense of getting caught in the crossfires.

There are larger themes at play that go beyond the individual carrying these placements. For some, this may play out at the level of generational patterns and for others, at a more collective level. In both cases, there is something that demands to be lived out and may be experienced as a powerful, all-consuming inner compulsion.

Psychologically, they may be understood as unconscious complexes—split-off pieces of psyche operating with tremendous force and autonomy. One the one hand, they express the nature and essence of the planet in its purest, most organic form and point to talents and gifts; on the other, they may cause much suffering both within and without, given the work it takes to make them conscious.

The Unaspected Sun in the Charts of Vincent Van Gogh and J.K. Rowling

J.K. Rowling has the sun unaspected in Leo (domicile) in her natal chart and Vincent Van Gogh has the sun unaspected in Aries (exalted). While the more positive expression of an unaspected sun in domicile/exaltation may be eminence (at whatever scale), the story that plays out behind the scenes is what makes the eminence so unique. JKR is certainly not the only famous children's author but the dramatic turn of events in her personal life—from 'as poor as it is possible to be in modern Britain without being homeless' to the phenomenal success of

Harry Potter—has a way of becoming mythologised (a solar quality) in the eyes of the public.

Van Gogh's story is even more dramatic. For starters, his fame was posthumous. And from the facts we have of his life (I'm going by the Van Gogh Museum here), the story of the unaspected sun emerges—on the one hand, lucid and brilliant; on the other, tragic and lost in its aloneness.

As a child, Vincent always felt different from others, always getting into trouble at home and at school. Unlike others, he also had zero clarity on who he wanted to be in terms of his vocation. So he shapeshifted frequently—from art dealer in Paris, and teacher in London, to priest in Belgium—before he found his true calling as an artist. Once he found his love for painting, he was consumed, obsessive and unstoppable. But he also had a drinking problem, suffered from a number of psychiatric disorders* and eventually shot himself at the onset of midlife at age 37. In the note he left his brother Theo, he says:

> 'I feel—a failure. I feel that that's the fate I'm accepting, and which won't change anymore.'

We could say that the real tragedy here is the inner experience of this sun that seems to shine so brilliantly to everyone but the one carrying it. But does this mean that everyone born with an unaspected sun is predestined to be the tragic, misunderstood artist? Or an easy hook for collective projections that on the one hand, elevates one to the level of the gods and on the other, 'cancels' them overnight, their whole life's contributions notwithstanding? You can see in these manifestations, the flight of Icarus (that we touched on in the discussion of the sun) and the madness of Herakles slaughtering his children or 'potential'

---

*https://www.bbc.com/news/world-europe-54780434

(that we saw in Leo); and any number of solar myths that warn us of the perils of the solar journey and flying too close to the sun, that are just as amplified in these individuals as the rags-to-riches stories that we so love.

The Unaspected Sun in My Chart

When I first came across the concept of unaspected planets in astrology and then found that I had, not any planet, but the sun itself unaspected (which is a little bit like the protagonist of the story deciding to go rogue), it put so many of my lifelong struggles—only some of which I've touched on in the memoir part of this book—into perspective.

The excessive preoccupation with the 'Who am I' question from a young age, the terror of ordinariness, the complete cluelessness about identity and vocation resulting in constant shapeshifting (from pursuing the humanities against everyone's wishes in college, to evangelical Catholicism, to advertising, to the world's shortest marriage that left me a single-parent at twenty-six, to writing novels, to astrology, to Jungian psychology), the extreme highs and lows of the twenties, the sense of not being able to recognise myself from one play act to the next ('How could I have possibly made this decision?', 'Why did I marry so young when it's so unlike me?', 'Who *was* that person masquerading as me?', 'How am I ever going to explain this to someone else when I cannot wrap my own head around it?'), the profound sense of inner aloneness that never goes away (this isn't quite loneliness though it can feel that way at times), the recurring theme of walking a solitary path or feeling like the one against the many, the list is endless.

But I had always felt like the outsider, desperately needing to belong, but unable to stop myself from rocking the boat every opportunity I got. Having the sun unaspected in a moon-ruled chart is like having the most fundamental aspects of your being always at war with each other. And just for the fun of it, the cosmos decided to saddle me with a yod as well, so my general blacksheep-ness was a predisposition any way you look at it. But until I discovered Jung (who also has a yod), no one told me about the healing power of the blacksheep for the family line. So I acted out my unaspected sun compulsively and unconsciously, and suffered a crippling sense of guilt and shame over who I was at a fundamental level.

I've struggled with moderation for as long as I can remember and while it never involved drug use or psychotic disorders (I'll get to those 'psychic' experiences in another section because they are not related to the unaspected sun), I have also had a way of attracting the extremes in others. As a child, I was either fawned over, put on a pedestal and told how 'extraordinarily brilliant' I was, or bullied, singled out and ganged up on, to the point that I still feel an inner terror about group involvements of any kind. In both situations, I had no awareness of what it was in me that elicited such extreme responses from others. It's not that I didn't enjoy being different and occasionally, admired, but it always came at the cost of my belonging. Over time, this made me withdraw into a shell and by my mid to late teens, I was an entirely different person. Since I rarely felt liked by others as an equal, romantic involvements became a great way to both belong and feel seen. Again, I would project my sun entirely on a literal man and then worship my own unintegrated luminosity as it showed up in him.

After I discovered astrology, I could see the specific parts that were being projected when I looked at how the other's chart interacted with mine. Typically, people whose planets fall on (conjunction) or in hard aspect to the sun and the moon in our charts, usually make an impact on us one way or another.

The more the aspects, the more intense the projection, and the psychological task ahead for the two involved. But imagine this in the case of an unaspected sun or moon, already so unconscious of itself. That unaspected planet, that Liz Greene describes as a tenant who's been living in your basement all along that you had no idea existed,* suddenly gets triggered awake by the partner's planets. And if it's a planet like venus or neptune, the potential for adoration and fusion become even more exaggerated; the partner idealised, and the sense of self, both redeemed and lost all at once.

That story about my first book is the other side of the unaspected sun—the often unlikely or unexpected success. My sun unlike Rowling's and Van Gogh's is not in its own sign or in exaltation and my 'success' (at least the one I'm referring to) was a modest one though for me, at the time, it was nothing short of a fairytale ending, and validation for a very long period of marching to my own drumbeat, with little to no approval from anyone around. But this is a difficult thing to explain when you are asked in an interview to share your 'struggles as a writer' or the 'long path to getting published' or the many 'rejection letters you collected before you made your debut' because that's the kind of story that inspires and encourages. Except it was not my story.

My first book was an experiment that happened to work out in my favour. And while a bestseller these days is objectively no big deal, back in 2011, for someone from my background, it was unreal. How was this happening when I hadn't even made a serious effort? The whole thing was an experiment because 'Well, I've failed at everything else, what have I got to lose?'

This can seem unearned and undeserved and maybe it

---

*Apollo's Chariot: The Meaning of the Astrological Sun, Liz Greene

was. Hell, I even lack the most basic level of commitment and discipline to call myself a writer. But that doesn't mean I haven't served my time and paid my coin (and will probably continue to for a lifetime) in isolation, self-doubt and an overwhelming sense of un-belonging.

Because the unaspected sun, like anything else in the chart that promises wonders, also extracts its price. And while there is an undeniable grandiosity that's always lurking beneath the surface in me, hungry for extraordinariness, the need to be different, and bringing me endless shame and embarrassment, I have learned to watch it with some level of amusement instead of taking it too seriously. I'm also more accepting of the aloneness, self-doubt and cluelessness that come with it; more aware of its unconscious tendency to be excessive and arrogant; and I have a bit more compassion and forgiveness for myself for those times, when having no guidance on my own psychology, I put myself in cruel and humiliating situations.

I wanted to discuss this placement in some depth because it explains so much of what is illustrated in the memoir. But though it's rarer for the sun, mercury and venus to be unaspected given how closely venus and mercury travel with the sun, any planet in the chart may be unaspected and it's often the part of the individual that is most visible.

A few examples: Monica Lewinsky has venus (the erotic aspect of the feminine) at 28 Leo making a sextile to saturn (government, authority, coming to maturity etc.) at 28 Gemini. The two form a duet as they make no other aspects in the chart. In Hitler's chart, the collective planets neptune and pluto are a duet in conjunction. This requires a lot more elaboration (please read Greene, Hamaker-Zondag) and I can't do it any justice here. In Thomas Edison's chart, uranus is unaspected (forming only a broad sextile with jupiter). Uranus is not only related to the Promethean urge for invention and progress, it also rules electricity. Ricky Gervais has a Yod involving the sun and mercury (individuality, thinking, communication), jupiter (comedy, exaggeration, the urge to broadcast, teach or amplify) and pluto (the urge to provoke, transform, expose what is buried and a general fascination with taboos).

Obviously we know very little about the inner experience of these individuals but I hope from what I've shared about the unaspected sun in my own life, you're able to get a more well-rounded picture.

For more on unhinged placements in the chart, read Richard Idemon's The Magic Thread: Astrological Chart Interpretation Using Depth Psychology

And now that we've covered the basic alphabet of astrology, let's see if we can look at the chart as a whole.

9

What Is the Story?
(aka Putting It All Together)

'The decisive question for man is: Is he related to something infinite or not?'

—C.G. Jung

I have a love-hate relationship with pop astrology. On the one hand, I recognise its purpose. And of course, it can be most entertaining. But the injustice it does to the depth, colour, texture and richness of the stories encrusted in those lines and squiggles that make up a natal chart, distresses my myth-and-fairytale-loving heart.

You are not just an assortment of astrological placements—'You have the sun in the twelfth house so you feel alone and unseen and your father was probably absent' is a dead-end. What are you supposed to do with that? I mean, even if it's true, where do you go from there?

Instead, if I told you how the placement of the sun in the twelfth house mirrors that part of dawn when the light is just beginning to stream in but it's probably not bright enough yet so you don't realise that you're standing at the threshold of a brand new day; and how, this is also the very early part of Harry Potter where he's still sleeping in a cupboard, feeling orphaned and alone, but the first Hogwarts letter has just arrived, and even though Harry hasn't got to read it yet, there is already the first sign of the hero's journey that is about to unfold. So is the twelfth house a place of exile where one must live out a sentence like Harry in the cupboard or is it a magical place where anything is possible for one who has the eyes to see it?

And suddenly, having located yourself in a myth or a story with archetypal themes, you now have a sense of being related to something larger; to the transpersonal layer of the psyche from which we derive meaning. And for some reason, unlike any other living being, we humans seem to need meaning.

Every single placement in the natal chart may be amplified (to use Jung's term) by fairytales (and I don't mean the PG rated Disney version but the early savage Grimms versions where Cinderella/Aschenputtel's step sisters chopped off their toes and heel to fit into the slipper, for example) and myths, which arise from the collective unconscious and are as Jungian analyst Edward Edinger puts it 'not simply tales of happenings in the remote past but eternal dramas that are living themselves out repeatedly in our own personal lives and in what we see all around us'.* There are differences between myths and fairytales which I won't get into here but if we are to get the most out of the Jungian/archetypal approach to astrology, we must immerse ourselves in the symbolic language of myth, religion and fairytales because they spring from the collective unconscious and without them, we exist in a vacuum, alienated and cut off from our own psychic depths.

But if you can see the vibrant images of mythology come alive in your own life's journey as portrayed by your natal chart, then you're not quite isolated or unmoored anymore. If you can

---

***The Eternal Drama: The Inner Meaning of Greek Mythology*, Edward Edinger

see yourself in a larger archetypal drama, then you have a sense of continuum.* Whether you're overcome with grief and wrath over the loss of a precious child (Demeter), been betrayed by a lover (Medea), facing an impossible struggle there is no way out of (Herakles), feeling the terror of being abducted into the dark recesses of your own unconscious where you're stripped of all naïveté by force (Persephone), facing the consequences of hubris (Icarus), confronting your inner gorgon through the reflective mirror of psychotherapy (Perseus) or learning to make your peace with life's shadow side by developing an acceptance for even meaningless suffering (Chiron), there is a god, goddess, hero or fairytale figure who has already been there and is eternally walking that path with you.

Archetypes exist outside of time. They are eternal, cyclical, having no beginning or end and part of the very essence of the cosmos.† They are not concepts or abstractions as many people assume 'Jungian archetypes' to mean. They are alive, embodied and have complete autonomy. We witness their range of expression from wondrous, life-giving and inspiring, to volatile, destructive and even bloodcurdlingly horrific, every day in headline news and (hopefully) to a lesser degree, in our own lives.

Kronos/Herod—the outworn system, authority or ruling power—terrified of the newborn who is destined to overthrow him, continues to swallow/slay his children—imprisoning, punishing and murdering the new idea or vision that threatens to destabilise the old order. This is a story as old as time but we don't recognise it when we see it playing out in the news. We make no connection between the unfolding drama and its mythic background. Because if we did, we'd know that Zeus/

Astrology, Myths and Fairytales: CPA Seminar Series, Liz Greene
†Ibid

Christ/the Divine Child is not dead though Kronos/Herod thinks he is. And horrifying as it may be to live through a time like this, we can live to fight another day because we know what comes after.

Will it happen tomorrow? Next year? In our lifetime? We don't know. All we know is that the birth of the Divine Child never takes place in a deluxe suite at a multi-specialty hospital with your doula present. It happens in a humble little manger because 'there is no room at the inn'.

The new principle that will ultimately overthrow the old order—whether this is playing out at a collective level or in your own psyche as two opposing forces—never looks like much when it first makes its appearance. But if you know the story, then you can consciously nurture this new spark of life which represents—among other things—the hope for redemption and a new vision arising within you. And in doing so, your free will allows you to play your part in altering the expression of the drama playing out in your life.

So using your chart as a map to guide you into the belly of your psychic space, you now have a sense of your personal myths or those archetypal images manifesting in an individual way through you.

Will you be an unconscious participant, where the gods and goddesses settle scores among themselves by dragging you into their dramas as they often do to mortals in myth? Or will you navigate this journey awake, present and taking responsibility for your own unconscious collusions?

This is the whole point of using the natal chart as a map of the psyche. It's a mirror, an MRI of your psychic terrain if you will, that gives you a clear sense of your archetypal nature—the ground from which your complexes originate. By studying it in relation to how you experience your life, you begin to understand where you may be out of balance; what you're really hungry for and possibly substituting with an addiction of some kind—from workaholism to fanaticism to substance abuse; which 'gods', archetypal powers or drives are meddling with your affairs and creating recurring themes and patterns because they don't feel honoured; how by becoming aware of your dark, unconscious side and making room for these 'others' in you, you not only have access to latent gifts and unlived potential but you stop needing others to play the gods and villains in your own drama; and most of all, by listening, or as Robert Johnson puts it, 'developing a ear for the psyche', by engaging with your natal chart in this way, you begin the journey of coming back home to your Self—your wholeness.

Keeping this as the basis for analysing the chart, I want to present here some ways of approaching your natal chart—what may be helpful to keep in mind, what questions you might want to bring, etc. This is not a chart interpretation handbook (there are many books on the basics of chart interpretation that you can easily find online) as much as a way to engage with the stories that you carry within you, that are seeking individual expression in your life.

Take this in slowly, at your own pace, make notes as you interpret, read what others have to say, and most of all, have fun. So let's get to it. One of the first questions anyone has when trying to interpret the chart is 'Where do I begin?' Every astrologer has their own favourite way and there is also value in approaching it through some kind of structure, such as the sun, moon and ascendant to begin with. But I present here, my answer which is 'anywhere'!

What is the first thing that you notice? And just let the patterns lead the way from there.

i) A Stellium

Pull up your natal chart. Zoom out. Scan the whole landscape. What is the first thing that catches your attention? Are your eyes drawn to any one area?

Do you see a cluster of planets for example, (known as a stellium—which is four or more planets in any one sign or house) anywhere? What planets form the stellium? How many personal planets are involved? As you know by now, personal planets represent those aspects of yourself that are most accessible to the ego so this is a huge chunk of your conscious personality that you would typically recognise in an instant. Notice the sign the stellium is in. Is it the same sign as your sun? If your knowledge of your natal chart has been restricted to sun signs so far, this alone should explain a lot.

Let's say you have the sun in Sagittarius which is a mutable fire sign that's always reaching for something 'more' than the limitations of reality, always keeping its options open, resisting any kind of finality or anything it perceives as a limitation on its freedom; but you have the moon, mars, saturn and the ascendant in Taurus, a fixed earth sign whose urge is to put down roots, create permanence and stability in the material world. This is a fundamental conflict, not unlike the marriage of Zeus and Hera, which if you remember, is part of the mythic pattern of Sagittarius.

I have seen a fair share of people with such combinations that go, 'Oh my god, that explains it. I've never really related so much to my sun sign. I mean, I see it in myself I guess, because I'm a doctoral candidate and that's a literal expression of Sagittarius but I identify wholly with the essence of Taurus.'

As I ask more questions, I may find out that despite their Taurean urge to 'settle down' and marry a stable partner, they are always attracting people who embody Zeus/Sagittarius—full of promise and adventure but either unavailable or unwilling to commit or 'earth' the relationship in any way. In this case, the Sagittarius sun is getting projected (at least in part) on a partner (usually a literal man) because there isn't sufficient consciousness around this aspect of oneself.

After much disappointment and heartbreak, this individual may decide to press pause on seeking a partner for a while and allow herself to be single. She may do something 'out of character' and start to travel (Sagittarius). She still identifies with the Taurean aspect of her nature but in the process of dealing with this 'problem', she's beginning to open up to another key aspect of herself—her Sagittarian sun. She may find that though she craves a sense of permanence in the material world as her primary lunar urge for safety, her adventurous side has a way of 'coming out' when she's traveling. And suddenly the world feels a lot bigger than the one she was living in (a classic sign that one has touched the jupiter/Sagittarian part of herself)— her problems seem a little smaller and she has this whole new perspective. As she begins this relationship with this unlived part of herself, she may find that her need for a partner is not nearly as compulsive anymore. She may even get to meet her inner commitment-phobe as her previously unconscious doubts about marriage and settling down, start to surface. This is great. Because she no longer has to tell herself that sad story about how no one really wants her. It was never about them to begin with.

I didn't even get around to interpreting the conjunction of planets in the stellium but you see how much we got just out of a simple thing like this? Now set your own personal story of your stellium (if you have one) in whatever sign or house, against its archetypal background. What does that tell you about the importance and relevance of this mythic pattern for your life? In many ways, this is a personal myth for you. It presents questions you must grapple with and live out in your own individual way.

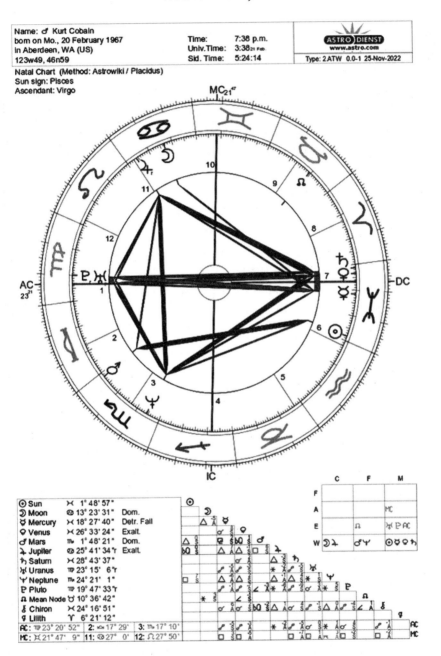

Figure 6. The Natal Chart of Kurt Cobain from Astro-Databank wiki

On the other hand, let's say you have the majority of your planets in the element of water but you don't see yourself as a feeling type. This is rare and can point to more serious issues because such a huge part of your nature has been repressed. Why? What was the early environment like? How did your family respond to your feelings? Do you experience others in your life as excessively emotional? What we're really trying to get at here is 'Where is all this energy going?' Maybe you're an artist or musician. Though you feel inhibited when it comes to expressing your feelings with others, it all pours into your work, which is great. But sometimes, you may need a handful of outlets. You may be a celebrated musician but it may not be enough to contain the water in your chart. I'm reminded of Kurt Cobain who had every planet save two (uranus and pluto in Virgo pinned to his Virgo ascendant) in the element of water. That's a record-breaking eight planets in one element. Of these, four planets including the sun and the chart ruler (mercury) are in Pisces.

Now pretend you know nothing of his biography (I know only the bullet points myself) and just imagine these placements as an image. If it were a painting, what would it look like?

To me, it's the ocean captured in all its magnificence and ferocity. It evokes a sense of awe but also terror of the depths. When I transport myself into this landscape imaginally, I feel vulnerable and inundated by feelings, images and dreams that are so vivid and textured, I cannot differentiate between the real and the imaginal. I must pour it all into a painting, a poem, or a musical composition because I cannot contain it. But even that's not enough. I feel hungry, and for what, I can't quite tell. I'm not sure if anyone can see this side of me though, because people tend to perceive me not as an ocean but as a wild fire (fire is a missing element in this chart, and I'll discuss missing elements/

singletons in the next point), to be admired and mythologised or feared, labelled arrogant or manic; or as a gust of cold wind (air too is a missing element), invigorating, clearing away the debris of outworn thinking, witty and sparkling but emotionally unreachable. Hell, I can't even really tell who I am, it all depends on what wants to take over the show on a given day—it's all too much, I'm on edge, I want to scream, I want to escape—and it's not that I'm ungrateful because I see everything I've been given. It's just that...I don't recall signing up for this.

> 'Perhaps we are here confronting an image of the transient yet sacred life of the individual soul, born out of the Mother and doomed to return to her, forever bound to her, yet for a brief season the fertiliser of the earth and the creative spark which renews life...The theme of redeemer and victim is very close to the heart of Pisces. Whether the individual Piscean identifies more with the victim and becomes the one whom life has dismembered, or with the redeemer who is the saviour of the suffering, there is not much to choose between them, for they are two facets of the same thing.'
>
> —Liz Greene

This is all just the water, Pisces emphasis and the two missing elements in Kurt Cobain's chart which in itself is quite striking and unusual. Does this mean he was doomed? I hope by now you know the answer to that (and it's 'no, absolutely not,' the chart cannot factor in free will or an individual's level of consciousness). But I hope this works as an example of how you can try 'getting into' the chart as a whole, as opposed to breaking down each placement in isolation.

ii) Unhinged Planets (Singletons, Unaspected Planets) and the Balance of Elements

What about the elemental balance in your chart? How many planets do you have in each element? Does any one element hog most of the space as in Kurt Cobain's chart? Are there two fighting for supremacy? Is there a missing element (no planets— and angles and nodes do not count—in a particular element)? Is there a singleton (only one planet in a particular element)? This can give you a broad sense of how you relate to the four functions—intuition, sensation, thinking and feeling. Which element has the most planets? If it's water, for example, you may immediately recognise feeling as your dominant function. Dominant in this sense is the one that's most developed and integrated and comes most naturally to you. Go back and read up on the particular element. Are they all concentrated in the same water sign or spread over two or all three signs? Does it resonate with you? Is this the element you would consider your dominant based on your knowledge of yourself? If not, make a note of the element you do think is dominant. Notice what you have here. If you see just one planet or no planets, there's a good reason you may be experiencing this as overwhelming your chart and by extension, your nature.

Singletons and absent elements have a way of hijacking the chart because they represent unconscious aspects of the psyche. Liz Greene says that a singleton, being the only one of its kind, fights for its survival like any living being. In this case, both the element (let's say earth) as well as the planet through which the element expresses itself (let's say mercury) may be quite jarring in the personality. It may operate as a pocket of energy that erupts every now and then, causing disturbances in the surface of consciousness, or it may repeatedly get projected because the person has no conscious relationship to the element.

A classic example of an unhinged singleton is my neptune in Sagittarius. Neptune is the only planet in the element of fire in my chart and I have always had a compulsive relationship with fire, which is one of the signs that something is operating unconsciously. My nearly lifelong craving for extraordinariness, freedom, excitement, constant stimulation and the need for something 'big' to the point of not being able to accept everyday life—all correspond to fire operating unconsciously.

This is further exacerbated by the unaspected sun which I've already talked about. Now neptune (the planet that represents the urge for transcendence and the mystical longing for God among other things) is the only mouthpiece for fire (the urge for greatness, immortality, for 'more'). When neptune first erupted in my life in a major way, I started seeing visions and receiving impressions and messages, and all those other 'spooky' experiences I've touched on here, that broadly fall under what we understand as 'psychic' or 'paranormal'. I would understand this as a heightened receptivity and sensitivity to anything that's floating around in the collective unconscious. For me, this happened through the Catholic Church (religion being one of the expressions of Sagittarius).

Later, I started writing fiction (another neptunian pursuit where the longing for 'another world' is found in the imaginal space) and getting published (Sagittarius). Eventually, I found in astrology and Jungian psychology—working with myth, fairytales and dreams—a fantastic outlet for those very urges, only this time, in a broader framework. My neptune is also part of the yod in my chart and stationary (this is when a planet comes to a standstill before it appears to change direction and said to 'stand out' in the person in some way), both of which add to its excessiveness and tendency to hijack and overwhelm. Had this part of me been left unattended, it would have typically manifested as illness, addiction or psychosis (among other possibilities). Even with all these outlets, it has a way of derailing my routine (it's in the 6th house) through binge-watching, day-dreaming and other forms of escapism when I take my eyes off it. I attribute many of the symptoms of ADHD to a neptune that's behaving unconsciously. When it's expressing itself consciously, however, it's right up there among my most rewarding placements.

So the singleton, like the unaspected planet, may point to extremely unconscious complexes that take time to emerge into consciousness and express themselves in a balanced way. If the singleton in question is an outer planet like mine, it's even more difficult for the ego to access and is therefore experienced as projected—as an event or something that 'happens' to the person. Unlike the unaspected planet however, the singleton may be well-aspected to other planets, making integration less difficult.

> *'Singletons are areas that focus. They are a point of nexus, of problem, of stress, of potential neurosis or complex based around what that planet archetypally connects with.'*
>
> —Richard Idemon*

iii) Aspects as Complex Pictures

When you look at aspects in the same way—as images, stories and psychodramas—it's suddenly not so overwhelming. Pick one aspect in your natal chart. Any one. Let's say you have the moon at 9° Taurus in a tight conjunction with venus at 11° Taurus. We know that a conjunction by definition means that the two planets are fused together, their energies blended and must be read as one. Sure, but that is not a story.

Magic Thread: Astrological Chart Interpretation Using Depth Psychology, Richard Idemon

What is the moon? It's a symbol of the Great Mother in her many manifestations. In Taurus, she is exalted, a fertile earth goddess. What is venus? The young, erotic aspect of the Feminine. Venus is dignified in Taurus in her own home. To me, they look like a cosy mother-daughter duo here. Do they get to remain in this blissful enmeshment or does some danger lurk just around the corner as it so often does in a story that begins this way? Ah, there it is. Pluto at 10° Scorpio makes a tight opposition to this moon-venus conjunction.

Pluto, whom we've already met, is the subterranean god, Hades, who abducts the floral maiden Persephone into the underworld.

Since everything in life operates in a pair of opposites, in a Jungian sense, the nourishing mother has a shadow side, which is the devouring mother. In other words, when one is identified with this archetypal principle and nourishes others in a compulsive way, she is also unconsciously feeding off of the other's dependency on her (we met this type of mothering in Cancer). If this is not made conscious, such a mother keeps her children infantile, dependent and helpless, in which case, initiation into adulthood and separation from the mother is always experienced as a terrifying abduction by Hades.*

So there you have it. We've interpreted not one aspect but an aspect pattern, which in this case is made up of one conjunction and one opposition. I still don't know how this plays out in your life. Are you Demeter or are you Persephone? Who are you more identified with? And who holds the other side for you? How has this story played out in your own life so far? It may have been quite literal—as a highly enmeshed relationship with your personal mother which got rudely interrupted when you

---

The Eternal Drama: The Inner Meaning of Greek Mythology, Edward Edinger

had your first boyfriend. This boy may have been experienced as Hades by a mother so possessive of her child. Unable to let go, the mother may have consciously or unconsciously punished you for leaving her by withholding love (this is typically the case when saturn is also involved in the pattern and you see the colder aspect of mother) or she may have manipulated, threatened or otherwise attempted to control you, making you feel guilty for such a 'betrayal'. If you succumbed and ended the relationship with your boyfriend, this dynamic may have continued in subtler ways to the point that as an adult, you may still be single, dependent on others and terrified of losing your mother or mother surrogate who is still the ultimate symbol of love, nourishment, safety and security.

On the other hand, you may have identified with Demeter, repressing your venusian side and projecting your unintegrated sexuality on venusian people you feel threatened by, in romantic relationships. In this case, Hades may erupt as a love triangle or a sexual betrayal when you are confronted with the piece of yourself that you've left out, through rivals who embody it.

Whatever the personal story (and there are many possible manifestations), this is an example of the archetypal layer of a complex at work in the individual life. We may also call this a mother complex since it involves the moon, whose sign, house and aspects, tell us something about your inner images of the archetypal mother, and those experiences that you are archetypally bound to run into, in relation to the mother principle.

So what happens when—after several cycles of loss, abandonment, grief and betrayal—you've managed to integrate all aspects of this particular complex? What happens when your inner Demeter and Persephone have made their peace with Hades? You begin to experience the life-giving side of Hades.

Anything that enters Hades (in this case Persephone who represents the naïve, the uninitiated, infantile aspects of self) undergoes a death-rebirth process, which is why in astrology, when we go through a pluto transit (the peak period of which takes about two years) we come out utterly transformed, often beyond recognition. The experience may be subjectively terrifying, intense and entail some kind of loss or ending. But the transformation that follows is so radical and empowering that you cannot imagine going back to how things were.

So if you have pluto in hard aspect to a personal planet in your chart, this suggests that you are destined to encounter Hades in the area of life related to the planet (in this case, the moon and venus). So it makes no sense to compare your emotional or sexual experiences to those who have no major pluto aspects. 'Why are my relationships always so messed up? Why can't I just have a stable relationship that so many people seem to have so effortlessly?' The far more useful question is 'What have I learnt and how have I been transformed through the alchemy of relationships so far? And how can I make room for the Shiva principle (which is a culturally closer image of Hades to me as an Indian) and the dance of creation and destruction that is endlessly taking place in this area of my life?'

Coming back to the aspect—moon-venus opposite pluto—we may amplify it with any number of myths, stories and fairytales that may shed a light on different aspects of the same themes. Many fairytales begin with the 'good' or innocent daughter who is left behind by the nourishing mother who dies, only to be mistreated by the wicked stepmother. But if we look at these aspects as pieces of ourselves, the good and terrible mother as two aspects of a whole, and use stories as a mirror to understand these patterns and trace them back to how they're showing up in our lives, astrology becomes alive, animated and fluid as opposed to static statements that fall flat, put you in a box or give you an excuse to continue living out your placements unconsciously.

iv) Your Natal Chart Is a Static Picture But Your Psyche Is Not

It's extremely important to remember this when attempting to understand the living, breathing human being who animates the chart. It is impossible to look at the natal chart alone and know where a person is currently at, in relation to the map. You are not the same person you were ten years ago and you're not going to be the person you are now, another decade from now. For this, we look at predictive astrology—the transits, progressions and other techniques—to understand the psychic processes you're currently undergoing, and what chapter you're in, in the book of your life.

But in this book, we are keeping the focus on the natal chart so I cannot emphasise enough that it's a symbolic portrayal— each placement having an impressive range of expression—and the more concretely you attempt to understand it, the more you lose sight of its magic and potential.

v) How Much Charge Does a Complex Have?

We talked about the 'charge' inherent in a complex. This charge describes how intensely a complex takes hold of a person's life. As Jung once said, 'Everyone knows nowadays that people have complexes. What is not so well known, though far more important theoretically, is that complexes can have us.' How compulsively does a complex operate in your life? Does it have a tendency to hijack your life or erupt as in aforementioned examples of singletons and unaspected planets which represent complexes that reside far away from consciousness, split-off and autonomous? Or are you more related to it? Are you in touch both with its light as well as its shadow?

Astrologically, anything in the chart may be understood as a complex or pockets of energy or charge around certain topics.

A stellium with several planets in conjunction, always points to a complex. In this case, the sign or house in which it is present, is going to carry the intensity of the complex. It's like the cosmos circled out this part of your life with a highlighter pen as an area where much of libido or psychic energy will invariably flow. There is work to be done here—much to be explored, unearthed, understood, integrated and embodied. Failing which, most of your 'symptoms' are likely to originate from the same place.

Planets conjunct or pinned to the angles which are points of manifestation, carry an enormous charge given their urgency to express themselves. A planet that is pinned to an angle also typically forms hard aspects (squares and an opposition) to all the other angles. So if you're unhappy with how it's expressing itself, digging deeper into its story both archetypally and in your own chart—looking at the houses it rules (for example, if mars is pinned to an angle, you'd want to study the houses that have Aries and Scorpio on the cusp), the sign and house it's placed in, as well as its aspects—can tell you how to work with it.

In general, the hard aspects—thanks to the discomfort, irritation and friction they cause—carry a high level of charge, the conjunction being the most intense. They demand action and some kind of resolution which is exactly how complexes operate. The trine and sextile are much weaker in terms of charge—they flow easily and there is no urgency to resolve anything.

So if you have two planets in opposition (let's say the sun at 16 Gemini opposite neptune at 21 Sagittarius) also forming a square to two planets that are conjunct each other in Virgo (let's say mars conjunct saturn at 20 Virgo), this is a picture of a highly-charged complex. The sun wants something, neptune is pulling it in the opposite direction, and mars and saturn who are already at war with each other (because they represent such contradictory principles, and forced to work together in a conjunction) are now further exacerbating this conflict by creating a confrontation or obstacle. This could go many different ways but once you understand its archetypal context and find its parallels in a story, you can begin to understand how it calls the shots in your own life.

You may, for example, identify with mars and project saturn. So you experience anyone in authority (saturn) as thwarting your will (mars). You may identify with the Gemini sun that tends towards a sort of compulsive, one-dimensional rationality where you reject neptune entirely. But find that you're always so riled up by religious, spiritual or 'irrational people' who seem to have the power to ruin your day. Or you may have a pattern of attracting con-artists, those who need rescuing or find that you get sucked into relationships (the opposition aspect almost always creates a projection and involves 'others') where you lose your sense of self (sun opposite neptune).

Understanding the power a complex holds can help you attend to its needs. The more unconscious a complex is, the more precious energy it holds up that is not accessible to you. Analysing these complex pictures in the chart can help the process of unraveling the stories they contain.

vi) Begin with One Placement and Try Personifying It

If interpretation is all too overwhelming, pick out just one placement. A planet in a sign. That's it. Put the two together and think, feel, sense and intuit your way into it. Who does this remind you of? Let's take the moon. You know by now what the moon represents but we're personifying it. So we're looking at a maternal figure, yes? A caregiver. Someone who seeks out emotional connection with others. Now the sign is going to modify how the moon behaves. In other words, the moon is going to be a caregiver but how does the moon in a particular sign go about doing this? Let's say the moon is in Capricorn. This is the polarity of Cancer on the zodiacal wheel, where the moon is in detriment. Capricorn is a cardinal earth sign ruled by saturn. Seasonally, it marks the winter solstice. How does this influence the way this person expresses their lunar nature? Would they feel comfortable asking for their needs to be met or would they want to take control (earth) by being self-contained and self-reliant (Capricorn)? How about vocalising their feelings? Would saturn (the planet that rules this moon)—the planet of restriction, lack, fear, insecurity and inadequacy—allow the moon to be emotionally expressive or would it see vulnerability as weakness? What about the way the moon goes about taking care of others in this sign? Would this be the kind of person who just listens to you rant about a problem, comforts you with a hug and distracts you with gossip or someone who may not have warmth and words of comfort to offer, but jumps right in and solves your problem by being practical, resourceful and efficient? Now if you do have this placement and you don't at all resonate with this, make a note of it but remember that we are currently interpreting just this one placement in isolation, not considering the conflicts and contradictions in your whole chart.

If this moon in Capricorn were the only placement in the chart, what would this person be like? If you're not familiar with myths and fairytales, that's fine for now. Think about your favourite fictional characters—whether in books, movies or TV shows. Who comes to mind? Why? How about people in your actual life? Play with this. When you have a sense of the person, add the house placement of the moon. If it's in the first house, this is going to be a very visible part of their personality. The moon in the first is going to be extremely receptive and sensitive to its environment and the needs of everyone around. It could be a compulsive nurturer too. But the fact that it's in Capricorn could mean that this urge to nurture plays out in one's career (Capricorn is the sign associated with the tenth house) where they may play an important administrative role or one where they strategise and look out for the interests of a whole company. But even if the person is a stay-at-home parent, they're going to nurture in a decidedly Capricorn way and it's going to be a big part of their personality (first house).

Now that you've got a sense of the planet in its sign and house, pick one of its aspects. Just one. The moon is conjunct uranus. This is a whole other story as uranus' urge is for progress and freedom, not safety and security which is what the moon, by nature, strives towards. The moon will always prioritise emotional connections, family and tribe over freedom, progress, individual goals and ambitions. Uranus sees this as a problem. It's holding the person back, keeping them fettered and stagnant and uranus won't have that. So we have a tension of the opposites, pulling the person apart from within. From our knowledge of how the psyche works, we know that this person is either going to feel this conflict powerfully within herself, in which case she may swing between the extremes or more ideally, make room for both parts of herself. But let's say she was raised in an environment and culture that harshly judges mothers who express any need for freedom or autonomy.

If she internalised this idea, she may identify wholly with the moon and repress her uranian needs. The repressed planet may then have to be acted out by a partner (projection) who decides to leave the marriage and family, seemingly out of the blue. Or it may be a mutual decision or an affair that helps release the tension that's accrued in the unconscious. It may produce phobias (fear of flying being a common one with moon-uranus), anxieties (around abandonment that are typically carried over from picking up on their own mother's ambivalence about mothering in childhood), nightmares or any of a number of symptoms that are basically uranus in disguise, begging for attention and integration.

Then you bring in the next aspect, working from the hard aspects to the softer ones. Examine the nature of the planet that's forming the aspect. Tell stories around each symbol. And finally, trace it all back to your own life to see how these universal patterns are expressing themselves in an individualised way through you.

vii) Empty Houses in a Natal Chart and Planetary Rulers of Houses

If you're looking at your natal chart for the first time and freaking out a little about the houses that have no planets in them ('I don't have any planets in the tenth house! Is this why my career seems to be going nowhere?'), please relax. As you know by now, there are only ten 'planets' but there are twelve houses, so everyone has empty houses. And while houses that are most tenanted assume particular significance in our lives, every house is coloured by a sign, which means that every house is ruled by the planetary ruler of that sign.

So if you want to understand a house better (let's say the tenth house), look at the sign that falls on the cusp of that house.

If it's Gemini, for example, you'd want to see what mercury is up to in the chart. It's in the fifth house in Capricorn conjunct the sun, saturn and squared by mars. This gives us a lot of information about your tenth house. You may want to ask how the public expression of who you deeply are (tenth) is tied to the fifth house, which is related to your inner child, play and creative self-expression. What does it mean that a heavy, exacting sign like Capricorn colours this house which is most associated with play and spontaneity? Could it be an inner pressure (saturn) to make something concrete (saturn, Capricorn) out of your need to bring forth your individuality in some creative act (fifth house)? And what does it mean that the midheaven ruler is tied to this? Could this have a big part to play in where you're headed in this lifetime? Perhaps a big part of your creative expression is being a parent. In which case, what kind of parent are you? You can play with the symbolism, turn the story around, look at it from every angle, from multiple points of view, to get a sense of how it works in your life and how you engage it with it.

Planets also make aspects to angles so even if you don't have something in a particular house—tenth, in this case—if you have planets in angular relationship to the midheaven—which would be planets in the first, fourth and seventh houses within 8-10 degrees of the midheaven—then they're going to be very much involved in your midheaven story arc.

viii) Everything Is Related

As you get deeper and deeper into the story of your chart, you start to notice how every placement or aspect pattern connects with each other. Anything of particular significance in a chart is also suggested over and over, at least three times, which is a magical number in myths and fairytales so keep an eye out for this. For example, you may have several planets in the first house, suggesting a particularly strong focus on the self. But all these planets may be in Libra, which is the seventh sign, presenting a me-versus-we polarity and an intense focus on the relationship axis. There is a balancing act that needs to happen here. The sun may be strong in Leo and conjunct mars, further amplifying the focus on selfhood and autonomy; but the moon may be in Cancer unaspected, so lunar needs may dominate the individual, and venus a singleton in water, also in Cancer, may hijack the chart, together creating a compulsive need for relationship and belonging. Now you're seeing a pattern that's repeatedly suggested. It presents questions and conflicts you must grapple with your whole life, in different ways, in varying degrees, so you can bring forth that 'something' that you 'must'.

'Free will is the ability to do gladly, that which I must do.'

—C.G Jung.

For more on chart interpretation, read Liz Greene's entire body of work particularly The Horscope in Manifestation, The Development of the Personality, Dynamics of the Unconscious, Relating: An Astrological Guide to Living with Others, Barriers and Boundaries: Defences of the Personality, *Richard Idemon's* The Magic Thread: Astrological Chart Interpretation Using Depth Psychology, *Karen Hamaker-Zondag's* Psychological Astrology *and Demetra George's* Astrology and the Authentic Self.

~ Onward ~

Opening your natal chart for the first time (or first several times) as you make sense of its strange language, is one of the most magical experiences you can have in this life. If you've ever left a fictional or fantasy world with that familiar void—that ache and yearning in your being for that 'something' that was possible in the world of story but is now so starkly missing in your 'real' life—you probably get it when I say that astrology is the closest I've come to bridging that gap.

I love and need story in one form or the other like most human beings, in order to function and make meaning. But if there is anything that upsets me about a good story, it is the part where I have to leave it. And I know I'm not really leaving it because it'll always be a part of me and that's the magic of story and yada yada, I get it *but*...that ache, that longing, that sense of this alternate realm being so close I can taste it, yet unable to anchor in my ordinary life which now feels outright lacking in salt. How can the thing that gives me meaning, also rob me of it?

I do what everyone else does and move on to the next show, the next book or if I've hit a low point, stalk the actors on social media, only to be further crushed by the fact that they were only temporarily the vessels for these imaginal beings—the 'people' I'm really missing.

Who are these beings that we universally respond to? Why do they move us so profoundly from a young age? How are we related to them? The study of astrology and Jungian theory not only answered these (and many more) questions for me, but showed me how I can permanently inhabit the world of Story in a way that elevates my own, and I never have to escape it.

We tend to describe most pleasurable things in life— holidays, hobbies, fiction, sex, even relationships—as an escape. And I don't know about you but I find this deeply saddening. Not the acknowledgment that reality can be hard and even feel downright impossible at times, but the idea that I must escape it.

What if our problem is not so much with reality but with our lack of understanding of those things we deem 'not real' (and therefore an escape)? And what if learning how this works, can help anchor us in the fantastical world of our own stories that we've projected a thousand times on those fictional worlds and beings?

Of the many treasures I've so far unearthed in this expedition of psyche and cosmos, this is probably the most precious. And it is one I hope you'll get to discover for yourself on this one-of-a-kind adventure.

I have so loved being your mercurial guide as you make sense of your chart. It's like getting to read a beloved book for the first time again.

I wish you endless enchantment on your way.

Reading List

1. *Relating: An Astrological Guide to Living with Others*, Liz Greene.
2. *Jung's Map of the Soul*, Murray Stein
3. *Psychological Astrology*, Karen Hamaker-Zondag
4. *Boundaries of the Soul*, June Singer
5. *The Psychology of C.G. Jung*, Jolande Jacobi
6. *How to Read Jung*, David Tacey
7. *The Horoscope in Manifestation*, Liz Greene
8. *Collected Works 13*, para 54, C.G. Jung
9. *Inner Work*, Robert Johnson
10. *Collected Works 8*, para 505, C.G. Jung
11. *The Archetypal Cosmos*, Keiron Le Grice
12. *Four Archetypes*, C.G. Jung
13. *The Luminaries: Seminars in Psychological Astrology Vol 1*, Liz Greene and Howard Sasportas
14. *The Inner Planets: Seminars in Psychological Astrology Vol 2*, Liz Greene and Howard Sasportas
15. *Development of the Personality: Seminars in Psychological Astrology Vol 3*, Liz Greene and Howard Sasportas
16. *Dynamics of the Unconscious: Seminars in Psychological Astrology Vol 4*, Liz Greene and Howard Sasportas
17. *The Art of Stealing Fire*, Liz Greene
18. *The Astrological Neptune and the Quest for Redemption*, Liz Greene
19. *The Astrology of Fate*, Liz Greene
20. *Hellenistic Astrology: The Study of Fate and Fortune*, Chris Brennan

21. www.carljungdepthpsychologysite.blog: *On the nature of four: Jung's Quaternity, Mandalas, the Stone and the Self.*

22. *Barriers and Boundaries: Defences of the Personality*, Liz Greene

23. *Astrology for Lovers*, Liz Greene

24. *The Twelve Houses*, Howard Sasportas

25. *The Yod Book: Including a Complete Discussion of Unaspected Planets and Duets*, Karen Hamaker-Zondag

26. https://www.bbc.com/news/world-europe-54780434

27. *Apollo's Chariot: The Meaning of the Astrological Sun*, Liz Greene

28. *The Eternal Drama: The Inner Meaning of Greek Mythology*, Edward Edinger

29. *Astrology, Myths and Fairytales: CPA Seminar Series*, Liz Greene

30. *Magic Thread: Astrological Chart Interpretation Using Depth Psychology*, Richard Idemon

31. *The Myth of the Goddess: Evolution of an Image*, Anne Baring and Jules Cashford

32. *The Interpretation of Fairytales*, Marie Louise von Franz

33. *Shadow and Evil in Fairytales*, Marie Louise von Franz

34. *Individuation in Fairytales*, Marie Louise von Franz

35. *Man and his Symbols*, C.G. Jung

36. *Memories, Dreams, Reflections*, C.G. Jung

37. *The Mythic Journey*, Liz Greene and Juliet Sharman Burke

38. *The Greek Myths*, Robert Graves

39. *The Gods of the Greeks*, Karl Kerenyi

40. *The Hero with a Thousand Faces*, Joseph Campbell

41. *Cosmos and Psyche*, Richard Tarnas

42. *Chiron and the Healing Journey*, Melanie Reinhart

43. *Incarnation: The Four Angles and the Moon's Nodes*, Melanie Reinhart

44. *Predictive Astrology: The Eagle and the Lark*, Bernadette Brady

45. *Leo in Myth and Psyche (webinar from Astrology University)*, Jason Holley

46. *Women Who Run with the Wolves*, Clarissa Pinkola Estés

47. *He: Understanding Masculine Psychology*, Robert Johnson

Acknowledgements

I have put off writing this section to the very last minute because there are too many people—dead, alive, close, don't-know-I-exist, from-the-past, from-the-present—to whom I owe a huge debt of gratitude. So if I've missed anyone out, it's not you. It's ADHD. Right, here goes. This is in no particular order.

My parents, for imparting just the right ratio of love and trauma to inspire my profound interest in the human psyche, as opposed to becoming a serial killer or worse, someone who subscribes to dubious concepts like normalcy.

I love you so much.

Kiara, my daughter, friend, noisy housemate, cockroach exterminator, Vrski-whisperer, affectionate-note-leaver, hug-dispenser, navigator, troubleshooter, best-big-sister-to-two-dog-bois, chatterbox, loner, shapeshifter, emo-teen-young-child-old-soul—I'm so lucky to have you on my team. Muah.

My brother, for being that one special human who had the same, yet entirely different childhood.

I'm so grateful for the love, friendship, unwavering support, dorkiness, conversation, laughter and the thousands of miles between us that make me miss you.

My dog-boys Vrski and Enzo who get me through everything—anxiety, panic attacks, sleep-deprivation, sensory overload, bad days, not-great-humans and book deadlines (by being non-judgemental and supportive when I'm procrastinating).

Liz Greene, who introduced me to two of my greatest loves: astrology and Jungian psychology. It pains me that there is a whole generation of astrology enthusiasts who have never read her and that many of her books are now out of print. This book is an effort to introduce people to the endlessly fascinating field that is psychological astrology and the many brilliant minds that have shaped it. I hope I've done justice.

Carl Jung, whose work helps me make sense of my madness and even enjoy it; for openly embracing astrology as 'the elder sister of psychology'—I can't imagine the courage it must have taken; and for opening up whole new worlds of interest to keep me busy for a lifetime. I hope nothing I've said here made him turn in his grave.

My tutor and mentor Beverly Martin from the Society for Psychology and Healing (SOPH, UK) who passed away unexpectedly last year. She was so excited about this book every time we discussed it, and I'm heartbroken that she isn't here to read it. Her encouragement and enthusiasm meant the world to me.

My analyst Faranak Mirjalili, who not only endured my incessant whingeing throughout the writing process but helped ground and deepen my engagement with the experiential aspects of Jungian theory.

Every person who has trusted me with their birth info in the last five years that I've been a consulting psychological astrologer. Thank you! One of the things I love about client work is the fact that I get to skip the small talk entirely and dive right into topics you couldn't otherwise have with strangers.

The following people for existing: Kirthi (and her whole family), Samit, Andy, Madhu, Ava, Chitra, Arjun, Kishore, Rhea. I love you.

There are too many aunts and uncles (especially uncle

Emmanuel and aunt Mala for being my rock), cousins and grandparents I am extremely grateful for and can only hope they know who they are. You have all inadvertently helped me write this book by just getting me through the last couple of years. Thank you!

My editor Himanjali for her patience and understanding as I missed several deadlines and for generally being a lovely human; and the entire team at Simon & Schuster—particularly, Tanvi, Megha and Mridu—for their time and energy.

Sukanya Ghosh, who designed this cover that I love so much. Thank you for capturing the essence of this book and the specific ideas in my head so beautifully.

You, if you feel drawn to read this book. I hope you enjoy it. And I hope it means something to you as it does to me.